CARBON DATES

ALSO BY DONALD F. GLUT

The Frankenstein Catalog
(McFarland, 1984)
Dinosaur Valley Girls: The Book
(McFarland, 1998)
Dinosaurs: The Encyclopedia
(McFarland, 1997)
*Dinosaurs: The Encyclopedia,
Supplement I*
(McFarland, 1999)

CARBON DATES

A Day by Day Almanac
of Paleo Anniversaries
and Dino Events

by Donald F. Glut

McFarland & Company, Inc., Publishers
Jefferson, North Carolina, and London

On the cover: Full-scale *Triceratops* model made by Elbert H. Porter in Orderville, Utah (courtesy State of Utah Division of Parks and Recreation).

Frontispiece: This full-scale model of a *Tyrannosaurus rex*, equipped with a moving lower jaw, was made by Louis Paul Jonas for the Dinoland exhibit, New York World's Fair (1964–65). The figure now resides at a famous dinosaur footprints site at Glen Rose, Texas (courtesy Sinclair Refining Company).

Library of Congress Cataloguing-in-Publication Data

Glut, Donald F.
      Carbon dates : a day by day almanac of paleo anniversaries and dino events / by Donald F. Glut.
          p.   cm.
      Includes bibliographical references and index.
      ISBN 0-7864-0592-9 (sewn softcover : 50# alkaline paper) ∞
      1. Paleontology — Miscellanea.   I. Title.
QE714.3.G54   1999
560 — dc21   99-29315
                                                                                CIP

British Library Cataloguing-in-Publication data are available

Manufactured in the United States of America

McFarland & Company, Inc., Publishers
   Box 611, Jefferson, North Carolina 28640
   www.mcfarlandpub.com

To Mike Brett-Surman
(aka "Dinosaur Mikey"),
who knows there are no dinosaurs
in "parallel time"

CONTENTS

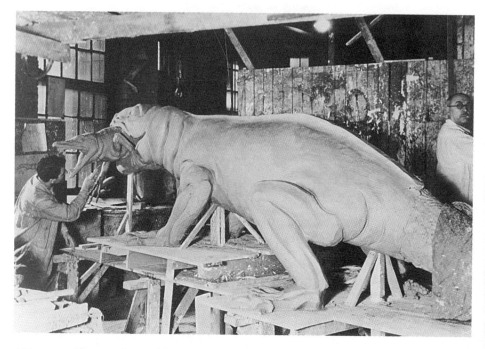

A Messmore and Damon sculptor models a mechanical fin-backed DIMETRODON *chomping on a* VARANOPS *for the company's "World A Million Years Ago" show at the 1933 Chicago World's Fair. Courtesy Francis B. Messmore.*

Drawing made prior to animating the STEGOSAURUS *versus* TYRANNOSAURUS *battle in the animated classic* FANTASIA *(1940).*

ACKNOWLEDGMENTS

I have been collecting dates relating to prehistoric life for decades. Many of these dates have come from the media, including radio and television and other sources. Good sources of usable dates have been in such diverse periodicals as the *News Bulletin* of the Society of Vertebrate Paleontology, scientific journals including the *Journal of Vertebrate Paleontology*, entertainment-industry trade publications such as *Variety* and *Hollywood Reporter*, monster-movie magazines, particularly *Famous Monsters of Filmland*, and specialty "fanzines" like *Dinosaur World*, *Space Academy Newsletter*, *Prehistoric Times* and *G-Fan*. The staff of the Margaret Herrick Library of the Academy of Motion Picture Arts and Sciences has provided many movie-related dates. Some dates have come simply from personal experiences and memories.

Many people have contributed to this project by supplying me with dates that I was not able to unearth on my own, and also by giving or lending me photographs and artwork to use herein. Among these people, to whom I am extremely grateful, are Forrest J Ackerman ("Mr. Science Fiction") of the Ackerman Archives and formerly of *Famous Monsters of Filmland*; Margaret Adamic and Howard Green of Disney Enterprises, Inc.; Robert R. Barrett and Sue Ann Bilbey of the Utah Field House of Natural History; Richard Blair; William J. Blair ("Bro-Mo"); Earle and Dee Bowman; Ronald R. Borst of Hollywood Movie Poster; Tom Burman of the Burman Studio; Danton Burroughs of Edgar Rice Burroughs, Inc.; Larry M. Byrd; Edwin H. Colbert, Museum of Northern Arizona; Daniel J. Chure of Dinosaur National Monument; Nina Cummings of the Photography Department, The Field Museum; Walter J. Daugherty; Mary Dawson and Elizabeth A. Hill of the Section of Vertebrate Paleontology, Carnegie Museum of Natural History; Allen A. and Dian E. Debus of Hell Creek Creations and *Dinosaur World*; Shel Dorf; Randy Epstein; Trish Exton-Parder of the

Calgary Zoological Society; James O. Farlow, Department of Geosciences, Indiana-Purdue University at Fort Wayne; John J. Flynn of the Geology Department, The Field Museum; Tracy L. Ford ("Dinosaur Hunter"); Mike Fredericks of *Prehistoric Times*; my mother, Julia Glut; Richard Hagopian; Jim Harmon ("Mr. Radio"); Eric L. Hoffman (the "Answer Man"); Charles L. Jackson II (the "Emperor"); Jack Janzen of *The E Ticket*; James I. Kirkland, formerly of Dinamation International Society, now State Paleontologist of Utah; J. D. Lees of *G-Fan*; Robert A. Long of the Museum of Paleontology, University of California, Berkeley; James H. Madsen, Jr., DINOLAB; Cathy McNassor of the George C. Page Museum of La Brea Discoveries; Michael L. Perry, formerly of the Museum of Western Colorado and currently of Dinamation International Society; Paul C. Sereno, Department of Organismal Biology and Anatomy, University of Chicago; Susan Shaffer; countless members of the Society of Vertebrate Paleontology (or SVP); Ed Summer of *The Dinosaur Times*; David A. Thomas; Pete and Andrea Von Sholly; Bill Warren; David B. Weishampel of the School of Medicine at Johns Hopkins University; and David Weisman.

Most helpful of all was Michael K. Brett-Surman of the National Museum of Natural History, Smithsonian Institution, who sent me many of the dates included in this project.

To all of the above — and any persons or institutions I may have inadvertently missed — I offer my sincere thanks.

TRICERATOPS family, brought to life through "Audio-Animatronics" developed by Walt Disney's technicians, which first appeared at the New York World's Fair on April 22, 1964, and can now be seen in the Primeval World at Disneyland® Park. © Disney Enterprises, all rights reserved.

INTRODUCTION

In a world where virtually every book publisher seems to have at least one title in their catalog dealing with paleontology (and usually focusing upon dinosaurs), it becomes increasingly difficult for an author to find a new or fresh approach to this very popular subject. I have tried to reach that goal with three earlier books — *The Dinosaur Dictionary* (1972), *The Dinosaur Scrapbook* (1980) and *Dinosaurs, Mammoths and Cavemen: The Art of Charles R. Knight* (1982, with Sylvia Czerkas). The format of this new book represents yet another such attempt by the present writer to treat the subject in a different way.

This project, however, began not as a book but as a standard calendar — the kind normally hung on a wall. More accurately, it started off as my own reaction to the myriad extinct animal–themed calendars that, with things prehistoric more popular than ever, have been coming out regularly for the past decade or more.

Most of these calendars have focused upon dinosaurs. Some of them have spotlighted a particular institution, reproduced illustrations from a single book or featured the work of a particular artist or group of artists.

What disappointed me about these calendars was their format. Invariably these calendars were basically the same. That is, except for the illustrations and their accompanying captions, usually one picture for each month, the individual *dates* of those months offered no information relating to paleontology. Never were there mentions of fossil discoveries, museum openings, birthdays of scientists, authors or artists, premieres of pertinent motion pictures or anything else — just the usual New Year's Day, Mother's Day, Halloween, Christmas and all the rest that can be found on any calendar, with or without a theme.

Also, once the year was over, the calendar, often graced by beautiful illustrations suitable for permanent display, was either filed or thrown away, perhaps never to be looked at again.

Frustrated — and at the same time sincerely wanting to *own* such a calendar — I decided to put one together myself, one that would be informative in ways the other calendars were not, while also being of use in the usual way regarding the passage of time, and one that could be kept and used year after year. With luck, perhaps I could unearth enough interesting and related events to fit at least most of the days in a single year.

I trusted that my assemblage of dates, some of them historically important, others more trivial, all of them hopefully interesting, would be fun to read. And if I left off the names of the days of the week my calendar could be used repeatedly.

I felt it would be interesting and even entertaining for the reader, on any given day, to be able to check out what happened in ancient life, in the worlds of science, the arts or media — on that date but in some previous year. Furthermore, I wanted to give the reader a feeling that the events they were reading about, though having occurred years ago, were happening while they read them. When a number of dates applied to a single major project, like the recovery of a Siberian mammoth in 1901, or Edwin H. Colbert's work at Ghost Ranch in 1947, the reader might even vicariously experience the passage of time by reading these dates in sequence.

As the project began to evolve, with most of the year's dates thankfully covered, I personally found fascinating how many similar kinds of events, though separated by years, decades or even centuries, coincidentally occurred on the same dates, this possibly constituting fodder for readers who enjoy making "connections" out of otherwise unrelated events.

And as this project took on form and substance (and most of the days of the year acquired entry material), I realized two important things: First, it was difficult, if not impossible, to interest any publisher of calendars in so specific a project as this one, especially when it is so much easier (and less expensive) for them to issue yet another dinosaur-themed calendar with the standard set of dates. And second, the project was growing to such a size that its information could never be squeezed onto a regular-sized calendar.

The only logical option was to forget the original calendar idea and revamp and expand the project into a book. A book that, unlike standard calendars, will never become — out of date.

Donald F. Glut
Burbank, California
Summer 1999

JANUARY

~ 1 ~

1822 Geologist and pioneer fossil hunter Gideon Algernon Mantell spends part of New Year's Day optimistically starting off his "Journal," the diary he will keep for most of his adult life: "I begin this new year with considerable apprehension; before the close of it should my life be spared I shall in all probability appear before the world as an author, and experience all the vexations and anxieties, inseparable from a first literary event." Mantell's "New Year's resolution" will come true. Early this year his book *The Fossils of the South Downs; or Illustrated Geology of Sussex* will be published. Important work with dinosaurs, particularly *Iguanodon*, is yet to come.

1929 Haruo Nakajima is born in Japan. Nakajima-san, a military pilot during World War II, will later become an actor best known to his fans for portraying the gigantic, mutated prehistoric monster Godzilla. Wearing uncomfortable rubber suits, he will play Godzilla and other fictional prehistoric creatures. He will also choreograph their battle scenes in Toho Co. films shot in Japan between 1954 and 1972. These include the following (English-language and release dates): *Godzilla, King of the Monsters!* (1956); *Rodan the Flying Monster* (1957); *Gigantis the Fire Monster* (1959); *Varan the Unbelievable* (1962); *King Kong vs. Godzilla* (1963); *Godzilla vs. the Thing* (1964); *Ghidrah the Three Headed Monster* (1965); *Frankenstein Conquers the World* (1966); *King Kong Escapes* (1967); *Godzilla vs. the Sea Monster* (1968); *Son of Godzilla* (1969); *Destroy All Monsters* (1969); *Monster Zero* (1970); *Godzilla's Revenge* (1971); *Godzilla vs. the Smog Monster* (1972); and *Godzilla on Monster Island* (1977). He will also play various prehistoric creatures on the Japanese television series *Ultra Q* and *Ultraman*, both debuting in 1966.

"Tiny" the TYRANNOSAURUS, first of a series of life-sized models built for Prehistoric Gardens near Port Orford, Oregon. Photo by Jack Janzen.

1955 The Prehistoric Gardens, a privately owned park displaying life-sized models of extinct animals, opens on Highway 101 between Port Orford and Gold Beach along the southern coast of Oregon. The 70-acre park, located in a small valley surrounded by the state's famous rain forest, is the brainchild of metalworker and paleontology enthusiast E. V. (Ernie) Nelson. Nelson's "Tiny" the *Tyrannosaurus*, based on the skeleton at New York's American Museum of Natural History, is the first "creature" to inhabit the park. The "BC" bestiary, which decades later will number more than 16 different kinds of extinct animals, will continue to grow. Among future additions, a giant *Brachiosaurus* will overlook the highway, this figure being the world's first full-scale model of one of the largest dinosaurs (measuring 86 feet in length).

1988 A float featuring big, "animated" dinosaurs (and "live" cave people) rolls through Pasadena, California's annual Rose Bowl Parade. The event is telecast live and in three dimensions, though seen "flat" without the required 3D glasses.

~ 2 ~

1857 Frederick Burr Opper is born in Madison, Ohio. Opper will become a writer and illustrator of books and children's stories, also one of the great pioneers of American newspaper comic strips, hailed as the "Mark Twain of cartooning." In the early 1900s he will begin writing and drawing the comic strip *Our Antediluvian Ancestors*. Satiric and often political, the strip will feature prehistoric people and animals in situations mirroring modern times. (Dies August 27, 1937.)

~ 3 ~

1983   Dinamation International Corporation, a company based in San Vicente, California, is incorporated. Founded by president Chris Mays, it originally distributes life-sized "animatronic" dinosaurs made in Japan by the Kokoro Company to museums, fairs and other places for exhibition on a temporary basis. Later Dinamation will move to Irvine, in Orange County, and expand, designing and manufacturing its own robotic dinosaurs and other prehistoric creatures. George Callison and Robert T. Bakker will number among the professional paleontologists employed by Dinamation Interna-

Full-scale robotic figure of the large carnivorous dinosaur ALLOSAURUS FRAGILIS designed, built and exhibited by Dinamation International Corporation. Courtesy Dinamation International Corporation.

tional Corporation as scientific advisors, with Callison eventually escalating to the position of Senior Scientist and Board Member. In the early 1990s, the company will create the Dinamation International Society, which in 1989 will become its own non-profit entity.

~ 4 ~

1939   Composer Igor Stravinsky signs a contract with Walt Disney allowing the producer to use his composition "Rite of Spring" for a sequence in Disney's full-length animated motion picture *Fantasia*. Stravinsky is paid $6,000. Although the composer had written this music to conjure up images of primitive tribes, Disney and his animators will reinterpret it as representing a young Earth and its progression of evolving life, climaxing with the extinction of the dinosaurs.

~ 5 ~

1884   Richard Owen, the foremost anatomist of his era, who will coin the word "Dinosauria," is knighted by his friend and sometimes "pupil," Queen Victoria of England.

Previously unpublished drawing by artist Russ Manning based on "The Reptile with a Heart," a story he illustrated for TARZAN'S JUNGLE ANNUAL no. 4 (published by Dell Comics in 1955), about a friendly TYRANNOSAURUS named "Wheek." Tarzan ® and © Edgar Rice Burroughs, Inc.

1929   Russ Manning is born in Van Nuys, California. Manning will become an artist and writer of comic books and strips, most of them starring Edgar Rice Burroughs' jungle hero Tarzan. He will start drawing *Tarzan* for Dell Comics in the 1950s, working with Jesse Marsh, then continue on his own when the title switches to Gold Key Comics in the 1960s. He will become a top artist and writer for the *Tarzan* newspaper strip in the 1970s, in addition to editing, writing and drawing original comic books for the foreign market in the late '70s. A lover of prehistoric animals and Burroughs' lost worlds, Manning will often bring dinosaurs and other extinct creatures into his plot lines, a Manning innovation being the revelation that one actually reaches Burroughs' lost land of Pal-ul-Don by passage back through time. (Dies December 1, 1981.)

1931   Paleontologist Bryan Patterson publishes a paper in which he describes the auditory region in toxodonts, large hoofed mammals that lived in South America from the Miocene through Pleistocene periods.

1982   Federal District Judge William Ray Overton overturns Arkansas Act 590, the so-called "creationism law," which stated that the biblical account of creation, with the world and its life forms being created over a six-day period, could be taught in school as an alternate scientific view. Says Overton, "Since creation science is not science, the conclusion is inescapable that the only real effect of Act 590 is the advancement of religion."

1993   At a news conference organized by the National Geographic Society, the University of Chicago/Field Museum of Natural History paleontologist Paul C. Sereno announces the discovery of *Eoraptor*, a 230 million-year-old carnivorous dinosaur found in Argentina in October of 1991.

~ 6 ~

1884 Abbott Gregor Johann Mendel, the discoverer of heredity, dies after a long illness in his monastery of Altbrünn, Austria.

1912 Geologist Alfred Wegener reads his paper proposing his new theory of "continental drift" before the Geological Association at Frankfurt-am-Main, Germany. According to his hypothesis, the Earth is a mobile planet on which the continents were once part of an enormous land mass that gradually split apart, the segments eventually drifting to their present locations.

1923 John S. McIntosh is born. Although a physicist by profession, "Jack" McIntosh will become a leading authority on sauropod dinosaurs, naming and describing new taxa and publishing revisions in classification. In 1978 he and Carnegie Museum of Natural History paleontologist David S. Berman will show that the sauropod *Apatosaurus* has had the wrong skull, actually the boxlike skull of *Camarasaurus*, for nearly a century and that the correct one is similar to the more elongate skull of *Diplodocus*. Consequently, museums change the skulls on their *Apatosaurus* skeletal mounts.

1947 Lev Alexandrovich Nessov is born in Tallin, Estonia. Nessov will become an internationally recognized paleontologist, much of his work dealing with fossil vertebrates found in the former Soviet Union. Nessov will author some 160 scientific papers on such diverse subjects as fossil fishes to mammals. He will name several hundred new genera and species and several higher taxa, and discover 80 new dinosaur localities in the USSR. Nessov will become senior scientific researcher at the Laboratory Palaeogeography, Institute of Earth's Crust, in St. Petersburg. His monograph, "Dinosaurs of northern Eurasia: New data about assemblages, ecology, and palaeobiogeography," naming numerous new taxa, is published in 1995 shortly before his death on October 1 of that year.

1992 The discovery of *Eoraptor lansensis*, what seems to be the most primitive known of all dinosaurs, is announced by the National Geographic Society. *Eoraptor* (or "dawn robber") was a small carnivorous animal, in life weighing about 25 pounds. Its almost complete skeleton had been found in October 1991 by Argentinean student Ricardo Martínez in Upper Triassic rocks (about 225 million years old) of the Ischigualasto Valley, during an expedition led by Paul C. Sereno of the University of Chicago and Alfredo M. Monetta of the National University of San Juan. According to Sereno, speaking earlier at a National Geographic Society news conference, "We are just a couple steps away from the ancestor of all dinosaurs."

~ 7 ~

1854 The *Illustrated London News* depicts the famous dinner that was held on New Year's Eve 1853 inside the "mould" of artist Benjamin Waterhouse Hawkins' giant *Iguanodon* sculpture on the Crystal Palace in London. The drawing, showing some of the famous guests inside the mold

and others apparently behind it as waiters serve the lavish meal, will be reprinted again and again in the next century. Designed when known only from meager fossil remains, the *Iguanodon* is incorrectly portrayed as a quadruped and possessing (according to Richard Owen's misinterpretation of what will later be identified as a spiked thumb) a nose horn.

The New Year's Eve (1853) dinner held inside the IGUANODON mold as depicted the next day in the ILLUSTRATED LONDON NEWS.

1934 Alex Raymond's comic strip *Flash Gordon* debuts in newspapers via King Features Syndicate. Most of the action occurs on the planet Mongo, where jagged mountain ranges and battling reptilian monsters suggest Earth in prehistoric times. Primitive Red Monkey Men, sacred Droks (resembling *Stegosaurus*) and theropod-like Horrorsaurs are among Mongo's primitive fauna. This ambience will carry over into the *Flash Gordon* radio series (Mutual, 1935) and also the movie serials made by Universal Pictures starring actor Larry "Buster" Crabbe. The first chapterplay *Flash Gordon* (1936) will feature photographically enlarged iguana lizards dressed up with horns and other appendages and also two theropod-like monsters. *Flash Gordon Conquers the Universe* (1940), the third chapterplay, will have giant iguanas called "iguanthions," their name based on the dinosaur *Iguanodon*.

1954   The Universal-International monster movie *Creature from the Black Lagoon*, having been shot in three dimensions, is successfully sneak previewed at the United Artists Theater in Los Angeles. The movie features the prehistoric "Gill Man," a "missing link" between various groups of animals (apparently fish, amphibian, reptile and human), a Devonian Era relic that has survived in a South American lagoon. The rubber Gill Man costume, made by Bud Westmore and Jack Kevan, is quite convincing compared to most film monsters of the 1950s.

1983   William J. Walker finds giant claws and other remains belonging to a new kind of fish-eating theropod dinosaur at the Ockley Brick Company's claypit near Ockley, Surrey, England. The media will nickname the dinosaur "Claws," after which the animal will be formally named *Baryonyx walkeri* after its discoverer.

1986   A half-scale flying model of the giant "Texas pterosaur" *Quetzalcoatlus northropi* is successfully test-flown at El Mirage Dry Lake, in Death Valley, California. The model, based on fossil remains found recently in Texas, was built for the Smithsonian Institution's Air and Space Museum in Washington, D.C. The figure was visually restored by paleo-artist Gregory S. Paul and the mechanics necessary to make it fly were designed by aerodynamics expert Paul MacCready and his firm AeroVironment, Inc., of Monrovia, California. It was constructed at a cost of $700,000 by MacCready's team of technicians. The model of "QN," with a wingspan of 18 feet and weight of 44 pounds, can reach flight speeds as high as 35 miles per hour, with forward flight activated by the flapping wings.

1993   Paleontologists Paul C. Sereno, Catherine A. Forster, Raymond R. Rogers and Alfredo M. Monetta publish a joint paper naming and describing the small carnivorous dinosaur *Eoraptor lunensis*, from the Upper Triassic Ischigualasto Formation of northwestern Argentina.

~ 8 ~

1823   Alfred Russell Wallace is born. Wallace will become a naturalist who, while working in Malaya (and by a barely credible coincidence), will propose his own theory of evolution, detailed in his essay "On the Tendency of Varieties to Depart Indefinitely from the Original Type," virtually identical to and simultaneously with that of naturalist Charles Darwin. (Dies 1913.)

1909 Pioneer paleontologist Harry Govier Seeley dies. At the time of his death he concurrently holds the titles of Professor of Geology and Professor of Geology and Mineralogy at King's College, London.

1993 The holotype skeleton of *Eoraptor*, partially prepared by William F. Simpson, Bob Masek and Joe Searcy, goes on temporary exhibition in Stanley Field Hall of The Field Museum. Following this relatively brief period of public display, the specimen will be sent to its permanent home, the Museum of Natural Science in San Juan, Argentina.

~ 9 ~

1928 David A. Thomas is born in Pocatello, Idaho. While looking for dinosaur fossils with his son during the 1960s, journalist Thomas will meet Utah State Paleontologist James H. Madsen, Jr., who suggests that Thomas sculpt some dinosaurs for him. This will lead Thomas into a new career of making full-scale dinosaurs, beginning in 1982 with the first life-sized bronze dinosaur model, a *Pentaceratops sternbergii* (nicknamed "Spike") for the about-to-open New Mexico Museum of Natural History in Albuquerque. For a while Thomas will work on the museum staff, after which he will make a full-scale *Gorgosaurus libratus* to face-off "Spike." Among future full-scale dinosaur commissions are: *P. sternbergii* and *Tyrannosaurus rex* for the National Museum of Natural Science, in Taichung, Taiwan; *Maiasaura peeblesorum* pair for the Museum of the Rockies in Bozeman, Montana; *Coelophysis bauri* for the Ghost Ranch Museum, Abiquiu, New Mexico; *Allosaurus fragilis* for the Mitsukoshi Traveling Exhibit, Japan; and *Utahraptor ostrommaysi* for the Utah Field House of Natural History, Vernal, Utah.

1948 Chemist Willard F. Libby, who with assistant E. C. Anderson had already announced his carbon-14 method of dating rocks to a small group of scientists at the University of Chicago, explains the method at an inter-science conference held at the university. As Libby details: Radioactive carbon (or carbon-14) is present, along with normal carbon (carbon-12), in all organic nature. After a plant or animal dies, its carbon-14 begins to disintegrate slowly and steadily, finally transforming into carbon-12. By measuring the amount of carbon-14 disintegration, one can, within limits, calculate the amount of time that has passed since an organism's death. This discovery will be hailed as one of the greatest scientific developments of the decade long before Libby dies in Los Angeles on September 8, 1980.

~ 10 ~

1956   Ernest Untermann, Sr., the "Artist of the Uintas," dies in Vernal, Utah, while working on an unfinished painting of Dyer Mine cabin where he and his son G. E. (Ernest) Untermann had once worked. Before his death he donates more than 100 paintings, murals and panels to the Utah Field House of Natural History in Vernal, Utah.

~ 11 ~

1613   The skeleton of a large mammal with downward curving lower tusks is discovered near the castle of Chaumont in the Dauphiné, near Lyons, France. Similar specimens found in the area over hundreds of years had been regarded as remains of human giants; hence, the surrounding area is known as Champ des Géants. A surgeon named Mazurier will identify this skeleton as that of the giant Cimbrian king Teutobochus. Later it will be correctly identified as *Dinotherium* or "terrible beast," an elephant-like animal of the Tertiary.

1880   Alfred Wegener is born in Germany. Wegener will become a geographer who proposes the theory of "continental drift." According to this theory, the Earth's continents have drifted, via viscous layers of the planet's interior, over millions of years, with different continents eventually being located near the North or South Poles. Wegener's pioneering work will be the foundation for later ideas regarding what will be called "plate tectonics" — that is, continents float along very slowly atop great sheets of the Earth's crust (or tectonic plates) which, in turn, seem to be powered by heat at the Earth's core.

1937   The San Diego Society of Natural History announces that a total of seven small dinosaur models by sculptor J. Elton Green, made under the guidance of paleontologist Charles H. Sternberg and donated by Captain Struan Robertson, will be exhibited at the San Diego Natural History Museum in Balboa Park. The models, five already completed, are to be placed beneath a mounted skeleton of the hadrosaur *Corythosaurus*, collected by Sternberg and his sons.

1986   The New Mexico Museum of Natural History, Albuquerque, opens to the public. Among its popular exhibits are skeletons (in the Hall of Giants) of extinct animals, including a Columbian mammoth; skeletal casts

of Morrison Formation (Upper Jurassic) dinosaurs acquired from DINOLAB; a mural depicting these dinosaurs in life by the Canadian artist Ely (or Eleanor) M. Kish and a "working model" of the inside of a volcano.

1988 "The Dinosaurs," a special exhibition of animatronic prehistoric animals — created by Kokoro, distributed in the United States by Dinamation International Corporation and sponsored by The Friends of the State Museum — opens at the State Museum of Pennsylvania, Harrisburg. All-time attendance records at the museum will be broken.

TYRANNOSAURUS, one of "The Dinosaurs," a 1988 exhibition of figures made by the Kokoro Company (but then distributed by Dinamation International), makes its roaring appearance at the State Museum of Pennsylvania, Harrisburg. Courtesy The Friends of the State Museum.

~ 12 ~

1890 The famous "fossil feud," active for nearly two decades between wealthy, egotistical paleontologists Edward Drinker Cope and Othniel Charles Marsh, erupts in the Sunday-feature pages of the New York *Herald*: "SCIENTISTS WAGE BITTER WARFARE. Prof. Cope of the University of Pennsylvania brings serious charges against Director Powell and Prof. Marsh.

Corroboration in plenty." The article resulted from Cope's outrage over being forced, by a law Marsh had put in the United States Geological Survey's contract, to surrender to the Smithsonian Institution all Cretaceous and Tertiary fossils he had collected while working for the Survey. The feud began in 1868 after Marsh pointed out that Cope had reconstructed a skeleton of the long-necked plesiosaur *Elasmosaurus* with neck and tail interchanged.

1951   Everett Claire Olson publishes a paper based on a study of growth and variation of *Diplocaulus*, a genus of Lower Permian amphibian with a large head shaped somewhat like a boomerang.

1974   "Invasion of the Dinosaurs," a multi-part adventure of the science-fiction series *Dr. Who*, begins airing on British television (BBC). The serial pits the Doctor (John Pertwee) against living prehistoric reptiles.

~ 13 ~

1956   Hans Dieter-Sues is born in Germany. Sues will go on to become a vertebrate paleontologist working on dinosaurs as well as other Mesozoic tetrapods, authoring and co-authoring numerous scientific papers, naming new taxa (including the small plant-eating dinosaur *Zephyrosaurus* and meat-eater *Saurornitholestes*), working for a while at the National Museum of Natural History and subsequently heading the Department of Vertebrate Paleontology at the Royal Ontario Museum in Toronto, Canada. In 1989 Sues and geologist Paul E. Olson will make a major find of mammal-like reptile specimens in Upper Triassic rocks of Richmond, Virginia.

~ 14 ~

1933   Myrl V. Walker of Englewood, Kansas, writes to paleontologist friend Charles Whitney Gilmore seeking employment as a National Park Ranger Naturalist. Walker will get the job and, in May, go to work collecting fossils in the Upper Triassic Chinle Formation at Petrified Forest National Monument in southeastern Arizona. Walker will recover many fossil specimens over the next five years.

1986   Dade County archaeologist Robert S. Carr announces the discovery, made three months earlier in a Florida sinkhole, of a major Ice Age fossil site, perhaps one of the most significant paleontological finds in North America and possibly 10,000 years old. Found here are thousands of well-preserved fossil bone fragments — a few Paleo-Indian, the majority animal (including mammoth, jaguar, dire wolf, bison, rabbit and condor). Evidence suggests that the primitive people ate well, killed with weapons made from limestone and cooked in a fire pit.

~ 15 ~

1961   "The Career of Charles R. Knight" art exhibition, presented by Knight's granddaughter Rhoda (Mrs. Richard Steel), opens at the American Museum of Natural History in New York. Included in this, the first major exhibition of this foremost restorer of extinct life, are original works including drawings, paintings and sculptures done for the American Museum under the direction of paleontologist Barnum Brown and sponsored by financier J. P. Morgan. Photographs of Knight and people with whom he worked are also on display.

1971   Mozambique, a province of Portugal in southeastern Africa on the Pacific, issues a series of nine postage stamps depicting indigenous fossils and also minerals. The fossils shown include the Middle Cretaceous ammonite *Lytodiscoides*, Permian seed-fern *Glossopteris*, Permian dicynodont *Endothiodon* and petrified wood.

1979   Yang Zhungjian (originally spelled Young Chung-Chien), among the most respected of all paleontologists from China, dies in Peking as a result of stomach bleeding.

~ 16 ~

1832   Charles Darwin reaches the Cape Verde Islands aboard the *Beagle*, a survey and research ship of the British government upon which young Darwin will travel around the world for five years. On the islands Darwin observes a white shell bed that was once part of an ancient sea bottom, physical evidence of a changing Earth through the long passage of time.

1968   The Wall Drug Dinosaur — the popular guardian of the South Dakota Badlands, a 37-foot tall, 80-foot long, 50-ton steel and concrete *Apatosaurus* model, construction of which was supervised by Rapid City sculptor Emmett A. Sullivan in the late 1950s — is moved by the Rapp Brothers Moving Co. 150 feet to its new location near Ted Hustead's famous drugstore. Now there will be no obstruction to extending Interstate 90.

The Wall Drug Dinosaur in 1968 being moved to its new and permanent location just outside South Dakota's Badlands National Monument. Courtesy Ted Hustead.

1970 Paleontologist Edwin H. Colbert receives the American Museum of Natural History's Gold Medal award for scientific achievement. For many years Colbert had been Curator of Fossils, Reptiles, and Amphibians at the museum.

~ 17 ~

1937 Dong Zhiming is born in China. A student of and successor to C. C. Young, Dong will become that country's foremost paleontologist specializing in dinosaurs, particularly those of Asia. Dong will work both in the field and in laboratories at the Institute of Palaeontology and Palaeoanthropology of Academia Sineca. During his career Dong will make numerous dinosaur discoveries and author many technical papers, some of them naming and describing new genera and species. He will be responsible for the recovery of a wealth of dinosaur material at the Dashanpu quarry in Zigong. In the early 1990s he will be one of the leaders of the Sino-Canadian Dinosaur Project.

~ 18 ~

1946   John H. Hanley, future invertebrate paleontologist, is born. Hanley will become a research paleontologist with the United States Geological Survey in Denver, Colorado. There he will be responsible for the development of various research programs using biostratigraphy, interpretation and lithofacies analysis. Hanley will be a specialist in fossil mollusks, although his main love will be in teaching paleontology. A major concern of his will be bridging the gap between scientist and layman. (Dies November 18, 1986.)

1989   "Dinosaurs Alive," an exhibition featuring a suite of Dinamation International Corporation's popular robotic dinosaurs, opens at the Palisades Shopping Center in Birmingham, Alabama. The exhibition is presented jointly by The DinoStore, the Red Mountain Museum and Dinamation. Groups are encouraged to visit the mall after hours and "camp out with the dinosaurs."

~ 19 ~

1869   Andrew H. Green, Comptroller of Central Park, responds to a petition, signed by 18 of New York's wealthiest men, promising that "the Commissioners will use their best exertions toward the establishment of a Museum of Natural History." That promised institution will become the American Museum of Natural History. Located on the city's west side across the street from Central Park, the museum will eventually house the world's greatest collection of original dinosaur fossils as well as thousands of other fossil specimens.

1890   The feud between O. C. Marsh and E. D. Cope brews hotter. The *Philadelphia Herald* publishes an entire page of denials by Marsh of various charges made against him earlier by Cope; then Marsh goes on to point out numerous scientific errors made by Cope.

1905   Georg Haas is born in Vienna, Austria. His studies at Vienna University will put him in the midst of many of the most noted Austrian and German paleontologists of his day. Haas will become both a zoologist and a paleontologist. In the early 1930s he will author a classic paper on the ciliate *Ichthyophthirius*, an invertebrate. Particularly interested in fossil reptiles of the Middle East, Haas will subsequently direct his research toward

Mesozoic reptiles and Pleistocene mammals. When Haas dies in Jerusalem on September 13, 1981, it is suddenly and in bed, a book in his hand.

1936   President Franklin Delano Roosevelt dedicates the Roosevelt Memorial Hall (for former President Theodore Roosevelt), a huge room more than 8,000 square feet at the American Museum of Natural History in New York. In November 1991 this hall will be home to the museum's *Barosaurus lentus* skeleton, mounted and displayed in 1991.

1949   Film Classics' *Unknown Island* enjoys its Hollywood premiere following showings in late 1948 in New York City and a minor publicity campaign in California. The first "lost world" type movie made in color, the picture features human actors in prehistoric animal costumes as well as "mechanical" models and puppets, courtesy of special-effects man Ellis Burman and (*very* loosely) based on paintings by Charles R. Knight published in the February 1942 issue of *National Geographic* magazine.

1955   The *Disneyland* television show (ABC) airs the black and white episode "Monsters of the Deep" during its first season. Walt Disney appears on camera with some model dinosaurs, then segues into *A World Is Born*, an edited-down version of the "Rite of Spring" sequence from *Fantasia* with an added informative narration track.
     Same day: Brian Franczak is born in New Britain, Connecticut. Franczak will begin his career as a professional artist around 1987. Having had a general interest in natural history for most of his life, Franczak will find it a logical step to focus upon reconstructing extinct forms of animals and plants. One of his earliest dinosaur-related assignments will be the book *Encyclopedia of Dinosaurs* (1990) for which he provides numerous paintings. In less than a decade Franczak will be regarded as one of the best among the relatively small group of illustrators of ancient life.

~ 20 ~

1934   *Newsweek* announces New York Justice Peter Schmuck's decision in a dinosaur lawsuit. Messmore and Damon, Inc., the makers of the original mechanical dinosaur in 1925, had sued New York stage show producer Earl Carroll for $7,500 in damages. According to Messmore and Damon, Carroll had examined "Dinah," their large *Apatosaurus*, for the purposes of buying the figure for his latest *Vanities* show, which was to include a prehistoric sequence featuring a dinosaur and pretty actress. Carroll then changed his mind and had a competing firm build their own non-mechanical *Apatosaurus*, which Carroll dubbed "Dinny." Messmore and Damon claimed that Carroll had infringed upon their patent; Carroll claimed that his dinosaur was different, being a male, and brought the finished product to court as evidence. Carroll's dinosaur would not fit through the courthouse doors and Justice Schmuck dismissed the complaint.

~ 21 ~

1991   The Japanese Kokoro Company, Ltd., which since the late 1970s has been manufacturing and distributing life-sized robotic prehistoric animals (and for which paleontologist John R. Horner is a consultant), opens a dinosaur exhibition at the San Bernardino County Museum in Redlands, California.

~ 22 ~

1875   D. W. Griffith is born (though some sources give 1874 as his year of birth). David Wark Griffith, who will become one of the key pioneer figures of film history and "invent" much of the visual language of the motion picture, directs two silent pictures set in the Stone Age — *Man's Genesis* (1912) and its sequel *Brute Force*, the latter including a full-sized, moving mock-up of a *Ceratosaurus* as well as some live reptiles dressed up to look prehistoric. After his career is essentially over, Griffith will be brought back to direct the movie *One Million B.C.* (1940), but then leaves, supposedly after a dispute with producer Hal Roach. Though legend will suggest that Griffith directed all or at least part of *One Million B.C.* (a movie similar in many ways to his silent Stone Age movies), he seems to have been involved only with working out the basic storyline and making some casting suggestions. (Dies 1948.)

~ 23 ~

1869   Elmer S. Riggs is born in Trafalgar, Indiana. Riggs will eventually become Curator of Paleontology at what is today The Field Museum. Intrigued by a letter written to him by a Colorado dentist about fossil bones found in the Grand Valley, Riggs will conduct field parties to that area and come back with an impressive collection of Late Jurassic dinosaur specimens. During his career at the museum, he will lead a dozen fossil-collecting expeditions to the southwestern United States, two to Canada and two to Argentina and Bolivia, recovering much fossil vertebrate material for the collections of The

Field Museum. He will be best remembered for naming and describing the new giant sauropod dinosaur *Brachiosaurus*, referring *Brontosaurus* to the genus *Apatosaurus* in 1903 and for the wealth of fossil mammal material collected in South America under his direction. (Dies March 25, 1963.)

1992   Excavation begins of an almost complete mastodon skeleton in Livingston County, Ohio.

1998   "Dinosaurs," an exhibit featuring 14 robotic life-sized dinosaur figures made by the Kokoro Company of Japan, is previewed — including on board a real paleontologist "at work" — for members at the Natural History Museum of Los Angeles County. The exhibit will officially open tomorrow and remain on public view through May 17.

~ 24 ~

1885   The British magazine *Punch* publishes the satiric poem "The Lay of the Trilobite." The nine-verse poem, critical of intellectual conceits, is accompanied by a cartoon depicting scientist Thomas H. Huxley, a champion of Darwin's theory of evolution, conversing with a eurypterid (not a trilobite, but another kind of fossil arthropod).

1954   The children's television series *Rod Brown of the Rocket Rangers* (CBS), a continuing space opera starring young Cliff Robertson in the title role, telecasts live the episode "Operation Dinosaur." A time machine sends Rod and a fellow Ranger back to the dinosaur age. Special effects are meager, but youthful and unjaded viewers believe what they see on their black and white screens.

1978   Roland T. Bird, fossil collector for the American Museum of Natural History and right-hand field man of Barnum Brown, dies at his Homestead, Florida, home.

1994   Cable television's Sci-Fi Channel and Turner Network Television ("Godzillabash 1994") offer a week's worth (a total of 10) of Toho monster movies.

~ 25 ~

1939   President Franklin Delano Roosevelt establishes Badlands National Monument in South Dakota. Petitions by the state legislature to establish this area as a national monument had started as early as 1909. Also known as the Big Badlands or White River Badlands, this mostly barren haven for fossil collecting lies mostly in the southwestern quarter of the state in the White, Bad and Cheyenne rivers drainages. Fossil treasures collected here include some excellent skeletons of Oligocene mammals like small oreodonts, giant pigs and the horned brontotheres, some of which are exhibited at the Museum of Geology at the South Dakota School of Mines and Technology in nearby Rapid City.

Woodcut made for Edward Drinker Cope depicting his ELASMOSAURUS as incorrectly reconstructed with neck and tail transposed.

1986 "Discovering Dinosaurs" opens officially at the Academy of Natural Sciences of Philadelphia, "the oldest institution in continuous existence in the western hemisphere devoted to research and education in the natural sciences." The highlight of this permanent exhibition is the thoroughly renovated dinosaur hall which had remained virtually unchanged for decades. The new exhibit features original skeletons and casts of skeletons remounted by paleontologist Kenneth Carpenter to reflect modern paleontological ideas. Included is Carpenter's dynamic mount of *Tyrannosaurus rex* (a cast of the American Museum of Natural History skeleton), considered by many scientists and laymen to be the best mounted skeletal display of *T. rex* in the world. Also featured are dinosaurs found and described during the earliest days of collecting in North America including *Hadrosaurus foulkii*, found and described by Academy curator Joseph Leidy in 1858. Another historical highlight is the famous skeleton of *Elasmosaurus platyurus* on which Edward D. Cope mounted the skull at the tail end. Computers and other high-tech presentations bring the old bones into the modern world.

~ 26 ~

1884 Roy Chapman Andrews is born. Andrews will become a member of the scientific staff of the American Museum of Natural History. Inspired by William Diller Matthew's theory that the origins of mankind are to be found in Asia, the flamboyant Andrews will have grand ideas to explore the Gobi desert. The mission will become the first Central Asiatic Expedition of the American Museum, led by Andrews. Though early hominid fossils are not found, the expedition makes significant Late Cretaceous discoveries including remains of the primitive horned dinosaur *Protoceratops* and the first verifiable dinosaur eggs. Andrews will author some scientific papers about fossil animals but will best be known to young readers as author of the book *All About Dinosaurs* (1953). In later years people will describe Andrews as a kind of real life "prototype" for movie hero Indiana Jones. (Dies 1960.)

1959 *Life* magazine publishes "Strange Creatures of a Lost World," an article about prehistoric mammals written by Lincoln Barnett. The article is illustrated with new paintings by Rudolph F. Zallinger, his first such work for the periodical in over half a decade.

1937 Bryan Patterson names and describes *Barylamda*, an eight-foot-long Paleocene pantodont (a kind of primitive hoofed mammal) from the late Paleocene of North America.

~ 27 ~

1881 J. W. Hulke, one of the early paleontologists who started his career as a doctor of medicine, names and describes the new armored dinosaur *Polacanthus* before colleagues in England. The dinosaur is unusual in possessing a "sacral shield" — a shield of bone over the back and hip region. Not until a century later will other kinds of dinosaurs be found possessing such a shield.

1851 The Academy of Sciences in Paris, France, receives the first bones and eggs of a giant (more than 10 feet tall) Pleistocene flightless bird from Madagascar. Isidore Geoffroy Saint Hilaire, who receives the material at the Academy, describes these fossils as belonging to a new genus and species which he names *Aepyornis maximus*, incorrectly believing it to be related to the modern ostrich.

1922 William J. Turnbull is born in Milwaukee, Wisconsin. Turnbull will become a paleontologist anchored at the Field Museum of Natural History (later The Field Museum) where he will specialize in fossil mammals and be instrumental in the mounting of some of the institution's fine fossil exhibits. Eventually he will be given the title Curator Emeritus at the museum.

~ 28 ~

Paleontologist Chester Stock with Ice Age fossils collected from the Rancho La Brea "tar pits." Courtesy George C. Page Museum of La Brea Discoveries.

1892   Chester Stock is born in San Francisco. Stock will become the major collector of Pleistocene fossils at the Rancho La Brea "tar pits" in Hancock Park, Los Angeles, California. In 1930 Stock will author the monograph *Rancho La Brea: A Record of Pleistocene Life in America*, the first comprehensive account of the fossils from the "tar pits," going through six revisions over the next three decades. He will supervise the construction of the Observation Pit and preparation of the short-faced bear and Harlan's ground sloth statues in Hancock Park. In 1949 he will become Head of the Science Division of the Natural History Museum of Los Angeles County where the Rancho La Brea collection was originally housed. Stock will die of a brain hemorrhage on December 7, 1950.

1921   Nicholas Hotton III is born in Michigan. Hotton will become a paleontologist specializing in amphibians and reptiles, particularly therapsids or mammal-like reptiles. In the 1960s he will be made Associate Curator and then Curator of Fossil Amphibians and Reptiles at the United States National Museum, where he becomes a driving force in the modernization of the museum's dinosaur exhibits. Hotton will author numerous technical papers, many of them focusing upon the role of functional anatomy in the evolution of amphibians and reptiles. Much of his work in the field will be in South Africa collecting mammal-like reptiles. Hotton's major dinosaur-related contribution will be the theory that dinosaurs migrated in and out of the Arctic Circle on a seasonal basis.

~ 29 ~

1915   Victor Mature is born (though some sources give 1916 as his birth date.) Mature will become a movie star specializing in active leading-man roles, his first important part being the lead character in the 1940 Stone Age epic *One Million B.C.* As caveman hero Tumak, Mature will create a classic role in a Hollywood-manufactured prehistoric world of dinosaurs, mammoths, giant lizards and an erupting volcano.

Caveman Tumak (Victor Mature) bravely protects his mate Loana (Carole Landis) from an attacking oversized iguana lizard in the movie ONE MILLION B.C. *(1940) © United Artists.*

1986   Scientists announce the discovery of the largest fossil find ever made in North America — over 10,000 pieces of fossilized bone found in Nova Scotia of Late Triassic to Early Jurassic age. Field work is carried out in cooperation with the Nova Scotia Museum, Halifax, and paid for by the National Geographic Society. Fossils that will be recovered here include 12 skulls and jaws of tritheledont reptiles, animals thought to be closely related to mammals. Other material from this site includes bones and teeth of early crocodiles, lizards, sharks and primitive fish. Most surprising will be a series of penny-sized dinosaur footprints, the smallest yet discovered. The fossils have been found at what is believed to be the Triassic-Jurassic boundary, described by Paul E. Olson and Neil H. Shubin, the scientists who made the discovery, as "a time of mass extinction" and also "the emergence of the modern world."

~ 30 ~

1998 "Dinosaurs," an exhibit featuring 14 robotic life-sized dinosaur figures made by the Kokoro Company of Japan, appears, is previewed — including on board a real paleontologist "at work" — for members at the Natural History Museum of Los Angeles County. The exhibit will officially open tomorrow and remain on public view through May 17.

~ 31 ~

1768 Resident agent for the Pennsylvania colony, Benjamin Franklin, who had been shipped some of the fossils collected in 1766 from Big Bone Lick in Kentucky, writes to astronomer Abbé Chappe d'Auteroche in Paris and discusses the material, asking if the teeth may be linked in some way to large ivory tusks being found in Siberia and then sold on the marketplace. The Abbé Chappe will reply that, although similar, the Big Bone Lick and Siberian specimens are different, though both undoubtedly are remains of creatures that had drowned during Noah's Flood.

Actors wearing uncomfortable CERATOSAURUS outfits (made from latex-covered canvas) on location in Palmdale, California, during the filming of UNKNOWN ISLAND (1948), using crew personnel as resting posts. The movie opened in Hollywood on January 19, 1949. ©Film Classics.

FEBRUARY

~ 1 ~

1900 Paleontologist John Bell Hatcher, a former field collector for O. C. Marsh, joins the staff of the Carnegie Museum of Natural History in Pittsburgh.

1906 Elmer S. Riggs, now Assistant Curator, Division of Paleontology at the Field Columbian Museum, names and describes *Basilemys sinuosus*, a new species of fossil tortoise, based upon a well-preserved (but somewhat flattened) shell discovered in the Laramie Beds of Montana.

1936 A monograph on *Apatosaurus*, written by United States National Museum paleontologist Charles Whitney Gilmore, is published. This major study includes some of the first accurate illustrations of the postcranial skeleton of this gigantic dinosaur.

1973 Zambia, a republic in south-central Africa, apparently in commemorating the geological survey of Zambia's collection of fossils from the (Late Paleozoic age) Luangwa Valley in 1972, issues five postage stamps depicting fossils, most of them from that region. The suite includes the (Permian Period) seed-fern *Glossopteris*; dicynodont *Oudenodon* versus gorgonopsid reptile *Rubidgea*; dicynodont *Zambiasaurus*; and carnivorous mammal-like reptile *Liuangwa* and the (Middle to Late Pleistocene) so-called Broken Hill Man, whose skull was found in 1921.

1991 The American Museum of Natural History closes its two dinosaur halls to the public for modern renovation. Plans to redo these halls date back to 1986 and will cost the Museum $48 million. The halls, arranged more or less chronologically, had remained virtually unchanged for almost half a century, during which time much of their information became dated. The halls will remain closed for four years, during which time they will be expanded upon and revamped to reflect modern paleontological knowledge and theories.

1997   "The Dinosaurs of Jurassic Park" exhibit, based on the blockbuster motion picture *Jurassic Park*, continues its tour, this time opening at the Cincinnati Museum Center, Cincinnati, Ohio. The exhibit, which has been approved by the movie's director Steven Spielberg, features such items from the film as props, full-size dinosaur reproductions, casts of skeletons, photographs and storyboard artwork.

Motion picture director Cecil B. DeMille with actress Anna Q. Nilsson in front of a fanciful TRICERATOPS skeleton on the museum set of the silent movie ADAM'S RIB (1923). © Paramount Pictures.

~ 2 ~

1844   Richard Owen, having evaluated two cases worth of bones belonging to a giant Pleistocene flightless bird, names the creature *Dinornis* (meaning "terrible bird") and lectures about it at the Royal Institution in London. At the same time Owen assigns six species to this genus.

1966   The Japanese television series *Ultra Q*, produced by Eiji Tsuburaya's new studio Tsuburaya Productions, debuts with the episode "Gomes vs. Litra," in which the giant monster Gomes is awakened by workers digging a railway tunnel. Gomes is a revamped and disguised Godzilla suit that was originally used in the movie *Godzilla vs. the Thing*.

1992   The video documentary *Dinosaur Movies* begins shooting in Don Glut's Burbank, California, home (the people outside observing Groundhog Day.) The documentary has evolved from the lecture "Fantasy Dinosaurs of the Movies" and song "Dinosaur Movies," the latter originally featured on the first *Dinosaur Tracks* cassette.

~ 3 ~

1790   Gideon Algernon Mantell is born in Lewes, England. Mantell, who will become both a physician and pioneer fossil hunter, will name and describe *Iguanodon*, the second dinosaur so treated in a publication. He will be instrumental in securing the purchase of the so-called Maidstone *Iguanodon* for the British Museum (Natural History) in 1834, see his book *The Wonders of Geology* published in 1838 and be awarded the Gold Medal by the Royal Society of London in 1849. (Dies November 10, 1852.)

1855   *Punch* publishes a cartoon titled "The Effects of a Hearty Dinner after Visiting the Antediluvian Department at the Crystal Palace." It shows a sleeping man having nightmares of prehistoric animals and other scary images after a trip to the park that opened in June of the previous year.

~ 4 ~

1923   *Adam's Rib*, a silent movie produced and directed by Cecil B. DeMille for Paramount Pictures, premieres in Hollywood, California, including scenes set among dinosaur skeletons in a museum and a flashback to cave people in the Stone Age. The film will officially open on March 5. (Two years later *The Vanishing American*, another DeMille-directed Paramount movie, will feature a sequence about prehistoric people.)

1973   "The World of Charles Robert Knight" exhibition opens at the Columbus Museum of Arts and Crafts in Columbus, Georgia. "An exhibition honoring the distinguished scientist, illustrator, artist and naturalist," the show includes paintings, sculptures, lithographs, drawings and color sketches by Knight.

~ 5 ~

1963   Paleontologist Barnum Brown, the American Museum of Natural History's greatest collector of dinosaur fossils, dies.

~ 6 ~

1973   The German Democratic Republic issues six postage stamps depicting fossils housed in the Natural History Museum in East Berlin. Images in this series include the trilobite *Odontopleura*; conifer *Lebachia* (Carboniferous and Permian period); fern-like plant *Sphenopteris* (Carboniferous Period); fern *Boytopteris* (Permian); pterosaur *Pterodactylus* (Upper Jurassic to Lower Cretaceous periods) and ancient bird *Archaeopteryx* (Late Jurassic).

~ 7 ~

1812   Charles Dickens is born in Portsea, England. Dickens' place in paleontological history will remain secure as the first author to mention a dinosaur in a work of fiction — *Bleak House*, published in 1853. (Dies June 9, 1870.)

1925   Raymond A. Dart, Professor of Anatomy at Witwatersand University in Johannesburg, South Africa, announces his opinion as to the identity of a small, human-like skull that he obtained the year before. "The specimen is of importance because it exhibits an extinct race of apes intermediate between living anthropoid race and man" in South Africa, he states. The skull, discovered by quarryman M. de Bruyn in a lime deposit near Taung, is that of an apelike creature about six years old at the time of death. The specimen will be named *Australopithecus africanus*. In popular vernacular it is the "Taung child" or "Taung baby."

1929   Edgar Rice Burroughs finishes writing the novel *Tarzan at the Earth's Core*, a "cross-over" between his Apeman hero Tarzan and Pellucidar series and destined to become one of the most popular entries of either. The Apeman journeys aboard a huge airship to Pellucidar, a subsurface world inhabited by various prehistoric creatures (including a *Stegosaurus* that can lower its dorsal plates to a horizontal position and glide through the air.)

1951   James O. Farlow is born in Greensburg, Indiana. Farlow will specialize in ichnology or the study of trace fossils, particularly footprints. Among his accomplishments will be authoring numerous scientific papers on fossil tracks (as well as other aspects of paleontology, including behavior). He will co-author a paper that gives the name *Brontopodus birdi* to the famous series of sauropod tracks collected in the 1930s by Roland T. Bird along the Paluxy River in Texas. *The Complete Dinosaur*, a major book edited by Farlow and Michael K. Brett-Surman, and featuring articles written by numerous dinosaur authorities, will be published in 1997.

1983   Paleontologists Alan J. Charig and Angela C. Milner visit Surrey, England, and find new remains belonging to the fish-eating dinosaur *Baryonyx walkeri*.

~ 8 ~

1828   Jules Verne, the "French Father of Science Fiction," is born in Nantes, France. Among Verne's fantastic novels will be *Voyage au centre de la terre* (English title: *A Journey to the Center of the Earth*), first published in 1864.

The tale is based somewhat upon earlier stories about a hollow Earth sometimes inhabited by monsters. In Verne's variation on this theme, explorers discover a vast subsurface lake where an ichthyosaur and plesiosaur battle each other. This scene was probably inspired by an engraving by Edouard Riou, who around the same time also illustrates Verne's stories published in Guillaume Louis Figuier's 1863 book *La Terre avant le Déluge* (*The Earth Before the Deluge*). Verne's story will be a popular one, reprinted and translated many times.

Artist Edouard Riou's ichthyosaur fighting plesiosaur illustration for Guillaume Louis Figuier's LA TERRE AVANT LE DÉLUGE *(1863), probably an influence on Jules Verne's novel* VOYAGE AU CENTRE DE LA TERRE *(A JOURNEY TO THE CENTER OF THE EARTH).*

It will later be adapted to various media including a well-made Hollywood movie released by 20th Century–Fox in 1959 and a television cartoon series from Filmation Associates. (Dies March 24, 1905.)

1855 The first public function, a trade exhibition, is held at the "Castle," the original building of the Smithsonian Institution.

1991 Mark International opens the Dino Gallery in Beverly Hills, California, displaying original paintings and sculptures by artists who specialize in restoring extinct animals. Opening night is a gala affair packed with celebrities in the dinosaur-art field. Other Dino Galleries are scheduled to open elsewhere, including Japan.

~ 9 ~

1856 The *Illustrated London News* alleges that a live pterodactyl has appeared in Culmont (Haute Marner), France. Supposedly the creature had emerged from a block of stone before a group of startled workers, who had been blasting out a tunnel to unite the St. Dizier and Nancy railways. "This creature," the story purports, "which belongs to the class of animals hitherto considered to be extinct, has a very long neck, and a mouth filled with sharp teeth. It stands on four long legs, which are united together by two membranes, doubtless intended to support the animal in the air, and are armed with four claws terminated by long and crooked talons. Its general form resembles that of a bat, differing only in its size, which is that of a large goose. Its membraneous wings, when spread out, measure from tip to tip three metres twenty-two centimetres. Its color is a livid black; its skin is naked, thick and oily; its intestines only contained a colorless liquid like clear water. On reaching the light, this monster gave some signs of life, by shaking its wings, but soon after expired, uttering a hoarse cry." The article goes on to say that the creature has been identified as a *Pterodactyl* and that the Lias-age rock which contained it "forms an exact hollow mold of its body, which indicates that it was completely enveloped with a sedimentary deposit." There will be no followup articles.

1928 Frank Frazetta is born in Chicago, Illinois. With his bold and romantic style, artist Frazetta will become one of the most respected and imitated artists of stories featuring heroic, powerful and savage characters. In 1952 he will create (both writing and drawing) the comic-book series *Thun'da*, about an American pilot stranded in a prehistoric land somewhere in Africa. The series, though short-lived, will inspire a less grandiose movie serial featuring cavemen but no dinosaurs, *King of the Congo*, made by Columbia Pictures in 1952 and starring Buster Crabbe. In the 1960s Frazetta will become the main successor to J. Allen St. John and be regarded as one of the top illustrators of Edgar Rice Burroughs stories (e.g., *Tarzan at the Earth's Core*, *Back to the Stone Age*, *Land of Terror* and *Savage Pellucidar*).

Much of Frazetta's art for Burroughs' and other writers' stories will feature dinosaurs and other extinct creatures.

1938   The movie *Bringing Up Baby*, considered by many film buffs as the all-time classic "screwball comedy," is previewed in New York, N.Y. The RKO picture stars Cary Grant as a flustered and frustrated zoologist, just one of his problems being a dog's theft of the only remaining bone required to complete his museum's "*Brontosaurus*" (or *Apatosaurus*) mounted skeleton. The museum set features prop dinosaur skeletons that will be recycled for various future pictures (e.g., *Once Upon a Time, On the Town, Zombies on Broadway* and *The Beast from 20,000 Fathoms*) and television shows (e.g., *Batman*). Some of the stop-motion models from *King Kong* and *The Son of Kong* can also be spotted in the museum set.

1990   Paleontologist Masahiro Sato discovers an incomplete tooth of the Early Cretaceous carnivorous dinosaur *Wakinosaurus* in Japan. The find is significant as being one of the very few dinosaurs known from Japan.

~ 10 ~

1825   Gideon Mantell recounts his discovery of *Iguanodon* in an address titled "Notice on the *Iguanodon*, a Newly-Discovered Fossil Reptile, from the Sandstone of Tilgate Forest, in Sussex" before the Royal Society of London and published in the *Philosophical Transactions of the Royal Society*.

The name for this animal, meaning "iguana tooth," was suggested by Mantell's friend and fellow English paleontologist Reverend William Daniel Conybeare. It was so named because its teeth appeared to Mantell to be those of a giant iguana lizard.

1906   Lon Chaney, Jr., is born Creighton Chaney in

Akhoba (Lon Chaney, Jr.), leader of the brutal Rock Tribe, is gored by a prop musk ox in the movie ONE MILLION B.C. *(1940). © United Artists.*

Oklahoma City, Oklahoma. Chaney will become a character actor best known for his starring and supporting roles in horror movies. His first major "make-up" role will be that of the older caveman Akhoba in *One Million B.C.* (United Artists 1940). Although Chaney, emulating his father Lon Chaney, Sr., creates his own make-up for this movie, union restriction will prevent its use. In the late 1950s the actor will play another caveman, this one thawed out of Ice Age ice to cause comedy havoc in a modern home in a live skit on *The Red Skelton Show*, telecast on CBS. (Dies July 12, 1973.)

1933 A radio presentation publicizing *King Kong* is broadcast over NBC, written by Russell Birdwell, featuring interviews with producer Merian C. Cooper and special-effects wizard Willis O'Brien, and including soundtrack bits from the 1933 movie.

1953 William F. Simpson is born in Bryan, Ohio. Simpson will become a paleontologist specializing in fossil mammals and work as a laboratory technician and chief preparator at The Field Museum. Much of his work at the Chicago museum, however, will involve dinosaurs, largely due to the public's enormous interest in the Mesozoic reptiles.

1961 *Gorgo*, a motion picture produced by the King Brothers, is released by Metro-Goldwyn-Mayer. Directed by Eugene Lourie (in his third go-round with this theme), the movie is about a gigantic prehistoric reptile that smashes her way through London to retrieve juvenile offspring "Gorgo," who has been captured and made a carnival attraction. The picture features spectacular special effects and one of the best-ever dinosaur-type monsters played by a human actor wearing a rubber costume. It will spawn a paperback novel plus a comic-book adaptation and series.

~ 11 ~

1904 Konstantin Konstantinovich Flerov is born in Moscow. Among his accomplishments, Flerov will be supervisor and main scientific organizer of various collective monographs on fossil mammals, including "Zoogeography of the Asian Paleogene" (1974) and "European Bison" (1979). Becoming an artist as well as a paleontologist, Flerov will also be noted for his reconstructions of extinct animals designed for the Palaeontological Institute Museum. (Dies July 26, 1980.)

1947 Seriozha (also Sergei) M. Kurzanov is born in the Soviet Union. Kurzanov will become a paleontologist specializing in the fossil vertebrates of Mongolia, particularly carnivorous dinosaurs. Among the new taxa to be named and described by him will be two new theropod genera — the tyrannosaurid *Alioramus remotus* and ostrich-like dinosaur *Avimimus portentosus*.

1993 "The Dinosaurs of Jurassic Park" exhibit opens at the Fort Worth Museum of Science and History, Fort Worth, Texas, this being the third destination for the touring exhibit.

~ 12 ~

1809 Charles Robert Darwin is born in Shrewsbury, England (sharing his birthday with future United States President Abraham Lincoln). Darwin is the son of Dr. Robert Darwin and grandson of Dr. Erasmus Darwin, both physicians, the latter believing that all life can be traced back to a single living filament. Charles will become a naturalist hailed as one of the greatest scientific thinkers of the 19th, or any, century. His theory of evolution through natural selection will have lasting and often controversial impact upon the world. Among his many published works will be the goundbreaking books *The Origin of Species* (1859) and *The Descent of Man* (1871). (Dies April 19, 1882.)

1873 Barnum Brown (named for showman P. T. Barnum) is born in Carbondale, Kansas. Brown will become a paleontologist famous as the greatest collector of dinosaur bones in history. He will begin his long-time association with the American Museum of Natural History in 1897 as the assistant of Professor Henry Fairfield Osborn, Curator of the Department of Vertebrate Paleontology. Diplomatic (and usually well dressed), Brown

Paleontologist Barnum Brown with the skeleton of TYRANNOSAURUS REX *he discovered in Montana in 1908, as mounted at the American Museum of Natural History. Courtesy Edwin H. Colbert and American Museum of Natural History.*

will travel the world hunting for dinosaur skeletons on behalf of the museum. Many classic dinosaurs, including the celebrated *Tyrannosaurus rex*, will be discovered and collected through Brown's efforts. His success in fossil-collecting in Canada will inspire that country to begin its own major collecting. The American Museum's Tyrannosaur Hall, dominated by the mounted skeleton of *T. rex* and showcasing many superb specimens collected under his supervision, will remain for decades a life-long monument to Barnum Brown. (Dies 1963.)

~ 13 ~

1988 A bigger-than-life sauropod dinosaur appears in the uncharacteristically cold environment of Calgary, Canada. In actuality it is a giant inflated float partaking, amidst chuck wagons and mounted cowboys, in the Winter Olympics parade.

~ 14 ~

1885 *Punch* publishes the eight-verse poem "Ballad of the Ichthyosaurus" in which the so-called "fish lizard" reptile laments the disparity between its eye and brain size. A cartoon showing the animal in a classroom wearing a graduation cap accompanies the poem.

The giant ground sloth, as apishly portrayed by Ray "Crash" Corrigan, makes its first appearance in the movie UNKNOWN ISLAND *(1948). © Film Classics.*

1907 Ray Corrigan is born (né Raymond Bernard) in Milwaukee, Wisconsin. The future athletic "Crash" Corrigan will become a motion picture actor known best for Westerns and serials, but also will enjoy a side career playing gorillas and other apelike creatures in costumes of his own design, some in films with prehistoric themes. He will play the gorilla in *Three Missing Links* (1938), *Dr. Renault's Secret* (1942) and *Captive Wild Woman* (1943), the former a Three Stooges comedy short, the latter two about mad scientists speeding up evolution by transforming apes into humans. *White Pongo* (1945) will feature Corrigan as a white-furred "missing link" between ape and man. In *Unknown Island* (1948) "Crash" will portray a prehistoric giant ground sloth that fights and kills a *Ceratosaurus*. As a turnabout, Corrigan will portray a human killed by a giant prehistoric man in *Killer Ape* (1953). (Dies August 10, 1976.)

1971   Russ Manning gives a Valentine's Day gift to prehistoric-creature fans as he starts off a new and lengthy storyline in the *Tarzan* newspaper comic strip in which the Apeman encounters dinosaurs — including the *Gryf*, a kind of evolved *Triceratops* possessing sharp teeth and *Stegosaurus*-type dorsal plates — and other prehistoric animals, primitive humanoid races and more primal threats in the lost land of Pal-ul-Don — which was originally featured in Edgar Rice Burroughs' novel *Tarzan the Terrible* (1921). In 1986, Blackthorne Publishing will reprint Manning's lovingly illustrated adventure in book form.

1987   "They're Alive! An Earthshaking Encounter with Real Dinosaurs," an exhibition of robot dinosaurs from Dinamation International Corporation, opens at the Cleveland Museum of Natural History. A score of "Dinosaur Happenings" is scheduled to coincide with the exhibition.

~ 15 ~

1986   "Dinosaurs Past and Present," a touring art exhibition featuring the best old and modern examples of restorations of extinct life, debuts at the Natural History Museum of Los Angeles County accompanied by a symposium in which artists and paleontologists participate. Among the artists represented are Sylvia Czerkas, Stephen A. Czerkas, Benjamin Waterhouse Hawkins, Charles R. Knight, Gregory S. Paul, Rudolph F. Zallinger, Jean Day Zallinger, Robert T. Bakker, John Gurche, Mark Hallett, William Stout, Douglas Henderson, Kenneth Carpenter, Margaret Colbert, Eleanor M. Kish and Archibald M. Willard. *Dinosaurs Past and Present*, edited by sculptor and exhibition organizer Sylvia Czerkas and paleontologist Everett C. Olson, will be published as a two-volume set in 1987 containing the formally written papers and reproductions of much of the art.

~ 16 ~

1877   Edward Drinker Cope names and describes the giant *Dystrophaeus*, the first sauropod dinosaur found in the New World and second dinosaur of any kind found in the western United States, before the American Philosophical Society in Philadelphia. It is based on well-preserved but scanty remains found in 1859 by geologist John S. Newberry at an unspecified site in Painted Canyon, Wayne County, Utah. Not until 1989 will the rediscovery of the site locality be announced by those who found it — David D. Gillette, Francis A. Barnes, Lynette J. Gillette and John S. McIntosh.

~ 17 ~

1970   The television special *The Man Hunters*, advertised as "a scientific detective story" that "probes the evolution of modern man," airs on NBC. Producers Nicolas Noxon and Irwin Rosten have based their script on the book *Early Man*. The program is narrated by actor E. G. Marshall.

1992   A special event is held at the *Coelophysis* quarry at Ghost Ranch, New Mexico. Paleontologist David D. Gillette of the New Mexico Museum of Natural History leads the event. Edwin H. Colbert, who led the American Museum of Natural History excavations at this site beginning in the late 1940s, recounts to an assemblage of scientists and other interested parties his experiences of that time.

~ 18 ~

1839   Harry Govier Seeley is born in England. Seeley will become one of the founding fathers of paleontology, specializing in fossil reptiles. In 1887 Seeley will publish a paper titled "On the Classification of the Fossil Animals Commonly Named Dinosauria," a revolutionary concept in dinosaur classification. In this Seeley writes that "the Dinosauria has no existence as a natural group of animals, but includes two distinct types of animal structure with technical characters in common, which show their descent from a common ancestry rather than their close affinity. These two orders of animals may be conveniently named the Ornithischia and the Saurischia." Seeley's idea that there are two separate "orders" of dinosaurs (the Ornithischia or "bird-hipped" and Saurischia or "lizard hipped," so named because the arrangement of their pelvic bones resemble that, respectively, in birds and lizards) will not be seriously contested — and found to be in error — for almost a century, when Richard Owen's Dinosauria is reinstated as a real group. Seeley's book on pterosaurs, *Dragons of the Air* (1901, to be reprinted by Dover in 1967), will become a classic. (Dies January 8, 1909.)

1928   John H. Ostrom is born. Ostrom will specialize in dinosaurs, go on to become Curator of Vertebrate Paleontology at the Peabody Museum of Natural History and become a key figure in modern interpretations of dinosaurs. During his years at Yale, Professor Ostrom will become an authority on the Jurassic bird *Archaeopteryx*. Research by Ostrom in the late 1960s through 1970s, primarily his work on *Archaeopteryx* and the sickle-clawed carnivorous dinosaur *Deinonychus*, will directly lead to conclusions suggesting that theropods are ancestral to birds, that at least some kinds of dinosaurs were quite active animals and that all or some may have been warm-blooded. Ostrom's groundbreaking work in these areas will stimulate other paleontologists to take these ideas even further, thereby planting the seeds for the so-called "Dinosaur Renaissance" of the 1970s.

~ 19 ~

1868 William Diller Matthew is born in Saint John, New Brunswick, Canada. "Will" Matthew will enjoy careers as both a geologist and paleontologist. Around the turn of the century he will become a collector and prolific writer about extinct life, particularly fossil mammals. In 1895 his work as a professional paleontologist will begin when he is appointed to a staff position at the American Museum of Natural History. His writings on fossil mammals and other topics will be published in both technical and popular journals, the latter intended to instruct the public on various topics ranging from new fossil finds to the museum's exhibits. Matthew will be best known for his most popular work *Climate and Evolution*, which he writes in 1915. (Dies September 24, 1930.)

Portrait of paleontologist William Diller Matthew taken in 1928. Courtesy Edwin H. Colbert.

1944 "Dinosaur" Don Glut is hatched ... that is, born on an Army base in Pecos, Texas. He will waste approximately six years of life before realizing and acting upon his love for dinosaurs. In later years he will author a book about dates relating to things prehistoric.

1989 Michael K. Brett-Surman receives the first "dinosaur" Ph.D. degree ever given at the Smithsonian Institution, Washington, D.C. His master's thesis — "A Revision of the Hadrosauridae (Reptilia: Ornithischia) and Their Evolution During the Campanian and Maastrichtian" — having been written while attending the Graduate School of Arts and Sciences of George Washington University, is a comprehensive study of duckbilled dinosaurs.

~ 20 ~

1824 Dean William Buckland announces *Megalosaurus*, the first dinosaur named and described, to the Geological Society of London. Buckland's description of this carnivorous animal appears later this year as "Notice on the Megalosaurus or Great Fossil Lizard of Stonesfield" in the *Transactions* of the Geological Society. Based on a leg bone, Buckland fairly closely estimates its size: "From these dimensions as compared with the ordinary standard of the lizard family, a length exceeding 40 feet and a bulk equal to that of an elephant seven feet high have been assigned by Cuvier to the individual to which this bone belonged."

1925 *The Lost World*, First National's silent-movie adaptation of the novel by Sir Arthur Conan Doyle premieres on Broadway highlighted by the special-effects work featuring dinosaur models sculpted by Marcel Delgado and animated by Willis O'Brien. The movie, including its "prehistoric lost land," "erupting volcano" and "giant monster loose in a city" themes, though new in 1925, will become fantasy-movie clichés in the years ahead.

1946 The PRC releases *The Flying Serpent*, a "potboiler" horror movie about a prehistoric feathered reptile once worshipped by the Aztecs as the god Quetzalcoatl. The creature now guards an Aztec treasure and is utilized by a mad scientist (played by George Zucco) to dispose of those he believes are out to steal "his" treasure. The prop monster was made by future make-up wizard Bud Westmore.

1985 Museum of Western Colorado director Michael L. Perry holds a news conference to announce the signing of a three-year lease-purchase for the old J. C. Penney building on Grand Junction's Main Street, a lease-purchase agreement with Dinamation International Corporation for six robotic prehistoric creatures and construction for the new Dinosaur Valley exhibit to be housed in the building.

~ 21 ~

1903 John Bell Hatcher names the new Jurassic sauropod dinosaur *Haplocanthus*, established on two partial skeletons found in Colorado. Upon discovering that the name *Haplocanthus* is preoccupied (or already in use) for a genus of fossil fish, Hatcher, in a note added to the original paper in which he describes this dinosaur, promptly renames it *Haplocanthosaurus*.

1933 The United States Patent Office grants George Messmore, the inventor half of Messmore and Damon (a company specializing in the manufacture and exhibition of animated prehistoric and also modern animals), a patent for the head-movement device he designed and built for the company's near life-sized mechanized *Apatosaurus*, the first moving dinosaur figure ever made. Until now, he had kept the inner workings of this creature a secret. Now, protected by law in the United States and Britain. Messmore will reveal his secrets in various published articles.

1949 Frank Brunner is born in Brooklyn, New York. Brunner's work as an artist will include book, magazine and comic-book illustration, animation, television and motion-picture storyboards, conceptual design and paintings. Much of his work will involve dinosaurs and other prehistoric creatures. He will become a character designer for the *Dino-Riders* television cartoons, an artist for the *Jurassic Park* trading cards, dinosaur illustrator for the movie *Dinosaur Valley Girls*, and creator of the *DinoForce* animation and live-action projects.

1954 The "Gill Man," star of the new movie *Creature from the Black Lagoon*, makes a surprise appearance on the *The Colgate Comedy Hour* live television show (NBC), menacing Lou Costello. Wearing the Creature suit is Ben Chapman, the tall ex–Marine-turned-actor who also played the character in the film in scenes shot on land.

~ 22 ~

1875 Charles Lyell, the "Father of Geology," dies in England. The inscription on his tomb at Westminster Abbey will include the following: "Throughout a long and laborious life he sought the means of deciphering the Earth's history in the patient investigation of the present order of Nature. Enlarging the boundaries of knowledge and leaving on scientific thought an enduring influence. 'O Lord how great are thy works and thy thoughts are very deep.'"

1925 *Iron Trade* magazine announces the world's first mechanical dinosaur, Messmore and Damon's *Apatosaurus* (usually referred to by its makers as an "amphibious dinosaurus Brontosaurus"). The creature is 48 feet 9 inches long, 9 feet 3 inches high, weighs 4,000 pounds and has been based on the skeleton at the American Museum of Natural History: "The body is made of rattan assembled with springs so it is flexible. Inside the body is a table that carries the 10 motors and speed reducers that operate the different parts. The legs of the table pass through the legs of the dinosaur. The head and neck are controlled by a heavy steel tubing working through a series of speed reducers, one section of which is worked by flexible shafts. All of these motions are controlled from one switchboard and the motions may be reversed if desired." The head and feet are made of specially prepared papier mâché; the coloring is green, gray and brown. The dinosaur, state-of-the-art by 1920s standards, goes on to thrill people at automobile shows, educational expositions and even the New York stage before becoming part of the prehistoric menagerie of "The World A Million Years Ago," an attraction premiering at the 1933 Chicago World's Fair.

~ 23 ~

1994 Geologists Carl Swisher and Garniss Curtis of the Institute of Human Origins, Berkeley, California, announce at an annual meeting of the American Association for the Advancement of Science that an advanced dating technique has pushed back the age of a key Asian hominid fossil — a juvenile specimen of what is commonly called Java Man — by a million years. Curtis' more precise argon-argon dating method more accurately sets the skull's age to be some 1.8 million years old rather than .9 million, as Curtis had dated it in the 1960s. This dating may shove *Homo erectus* down a dead-end branch of his family tree.

~ 24 ~

1871 Charles Darwin's book *The Descent of Man, and Selection in Relation to Sex*, written over a period of three years and dealing with some of the revolutionary issues implied by his theory of evolution through natural selection, sees first publication. Darwin, at last deciding to deal with the subject of human origins, has concluded in the new book that man has indeed descended from an earlier life form: "He who wishes to decide whether man is the modified descendant of some pre-existing form would probably first inquire whether man varies, however slightly in bodily structures and in mental faculties; and if it is so, whether the variations are transmitted to his offspring in accordance with the laws which prevail with the lower animals."

1961 *The Twilight Zone* (CBS), Rod Serling's fantasy-anthology television series, airs "The Odyssey of Flight 33," in which an airplane inadvertently breaks the time barrier and finds itself in the Mesozoic Era. The dinosaur spotted from the air is really the *Apatosaurus* from the movie *Dinosaurus!* (1960) but in new stop-motion footage.

1967 *Time Tunnel* (ABC), producer Irwin Allen's continuing science-fiction television series made for 20th Century–Fox, runs the episode "Chase Through Time," pitting time-traveling heroes Tony Newman (James Darren) and Doug Phillips (Robert Colbert) against giant prehistoric reptiles. It is not surprising that the creatures look familiar, appearing in stock footage from Allen's remake of *The Lost World* (20th Century–Fox, 1960).

~ 25 ~

1868 William Hunter, London's leading obstetrician, gives his opinion to the Royal Society of London that the fossil remains collected in 1866 at Big Bone Lick pertain to a kind of carnivorous elephant that is "thank heavens ... probably extinct."

1915 Evgeny (also Eugene) A. Maleev is born in the Soviet Union. Maleev's work as a vertebrate paleontologist will mostly involve dinosaurs he collects and describes from Mongolia. Among his discoveries will be the giant theropod which, in 1955, he names *Tyrannosaurus bataar*, for many years known as *Tarbosaurus*. (Deceased.)

1996 The television special *The Mysterious Origins of Man* (NBC), hosted by Charlton Heston, purports that dinosaurs and man co-existed. The evidence includes alleged "man tracks" found along the Paluxy River, near Glen Rose, Texas (now known by paleontologists to be either misinterpreted dinosaur tracks or carved fakes). No paleontologists are interviewed.

~ 26 ~

1874 Albert Thomson is born. "Bill" Thomson will become a paleontologist at the American Museum of Natural History where he will be regarded as one its most valuable fossil collectors. His professional work will begin in summer 1898 at Como Bluff, Wyoming (the museum's second season at this locality), digging up dinosaur bones for Barnum Brown. (Deceased.)

1911 Walter Georg Kühne is born in Berlin, Germany. He will become a paleontologist specializing in Mesozoic mammals. Among Kühne's accomplishments will be co-discovering the coal mine locality of Mesozoic mammals at Guimarota in Portugal, which will eventually yield thousands of skeletons and teeth of fossil amphibians, reptiles and mammals. Significantly, he will be among the first paleontologists to embrace the theory of phylogenetic systematics as proposed by Willi Hennig. (Dies March 16, 1991.)

~ 27 ~

1993 Barney, the friendly purple dinosaur of PBS television and home-video fame, appears on the cover of *TV Guide*. Sharing the spot of honor is television news personality Jane Pauley.

~ 28 ~

1961 Edwin H. Colbert names and describes the small, bipedal, Triassic reptile *Poposaurus*, which he believes to be a primitive dinosaur of the new family Poposauridae. In later years this genus will be reclassified as a more primitive non-dinosaurian reptile.

1972 Julia Golden and Matthew H. Nitecki publish a catalogue of type specimens of fossil brachiopods housed at the Field Museum of Natural History.

~ 29 ~

1920 Arthur Franz is born a leap year baby. Franz will become an actor best known for leading man–scientist roles in science fiction movies and television shows of the 1950s. He will portray one such scientist who witnesses an example of Darwinian evolution in "Marked Danger," an episode of television's *Science Fiction Theatre* (1955). In the movie *Monster on the Campus* (Universal-International 1958), Franz will play college biology professor Dr. Donald Blake, who, upon smoking a pipe containing the blood of a thawed out coelacanth, transforms into a hatchet-wielding prehistoric apeman (change-over courtesy of the special effects department and make-up by the Bud Westmore team).

MARCH

~ 1 ~

1872 The "fossil feud" continues. Edward D. Cope delivers a paper to the American Philosophical Society in Philadelphia describing fossils of Late Cretaceous North American pterosaurs he had collected the previous summer from Niobrara chalk deposits of Kansas — at dig sites recently vacated by rival Othniel C. Marsh, who had also collected pterosaurs. Cope names his largest pterosaur genus and species *Ornithochirus umbrosus*. Less than a week later Marsh's name for a new species of *Pterodactylus*, *P. ingens* (later referred to *Pteranodon*) is proposed for remains representing the same animal.

1957 Dougal Dixon is born in Dumfries, Scotland. Dixon will become a paleontologist, sculptor and prolific writer who will travel the world lecturing on dinosaurs. Among the more unusual of the many books he will author are *After Man: A Zoology of the Future* and *The New Dinosaurs: An Alternative Evolution*, these being "what if?" looks at the different courses evolution might have taken had the dinosaurs not gone extinct.

1987 Entrepreneur "Lucky" Murdock opens The Las Vegas Museum of Natural History (advertised as "The Greatest Show Unearthed!") to the public amid the usual glitter on Las Vegas Boulevard. Casts of fossil specimens from Mary Jean Odano's Valley Anatomical Preparations of Canoga Park, California, mechanical prehistoric creatures and exhibits of modern animals are among the items displayed. But "Lucky's" luck is not the best; the museum will close, then be sold to new owners and relocated to the front building of what was once the Jockey Club in northern Las Vegas.

~ 2 ~

1866 Willis H. (Harold) O'Brien is born in Oakland, California. "Obie" (as he will be nicknamed) will develop the stop-motion technique of movie special effects (moving an articulated model a fraction of an inch, photographing each increment of movement one frame at a time, then projecting the full sequence of exposed frames) to an art form. As an amateur paleontologist and fossil collector, he will apply these interests to many of his movie projects, among them *The Dinosaur and the Missing Link*, *Morpheus Mike*, *RFD 10,000 B.C.* and *Prehistoric Poultry* (all 1917); *The Ghost of Slumber Mountain* (1922); *The Lost World* (1925 original and 1960 versions); his masterpiece *King Kong* and its sequel *The Son of Kong* (both 1933); *The Animal World* and *The Beast of Hollow Mountain* (both 1956) and *The Giant Behemoth* (1959). Unfortunately some of his planned prehistoric-animals projects (e.g., *Creation*, *War Eagles* and the original *Gwangi*) will not be made or completed when he dies from a heart attack on November 8, 1962.

Special-effects artist Willis O'Brien photographed by surprise while animating the horned dinosaur AGATHAUMAS for CREATION (1931), a film that was never completed.

1933 *King Kong* opens in New York City simultaneously at the Roxy and Radio City Music Hall on the birthday of Willis O'Brien who created its special visual effects. In addition to the titled giant gorilla, the film offers a supporting cast of prehistoric actors sculpted by Marcel Delgado (based on artwork by Charles R. Knight) and expertly animated a frame at a time by O'Brien. Its Mesozoic menagerie includes the dinosaurs *Stegosaurus*, *Apatosaurus* and *Tyrannosaurus*, the plesiosaur *Elasmosaurus* and pterosaur *Pteranodon*, as well as miscellaneous other creatures. The film is such a hit that its studio, RKO, rushes out a charming but inferior sequel *The Son of Kong*, released later this year. *King Kong* will achieve classic status. Remakes, imitations and rip-offs follow over the next six decades or so.

~ 3 ~

1849 The Department of the Interior is established to develop and conserve the natural resources of the United States of America and its territories. The job of this government branch is to supervise public affairs relating to such offices as the Bureau of Land Management, Geological Survey, National Parks Service and Bureau of Mines, all of which will occasionally be involved with the collection and preservation of fossils.

1914 Akira Ifukube is born to a distinguished family in the village of Kushiro, Hokkaido, Japan. Ifukube-san will become a major composer of film music, best known for scoring the Toho Co.'s Godzilla motion picture series filmed in Japan from the first, released in Japan in 1954, through the modern series of the 1990s. Much of his work for these movies (as well as other non–Godzilla prehistoric-creature epics made by Toho) will be recycled for sequels in the Godzilla series and be made available on numerous soundtrack albums.

1959 The film *The Giant Behemoth* (original British title: *Behemoth the Sea Monster*) is released. The movie was directed by Eugene Lourie who had previously directed *The Beast from 20,000 Fathoms* (1953) and would go one to direct *Gorgo* (1961), all three movies having similar plots. In the case of *Behemoth*, the long-necked (and radioactive) dinosaur attacks London. Special effects were designed and directed by Willis O'Brien, stop-motion models animated by Pete Peterson.

Ann Darrow (Fay Wray) watches the "Eighth Wonder of the World" battle a Tyrannosaurus *in the classic* King Kong *(1933), models sculpted by Marcel Delgado and animated by Willis O'Brien. © RKO Radio Pictures.*

1986 Robotic dinosaurs provided by Dinamation International Corporation, having ended a promotional tour to various Eastern museums, return to their permanent home at Dinosaur Valley, Mesa County, Grand Junction, Colorado.

~ 4 ~

1839 Gideon Mantell, suffering financial woes, reluctantly sells his fossil collection to the British government for a sum of £4,000 (he had hoped to get £1,000 more). The collection will subsequently be entrusted to the British Museum (Natural History).

~ 5 ~

1906 William Diller Matthew arrives in Boston and prepares to dismantle the famous Warren *Mastodon* skeleton for relocation to the American Museum of Natural History. The specimen had been bought in 1846 by Professor John Warren of the Harvard University medical school for his private museum. Urged by Henry Fairfield Osborn, wealthy benefactor J. P. Morgan purchases the skeleton and the rest of Warren's collection for the

One of the pieces in the touring exhibit "Dinosaurs, Mammoths and Cavemen: The Art of Charles R. Knight," this scene of early hunters fighting a mammoth originally done for the book LIFE THROUGH THE AGES (1946), which Knight also wrote. Photo of an original charcoal by Robin Robin.

American Museum in 1906. Matthew is not overly impressed by the collection and expresses his opinion that Morgan was overcharged.

1965   Poland issues 10 postage stamps of extinct reptiles, mostly dinosaurs, images including the herbivorous, "sail-backed" pelycosaur *Edaphosaurus*; freshwater reptile *Mesosaurus*; long-necked plesiosaur *Cryptocleidus*; small pterosaur *Rhamphorhynchus*; gigantic sauropod dinosaur *Apatosaurus*; bigger sauropod *Brachiosaurus*; plated dinosaur *Stegosaurus*; spike-frilled ceratopsian dinosaur *Styracosaurus*; helmet-crested hadrosaur *Corythosaurus*, and giant theropod *Tyrannosaurus*. The artwork is mostly adapted from paintings by Czech artist Zdenek Burian.

1982   "Dinosaurs, Mammoths and Cavemen: The Art of Charles R. Knight," a touring exhibition organized by Sylvia Massey Czerkas, has its gala debut at the Natural History Museum of Los Angeles County, featuring myriad drawings, paintings and sculptures by Knight, plus personal memorabilia. It coincides with the release of *Dinosaurs, Mammoths and Cavemen: The Art of Charles R. Knight*, co-authored by Czerkas and Don Glut.

1989   The Dinosaur Club of Southern California has its first meeting in Burbank. The group — membership including paleontologists, writers, artists and movie special-effects creators — is a new incarnation of the Dinosaur Society (not the later organization bearing this name), which was started in 1978 by sculptor Sylvia Czerkas (then Massey).

1997   Milestone Film & Video releases a "restored," slightly longer version of *The Lost World* (1925). Following the advent of talking pictures in the late 1920s, the 108-minute film was edited down to almost half its original length for distribution to the 16mm home-movie market. A fully restored and complete version of the movie has yet to surface.

Carnivorous ALLOSAURUS *versus herbivorous* APATOSAURUS *in* THE LOST WORLD *(1925). © First National.*

~ 6 ~

1946 The Mutual radio network's serialized *Superman* program has cub reported Jimmy Olsen (voiced by actor Jackie Kelk) rocket to the moon with an absent-minded scientist, only to be attacked by a flock of prehistoric "winged mammals" which he fights off with a fire extinguisher. Later, Superman (Clayton "Bud" Collyer) will fly to the rescue, saving the two earthlings from primitive apemen and a group of lizard-like animals that glow in the dark.

~ 7 ~

1872 Othniel Charles Marsh refers his *Pterodactylus ingens*— an 80-million-year-old, toothless flying reptile — to the new genus *Pteranodon*. Marsh calculates the animal's wingspan to measure more than 20 feet from tip to tip.

1877 Union Pacific Railroad worker William ("Bill") H. Reed discovers an enormous Upper Jurassic bone bed at Como Bluff, Wyoming. Soon collector O. C. Marsh's collector Samuel Wendell Williston describes the site in a letter to Marsh: "[The bones] extend for *seven* miles and are by the ton."

1956 Author L. Sprague de Camp's science-fiction story "A Gun for Dinosaur" is dramatized on the acclaimed *X Minus One* radio anthology series sponsored by *Galaxy* magazine. The story, published this same month in that periodical, is about a safari guide who takes clients back through time to hunt *Tyrannosaurus*.

1991 Jean Piveteau, among the most notable paleontologists of France, dies at the age of 92. Born in Rouillac (Charente), France, Piveteau is remembered for his work involving a variety of fossil vertebrate groups including fishes, amphibians, reptiles and mammals. His main interests were the problems of the organization and evolution of vertebrates and those of human evolution. Piveteau authored over 250 scientific papers and books. His classic work was the *Traité de Paléontologie*, an enormous 10-volume synthesis which appeared between 1952 and 1969, featuring chapters by 51 internationally reknowned authors. Professor Piveteau completed editing *La Main et l'hominisation*, his last book, just weeks before his death.

~ 9 ~

1887 Harry Govier Seeley reads his paper on *Poikilopleuron pusillus*, a theropod dinosaur named and described earlier by Richard Owen, before the Geological Society of London. In this paper Seeley renames Owen's dinosaur *Aristosuchus*. This name, however, is not meant to last. In later years the type species *A. pusillus* will be generally considered to be a junior synonym of *Calamospondylus oweni*.

~ 10 ~

1791   United States President Thomas Jefferson, himself an ardent student of "natural philosophy" with an interest in fossils, announces the discovery of an approximately cow-sized ground sloth (later named *Megalonyx*) to the American Philosophical Society in Philadelphia.

1909   Bryan Patterson is born in London, England. "Pat" will become a paleontologist specializing in fossil mammals. Starting in the early 1930s, he will for many years be associated with the Field Museum of Natural History. During the 1950s he will work jointly with the Texas Memorial Museum to collect huge quantities of Early Cretaceous mammal material from a site found by an earlier Field Museum party. (Dies December 1, 1979.)

1966   *The Munsters*, Universal Pictures' spoof of television situation comedies and old horror movies, airs the episode "Prehistoric Munster." Herman Munster (Fred Gwynne), the Frankensteinian head of the family, is mistaken for the "missing link" by a pair of university anthropologists.

1986   Dinosaur Pizza, a restaurant owned by Warren Harrison and managed by Sherry Tice, opens in Loma, Colorado. Harrison does the cooking. (Before Harrison took over the property, it was a tourist shop called the Dinosaur Store.)

~ 11 ~

1874   Charles Whitney Gilmore is born in Pavilion, New York. Gilmore will become one of the great authorities on dinosaurs. Though his early years as a paleontologist will be spent at the Carnegie Museum of Natural History, most of his professional career will be based at the United States National Museum. At home in both the field and museum, Gilmore's work on dinosaurs will include collecting numerous specimens, organizing data (especially information pertaining to Dinosaur National Monument) and authoring some 43 papers, some in which he names and describes new taxa, some offering complete osteologies. (Dies September 27, 1945.)

1991 Writer Don Lessem and paleontologists David B. Weishampel and Peter Dodson establish The Dinosaur Society, an international, not-for-profit organization dedicated to furthering paleontological research and education. The Dinosaur Society will provide research grants, publish technical and popular works, arrange traveling dinosaur exhibits, offer a catalog of approved dinosaur-related products and underwrite dinosaur-related articles appearing in the *Journal of Vertebrate Paleontology*. A prime interest of The Dinosaur Society is being a source of education and inspiration to children.

~ 12 ~

1784 William Buckland is born in Axminster, England. Buckland will become both minister and geologist, eventually achieving such titles as President of the Geological Society of London and Reader in Geology at Oxford University for his scientific achievements. Among Dean Buckland's achievements, he coins the generic name *Megalosaurus* (after a suggestion by his colleague and fellow minister, the Reverend William Daniel Conybeare), assigned to the first dinosaur ever to be named and described. (Dies 1856.)

1872 Edward Drinker Cope's paper naming *Ornithochirus* is quickly published and distributed. Alas, neither Cope nor his publisher is quick enough, as Pteranodon, Marsh's name for the same animal, is already in print and therefore has priority. The Cope vs. Marsh "bone war" continues...

1953 Barnum Brown replies to a letter written to him by Pauline Wischmnann, a local historian in Jordan, a town in eastern Montana. Brown recounts his discovery and later mounting of the first two skeletons of the classic dinosaur *Tyrannosaurus rex*. The skeleton displayed at the American Museum will be considered by many scientists to be the most famous of all dinosaur specimens.

~ 13 ~

Artist Benjamin Waterhouse Hawkins, who made the first full-sized figures of dinosaurs and other prehistoric animals. Courtesy Ewell Sale Stewart Library, The Academy of Natural Sciences of Philadelphia.

1868 Sculptor Benjamin Waterhouse Hawkins arrives in New York and will soon be approached by city officials to repeat in the United States his success with building life-sized statues of prehistoric animals similar to those at Crystal Palace.

1949   Philip J. Currie is born in Ontario, Canada. Currie will become one of leading paleontologists specializing in dinosaurs, particularly theropods, and in 1985 be made Curator of Dinosaurs at the new Royal Tyrrell Museum of Palaeontology in Drumheller, Alberta. In the late 1990s he will be a leader of the Sino-Canadian Dinosaur Project, during which he and colleagues will discover, name and describe numerous new vertebrate taxa. Among Currie's most spectacular discoveries during this expedition will be skeletons of the theropod *Oviraptor* atop their eggs in the nests exhibiting what seems to be the first hard evidence of avian-like brooding behavior in dinosaurs. Frequently on camera for documentaries and news shows about dinosaurs, he will become one of the relatively few paleontologists known to

Paleontologist Philip J. Currie working in a ceratopsian bone bed in Alberta, Canada. Photo by Florenco Manovern.

the public. Currie will also be well known as an expert on Edgar Rice Burroughs and that author's stories, some of them about prehistoric creatures, publishing and co-editing the Burroughs "fanzine" *ERBivore* in the 1970s. *The Encyclopedia of Dinosaurs*, a major work co-edited by Currie and paleontologist Kevin Padian, featuring entries written by the world's most noted dinosaur authorities, will be published in 1997.

~ 14 ~

1942   Peter M. Galton is born in England. Galton will become a paleontologist specializing in virtually all major groups of dinosaurs, particularly prosauropods and stegosaurs. Based at the Department of Biology, University of Bridgeport, in Bridgeport, Connecticut, Galton will also be an extremely prolific author, publishing myriad scientific papers about dinosaurs, many of them naming and describing new taxa or redescribing established taxa.

~ 15 ~

1876 Othniel Charles Marsh takes delight in referring rival Edward Drinker Cope's pterosaur *Ornithochirus* to his own *Pteranodon*, thereby putting into effect the rules of priority in scientific naming. Cope suffers the "nomenclature blues."

1961 Artist Charles R. Knight is cover-featured in the scholastic magazine *News Time*.

1995 Peter Larson, President of the Black Hills Institute of Geologic Research, is sentenced to 43 months in prison for failing to report correctly money brought into and out of the United States and for removing fossils from private lands in South Dakota and Montana.

~ 16 ~

1868 Benjamin Waterhouse Hawkins lectures to the New York Lyceum of Natural History about his recreations of ancient forms of life.

~ 17 ~

1877 William H. Reed finds a large dinosaur bone at Como Bluff, Wyoming. The same day O. C. Marsh, at Yale, draws up an agreement between him, Reed and the latter's fellow Union Pacific Railroad ex-employee William E. Carlin. The document calls for Reed and Carlin to collect fossils exclusively for him for at least a year and to do whatever they can to keep other collectors away from the area. Furthermore, Marsh retains the right to hire superintendents of his own choice to oversee Reed and Carlin's work. All of this work will bring the two men $90 per month each. Though Reed and Carlin are not fond of this last stipulation, they sign.

1910 The United States National Museum, belonging to the Smithsonian Institution in Washington, D.C., opens to the public in a new building. The Smithsonian's collections having outgrown the original building, the

United States Congress had, in late 1909, appropriated $3.5 million for the new structure to house the natural history collections. In the 1920s, largely due to the work of Charles W. Gilmore, the museum will house and display much of the fossil material collected at Dinosaur National Monument.

1966 Rainer Zangerl names and describes *Ornithoprion hertwigi*, a new genus and species of edestid shark from the Pennsylvanian Mecca and Logan Quarry Shales of Indiana.

~ 18 ~

1856 Joseph Leidy names and describes four new dinosaurian genera and species at the Academy of Natural Sciences of Philadelphia. These taxa include *Deinodon horridus*, a giant theropod, based on teeth, and *Trachodon mirabilis*, originally based on a mixture of hadrosaur and ceratopsian teeth.

1899 Othniel Charles Marsh dies of pneumonia in New Haven, Connecticut. According to the terms of his will, all of his fossils at the Peabody Museum of Natural History, an institution he was instrumental in establishing, become the property of Yale University.

1913 Edwin Carter Galbreath is born in Ashmore, Illinois. As a pale-ontologist his interests will be wide ranging, though his work in vertebrate paleontology will mostly focus upon the Quarternary of the Midwest, par-ticularly the continental Tertiary of northeastern Colorado. In addition to authoring some 45 professional papers, Galbreath will from 1963 to 1967 edit the *Transactions of the Illinois Academy of Sciences*. (Dies January 20, 1989.)

1945 Edgar Rice Burroughs' Apeman, in the *Tarzan* Sunday comic strip written and illustrated by Burne Hogarth, begins a new adventure in which he encounters an idol made in the image of a meat-eating dinosaur, then battles the live model. In 1996 this continuity will be reprinted in a qual-ity hardcover book (Flying Buttress Classics Library).

1966 Robert E. DeMar names and describes *Longisctula houghae*, a new genus and species of dissorophid amphibian from the Permian of Texas.

~ 19 ~

1853 The first part of Charles Dickens' serialized novel *Bleak House* is privately published. It is significant as the first known piece of fiction to mention a dinosaur. In the opening paragraph Dickens writes: "Implacable November weather. As much mud in the streets as if the waters had but newly retired from the face of the earth and it would have been wonderful to meet a Megalosaurus, forty feet long or so, waddling like an elephantine lizard up Holborn Hill...."

1988 "Chinasaurs: The Dinosaurs of Sichuan," a touring exhibition displaying dinosaur bones and other fossils from Sichuan, China, and already popular in Japan and France, has its North American debut at the Burke Museum, University of Washington, Seattle, Oregon. The opening is appropriately timed in China's "Year of the Dragon," as "kong long," the Chinese word for dinosaur, translates as "terrible dragon."

1998 Once again the Academy of Natural Sciences of Philadelphia opens a newly renovated "Dinosaur Hall," this one in conjunction with the third Dinofest International event (which will open nine days later.) Many new exhibits join the old in this latest presentation — among them, a skeletal cast (made by Valley Anatomical Preparations in California) of the gigantic carnivorous dinosaur *Giganotosaurus carolinii*, apparently bigger than the biggest *Tyrannosaurus rex*.

~ 21 ~

1931 Al Williamson is born in New York City. Williamson will become an artist drawing numerous comic strips and comic books featuring prehistoric and other exotic creatures. In the late 1940s, before eventually achieving fame in these fields, he will be Burne Hogarth's assistant on the *Tarzan* newspaper strip. Williamson will go on to illustrate various *Flash Gordon* projects where he has many opportunities to work a variety of alien prehistoric animals into his artwork.

~ 22 ~

1920 Anatoli K. Rozdestvensky is born in the Soviet Union. Rozdestvensky will become a paleontologist specializing in Asian dinosaurs, particularly those of the Upper Cretaceous of Mongolia. Among his accomplishments will be identifying some large fossil claws, named *Therizinosaurus* and originally regarded by their describer Evgeny A. Maleev as those of a turtle, as belonging to a theropod dinosaur.

1947   Malcolm J. Heaton is born in Toronto, Canada. Like many future paleontologists, he will become interested in dinosaurs as a child. Most of his professional career he will work at the Royal Tyrrell Museum of Palaeontology where he takes a research position in 1982. He will produce 10 manuscripts during his brief career and leave behind manuscripts and notes for many more when he dies on August 2, 1984.

1995   Preliminary scenes for the movie *Dinosaur Valley Girls* are shot before a "green screen" at HES studio in Studio City, California. In post-production, these shots will be composited with other footage.

~ 23 ~

1973   Robert M. West publishes a study on the geology and mammalian paleontology of the New York–Big Sandy area of Sublette County, Wyoming.

~ 24 ~

1912   *The Lost World* bows as a serial (continuing through July 21) in the Sunday supplement of the *Philadelphia Press*, this being the first publication anywhere of Sir Arthur Conan Doyle's novel. In April through November, again serialized, it will have its first printing in Conan Doyle's native England in *The Strand* magazine, this to be followed by the first hardcover book edition (with photographs of Conan Doyle made up as lead character Professor George Edward Challenger) in October or November. The story — about explorers journeying to a prehistoric world of live dinosaurs and other supposedly extinct creatures surviving atop an isolated South American plateau — becomes the prototype for countless future adaptations, sequels and imitations.

1933   The Hollywood premiere of the movie *King Kong* is held at Grauman's Chinese Theatre. The event includes a live stage show complete with "native" dancers. Outside the theatre a full-scale mechanical bust of the giant prehistoric ape Kong, a prop used in the movie, leeringly greets attendees.

1939   Bryan Patterson names and describes new taxa belonging to the mammalian groups Pantonta and Dinocerata from the Upper Paleocene of western Colorado.

The fictional (also radiactive) PALEOSAURUS *in the science-fiction movie* THE GIANT BEHEMOTH *(1959; original British title,* BEHEMOTH, THE SEA MONSTER*). © Diamond/Allied Artists.*

1945 Robert T. Bakker is born in Teaneck, New Jersey. Bakker will become one of the most significant (and sometimes controversial) of modern paleontologists specializing in dinosaurs. He will enter the field at a time when dinosaurs are generally regarded by scientists as dead-end curiosities not worthy of much serious consideration. A self-styled "maverick," Bakker will frequently propose new and often revolutionary ideas about dinosaurs and their behavior which prompt the so-called "Dinosaur Renaissance" of the 1970s and '80s. Bakker's ideas will dramatically alter the way dinosaurs are perceived by fellow scientists and the public and sometimes inspire other paleontologists to pursue new lines of research. Indeed, he will become the main champion of the theory that dinosaurs were not the sluggish cold-blooded reptiles they had usually been regarded as, but rather active, warm-blooded animals. Cultivating an identifying image, including beard, long hair and trademark cowboy hat, Bakker will become one of the relatively few paleontologists whose name and face are known to the public, inspiring a character in the movie *The Lost World: Jurassic Park*. Among Bakker's many accomplishments, he will name and describe many new dinosaurian taxa, become a staff paleontologist at Dinamation International Corporation and author as well as illustrate two best-selling books, *The Dinosaur Heresies* (1986) and the novel *Raptor Red* (1996).

1985 The author begins a month-long tour for Disney Studios to promote Touchstone Pictures' forthcoming dinosaur movie *Baby … Secret* *of the Lost Legend.* The tour includes radio, television and print interviews and giving the lecture "Fantasy Dinosaurs of the Movies."

1994   The first Dino Fest (later renamed Dinofest) International begins at Indiana University/Purdue University, Indianapolis, Indiana. More than 30 paleontologists and numerous dinosaur buffs attend. Topics for discussion include dinosaur origins, excavations, evolutionary trends, possibilities of cloning and DNA replication and extinction theories. There is also a "Dino Feast" and exhibits. The event proves popular and more are scheduled, one every two years.

~ 25 ~

1963   Elmer S. Riggs, who gave the world the name *Brachiosaurus* and changed *Brontosaurus* to *Apatosaurus*, dies in Bartlesville, Oklahoma.

~ 26 ~

1934   Akemi Nagishi is born. Ms. Nagishi will become a performer in motion pictures perhaps most fondly remembered as the dancing native girl in the movie *King Kong vs. Godzilla* (1963), her gyrations helping to summon the giant prehistoric ape Kong.

~ 27 ~

1956   The Chicago Natural History Museum "unveils" its new exhibit to museum members on "Dinosaur Night"— the skeleton of the large carnivorous dinosaur presently named *Gorgosaurus* looming over that of the crested duckbilled dinosaur *Lambeosaurus*. The skeletons, both found in the Upper Cretaceous of Alberta, Canada, have been prepared by Chief Preparator Orville L. Gilpin. Gilpin (known to co-workers as "Gilly") has mounted the *Gorgosaurus* (nicknamed "Gorgy") entirely from within, this being the first dinosaur skeleton ever mounted with no external supports.

~ 28 ~

1962   Paleontologist Robert H. Denison publishes a paper in which he reconstructs the shield of *Bryantolepis brachycephalus*, a species of arthrodire, or archaic armor-bearing fish of the Devonian Era.

~ 29 ~

1981 On a fossil dig in Orange County, California, led by paleontologist George Callison as an outing of the original Dinosaur Society, Donald F. Glut discovers the snout of a previously unknown species of extinct dolphin. The skull itself, buried in a nearby hill, will subsequently be found by professionals. The new species will *not*, however, be named for its discoverer.

~ 30 ~

1940 *Monkey into Man,* an independently produced, feature-length British documentary motion picture about evolution, is previewed in a New York projection room for film critics. The movie "traces animal life from the stone age up to the present time and manages to prove quite interesting despite the tedious development and its comprehensive scope," according to the review in *Variety*. The movie will soon be forgotten.

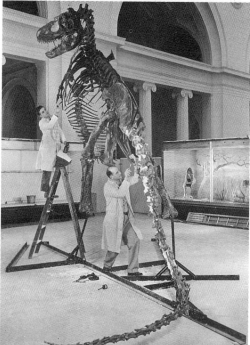

Top: *Donald F. Glut on March 29, 1981, approximately a minute after finding the piece of fossil snout that would represent a new species of Cenozoic dolphin. Photo by George Callison.* Bottom: *Chief Preparator of Fossils Orville L. Gilpin (on floor) and assistant Cameron Gifford "touch up" the skeleton originally labeled "GORGOSAURUS LIBRATUS" (probably actually the similar DASPLETOSAURUS), the first to be mounted from within with no external supports, close to its 1956 unveiling in Stanley Field Hall, at the formerly named Chicago Natural Museum. Courtesy The Field Museum (neg. #GEO81671).*

APRIL

~ 1 ~

1885 Wallace Beery is born. During the silent days of Hollywood the burly actor will appear in two movies having prehistoric themes. In 1923 he will play an antagonistic caveman opposite hero Buster Keaton in *The Three Ages*, a comedy with a long prehistoric sequence complete with *Apatosaurus* and mammoth. More significantly, two years later Beery will portray the first and definitive Professor Challenger in *The Lost World*.

1962 Christopher A. Shaw is born in Los Angeles. Shaw will become a paleontologist specializing in Pleistocene mammals. Shaw will be employed at the George C. Page Museum of La Brea Discoveries and become Collections Manager. Having access to the museum's unsurpassed collection of Ice Age fossils, Shaw will become a leading authority on the sabretooth cat of the "tar pits," *Smilodon fatalis*.

Actor Wallace Beery playing a bully caveman riding an Indian elephant playing a prehistoric mammoth in the silent comedy film THE THREE AGES *(1923). © Metro-Goldwyn-Mayer.*

1989 Charles Cockell, an undergrad at Bristol University in England, announces his experiments that may lead to cloning a living mammoth. Cockell has pieces of mammoth tissue with which, through bio-technology and genetic engineering and the participation of a live female elephant, he hopes to bring the extinct mammal back to the modern world. He has already extracted mammoth DNA from this tissue.

1999 A living *Tyrannosaurus* is cloned from preserved DNA, extracted from blood consumed by a pesky bug preserved in amber. (April Fool!)

~ 2 ~

1973 The NTV/Toho series *Ryusei Ningen Zone* (better known as *Zone Fighter*) premieres on Japanese TV. Godzilla is guest-starred and will return in future episodes to assist superhero Zone Fighter in his battle against the evil Baron Garoga. The juvenile series will continue through September 24.

1978 A menacing *Tyrannosaurus* robot enters the storyline of the *Star Hawks* newspaper comic strip, written by Ron Goulart and illustrated by Gil Kane. The mechanical creature is part of a futuristic theme park. In 1986, the adventure will be reprinted as a book (Blackthorn Publishing).

~ 3 ~

1995 Principal photography begins shooting on *Dinosaur Valley Girls* at Delfino Sound Stage in Sylmar, California.

~ 4 ~

1914 *The Lion, the Lamb, the Man*, a silent movie made by the Rex film company, opens. Lon Chaney, famed for offbeat character roles and original make-ups, portrays a caveman in a prehistoric flashback sequence.

1916 Zdenek V. Spinar is born at Cáslav in central Bohemia. Spinar will become a vertebrate paleontologist specializing in Permo-Carboniferous labyrinthodont amphibians, publish at least 80 papers and author four books (including *Life Before Man*). In 1962 he will receive the Czechoslovakian National Prize of Klement Gottwald for his scientific achievements. Later he will be made Professor of Zoology at St. Charles University in Prague. (Dies August 14, 1995.)

1988 The United States Postal Service launches its "Readasaurus" project, starting a 21-city run in Anchorage, Alaska. The project is "designed to delight and stimulate millions of American kids to read millions of books in the summer of 1988." It starts with the discovery by "two heretofore unknown paleontologists, Drs. Schmidt and Zonian," of the egg of a "Readasaurus," a rare breed of dinosaur, on the North Slope of Alaska. The egg is supposed to hatch in 33 days.

~ 5 ~

1990 "Prehistoric Sea Monsters: Dinosaurs and the Deep," an exhibition of robotic extinct sea creatures from Dinamation International Corporation, opens at the Chicago Academy of Sciences in Illinois. Among its denizens of the ancient deep is a 50-foot long replica of the giant mosasaur *Tylosaurus*.

1996 Kraft's *Adventures in Cheese & Macaroni Land*, "A Fun-Filled Musical Revue Starring Cheesasaurus Rex!" opens at The Brickyard in Chicago. The children's show, featuring a friendly dinosaur, includes contests and games.

~ 6 ~

1869 The American Museum of Natural History is given its charter of incorporation in a bill signed by John T. Hoffman, Governor of New York. This act may invalidate Benjamin Waterhouse Hawkins' earlier agreement to supply prehistoric-animal figures for the city's proposed Paleozoic Museum.

1985 "Spike," the *Pentaceratops sternbergii* sculpted by David A. Thomas, is installed outside the New Mexico Museum of Natural History. The model is distinguished as the world's first life-sized bronze dinosaur cast by means of the "lost wax" method.

"Spike" (scientific name: PENTACERATOPS STERN-BERGII), a full-scale bronze model sculpted by David A. Thomas, makes its dramatic arrival outside the New Mexico Museum of Natural History. Photo by David A. Thomas.

~ 7 ~

1939 V. T. Hamlin introduces the science fiction story element of time travel into his popular *Alley Oop* comic strip which until now has had a strictly "Stone Age" setting. Dr. Elbert Wonmug has invented a time machine which will bring Oop and girlfriend Oola into the modern age. It can also send them anywhere or "anywhen" in history, thereby expanding the strip's horizons.

1954 The Fossil Fish Alcove, showing the evolutionary history of fishes over time, opens in the west end of the American Museum of Natural History's former Early Dinosaur Hall.

~ 8 ~

1981 Griffith Park Observatory in Los Angeles, California, opens its "Death of the Dinosaurs" planetarium show, presented by Observatory Program Supervisor John Mosley. The show, with slides and special effects, dramatically illustrates the new Alvarez theory that the last dinosaurs may have died out after a giant celestial object crashed into the Earth.

~ 9 ~

1987 An airlift under the direction of Museum of Western Colorado paleontologist Harley J. Armstrong removes the fossilized remains of a *Stegosaurus* from its excavation site in Rabbit Valley. The site had been found a decade earlier by Harold Bolian, an industrial arts professor at Mesa College and an amateur paleontologist. The specimen was found including some skin impressions and with plates overlapping.

~ 10 ~

1977 An animal, believed by some people to be the recently dead carcass of a Mesozoic marine reptile called a plesiosaur, is recovered underwater by Japanese fishermen near Christchurch, New Zealand. Most scientists, however, are skeptical, interpreting the remains as those of a decomposing shark.

~ 11 ~

1755 James Parkinson is born in England. Parkinson will become a medical practitioner, but also be one of the scientists to establish British paleontology in the early 19th century. Among his future accomplishments are important chemical investigations of fossil wood and "fossil objects," his work contributing to the demonstration that fossils are not, as commonly believed, products of some "plastic" force of nature. He will be the first to publish the name *Megalosaurus* and also will write the three-volume *Organic Remains of a Former World* (1804, 1808 and 1811, the third volume dealing largely with fossil vertebrates). (Dies December 21, 1824.)

1907 The Gallery of Vertebrate Paleontology, or Dinosaur Hall, opens at the Carnegie Museum of Natural History during dedication of the greatly enlarged building. The opening will span three days. Displayed are skeletons of some of the dinosaurs — including *Apatosaurus louisae*, *Dryosaurus altus*, *Diplodocus carnegii*, *Allosaurus fragilis* and *Stegosaurus ungulatus* — recovered at what will become Dinosaur National Monument.

1934 Having wintered in Kansas, Myrl V. Walker and his wife begin a second season of fossil collecting at Petrified Forest National Monument. They will soon find the skull of the large phytosaur *Leptosuchus*, later to become an exhibit at the Rainbow Forest Museum in the Forest.

~ 12 ~

1897 Edward Drinker Cope, one of the great personages in the early days of paleontology, dies after a long illness. He is found at his Pine Street, Philadelphia, home atop his office cot amid a clutter of fossil bones. Henry Fairfield Osborn will be present at the funeral services at Cope's house where he will read these lines from the Book of Job: "Where was thou when I laid the foundations of the earth? Declare, if thou has understanding...." Then Osborn will comment, "These are the problems to which our friend devoted his life." As per Cope's request, his remains will be buried beside those of his late mentor and friend Joseph Leidy — that is, most of them. As per another of Cope's requests, one less traditional but certainly in keeping with his personality, he has willed his skull to the collections of the University of Pennsylvania, where he spent his last days, as the type specimen of *Homo sapiens*, left to inspire future students and scientists.

1997 "The Ceratopsia: The Life and Times of the Horned Dinosaurs" exhibition, organized by James I. Kirkland for Dinamation International Society, opens at the Tampa Science Museum in Florida. Exhibited are skull and skeletal casts of all ceratopsian dinosaurs, as well as scientifically accu-

Previously unpublished photo showing James I. Kirkland (right) in 1992 at the site of the UTAHRAPTOR discovery, having just received Edward Drinker Cope's skull from Louie Psihoyos (author of the book HUNTING DINOSAURS), who was then taking the remains on a nationwide tour. Photo by Michael L. Perry, courtesy James I. Kirkland and Dinamation International Society.

rate life models supplied by Saurian Studios (most of them sculpted by Mike Jones) and the Dinosaur Studio.

~ 13 ~

1726 Nikolaus Hehn, his brother Valentin and Christoper Zänger, all youths from the village of Eibelstadt on the Main, near Würzburg, Germany, are formally charged in court with having faked, buried and then sold various "figure stones" — supposedly fossils — including those "discovered" the previous year by Professor Johannes Bartholomaeus Adam Beringer. The boys will testify that the plot of deception was concocted by two Würzburg professors, Johann Georg von Eckhart and his assistant Ignaz Roderique, both of whom bore grudges against Beringer. Following these revelations, Beringer will have the first edition of his tome *Lithographiae Wirceburgensis* bought up by a bookseller, then reissued with a new preface, believing most of the curious stones to be authentic despite the confessions of forgery: "That does not make all the found figure stones false, any more than all old coins or all old works of art are false because counterfeiting and art forgeries exist." Beringer will maintain this belief up to the time of his death 14 years later.

1743 Thomas Jefferson is born (on April 2, "old style") at Old Shadwell in Goochland (now Albemarle) County, Virginia. Although he will be best remembered as one of the authors of the Declaration of Independence and third President of the United States, Jefferson will also be a student of natural philosophy and an amateur paleontologist. Refusing to accept that God would allow any species to become extinct, he will believe that giant animals—including what will become known as the American mastodon—represented by fossil bones being discovered still roam the wilderness of North America's Far West. In the late 1790s Jefferson will be elected president of the American Philosophical Society of Philadelphia. During the early 1800s his involvement in the Lewis and Clark Expedition will result in the collection of many fine fossil specimens. Jefferson will die on July 4, 1826, the fiftieth anniversary of the signing of the Declaration of Independence.

1977 The George C. Page Museum of La Brea Discoveries, located at the site of the famous "tar pits" in 23-acre Hancock Park, opens to the public in Los Angeles as a satellite facility of the Natural History Museum of Los Angeles County. The museum, bought for the County by entrepreneur and philanthropist George C. Page, houses the heritage of Rancho La Brea—thousands of well-preserved specimens from 4,000 to 40,000 years ago, representing some 140 species of plants and 420 species of animals and the world's best collection of Ice Age fossils. Large glass windows allow visitors to look into the laboratory to observe paleontologists at work.

1990 "The Age of Dinosaurs in Japan and China," a major exhibition organized by Dong Zhiming of Asian dinosaur and other fossil specimens, opens at the Fukui Prefectural Museum, Fukui City, Japan.

~ 14 ~

1933 In the *Alley Oop* comic strip, Oop constitues "proof" that cavement and dinosaurs coexisted.

1988 Precious stones meet historic bones at a Page Museum lecture.

~ 15 ~

1845 James Rawlins Johnson of Hotwells, Bristol, England, one of the most important early collectors of ichthyosaur specimens, auctions off his treasures which include skeletons recovered from Lyme Regis and other areas. The auction spans five days. The items include beautifully intact specimens clearly preserving evidence of paddle-like limbs.

1952 Having already dealt with dinosaurs on television the previous year, Astro (voice of actor Al Markham) and his Space Academy pals encounter more dinosaurs in the prehistoric swamps of his native planet Venus on the *Tom Corbett, Space Cadet* radio serial. There, thanks to the listeners' imaginations, the special effects can be far superior. The story will resume on April 17.

1953 After saying to his daughter Lucy, "Don't let anything happen to my drawings," Charles R. Knight dies peacefully in a Manhattan hospital.

~ 16 ~

1960 Audiences feel cheated by *The Incredible Petrified World*, an incredibly dull motion picture from Governor Films, released today to theatres. Despite the implications of word "Petrified" in the title and advertising promising (presumably prehistoric) "Monsters" at "The Center of the Earth," the main threats consist of being stranded in a vast cave, surviving the eruption of a subterranean volcano and the seeming possibility that the film will never end. Audiences are petrified by boredom.

~ 17 ~

1942 Douglas Ralph Emlong is born in St. Joseph, Michigan. Emlong's later discovered ability to find fossils will lead to employment in 1967 with the Smithsonian Institution. A nonconformist, he will collect in his own way, neither keeping a standard field notebook nor learning how to make the standard plaster jacket for protecting specimens. Eventually Emlong will acquire a collection of marine-mammal fossils second to none in terms of number, variety and quality. In 1966 he will publish a major paper describing the extinct whale *Aetiocetus cotylalveus*. On June 8, 1980, while collecting fossils, his career will be terminated by a fatal plunge from a high overlook in Lincoln County, Oregon.

1981 *Caveman*, a comedy movie starring Ringo Starr and Barbara Bach as prehistoric sweethearts, opens in the United States and Canada. A send-up of movies like *One Million Years B.C.*, it features a menagerie of prehistoric animals including an overweight *Tyrannosaurus*, a *Pteranodon* and a bug-eyed giant lizard designed by Jim Danforth and animated by David Allen.

~ 18 ~

1939   The American Museum of Natural History's new Jurassic Dinosaur Hall, curated by museum paleontologist Barnum Brown, opens. The room, designed by the Trowbridge and Livingstone architectural firm and finished in 1932, displays mounted skeletons of some of the museum's best Jurassic dinosaur skeletons, including those of *Apatosaurus*, *Stegosaurus*, *Ornitholestes* and *Allosaurus*. Also displayed are specimens of the Triassic dinosaur *Plateosaurus* and various reptiles predating the Mesozoic Era.

1957   The Three Stooges (Moe Howard, Larry Fine and Joe Besser) are almost killed by a dinosaur (a "giant lizard" stock shot from *One Million B.C.*) on the planet Sunev (spell it backwards) in the comedy short *Space Ship Sappy*.

1958   A composite skeleton of *Apatosaurus excelsus*, mounted by Orville L. Gilpin, is unveiled to museum members this evening at the Chicago Natural History Museum. Most of the back half has been on exhibit for decades, having been collected in 1901 from the Grand River Valley near Fruita, western Colorado, by a Field Columbian Museum field team led by Harold W. Menke. The front half consists of bones from another individual found in Utah in 1942. The skull is a cast of a *Camarasaurus lentus* skull and will be replaced with the correct one about three decades hence.

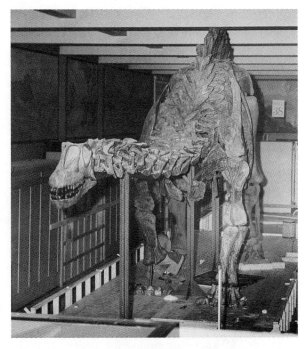

Composite skeleton of Apatosaurus excelsus, *not yet completed, prior to its official 1958 unveiling in Hall 38 at the (formerly named) Chicago Natural History Museum. Courtesy The Field Museum (neg. #GEO84054).*

~ 19 ~

1882 Charles R. Darwin dies peacefully at Down House, his quiet country home in Kent, England, two months after suffering a slight heart attack. "When I am obliged to give up observation and experiment," he once said, "I shall die." Indeed, Darwin worked until two days before his death. Darwin may, in fact, have predicted his death, for on his last birthday he told a friend, "My course is nearly run." Darwin's remains will reside among the greats in Westminster Abbey, his funeral attended by some of the foremost thinkers, artists and leaders of his day.

1956 *Godzilla, King of the Monsters!* is released in the United States, two years after the movie's original release in Japan as *Gojira*. In order to make the film more acceptable to an American audience, new footage had been shot and edited into the movie featuring actor Raymond Burr as a reporter who, functioning as a kind of "Greek chorus," comments on the action. American audiences respond positively to the result.

~ 20 ~

1959 The Chicago *Sun-Times* Sunday supplement publishes the start of a poem written by Eugene S. Richardson, Curator of Fossil Invertebrates at the Chicago Natural History Museum, about the museum's *Gorgosaurus-Lambeosaurus* exhibit. The verse describes how the *Gorgosaurus* was interrupted before having finished its meal of *Lambeosaurus*.

~ 21 ~

1922 Led by Roy Chapman Andrews, the first Central Asiatic Expedition of the American Museum of Natural History sets out from Kalgan, on the Chinese border, for the unknown wilds of Mongolia in the Gobi Desert, searching for fossils supposedly linking the origins of man to Asia. Transportation comprises a train of camels and a fleet of automobiles.

~ 22 ~

1923 Paleontologist Charles Lewis Camp starts collecting fossils in the Petrified Forest in the first expedition sponsored by the Museum of Paleontology at the University of California, Berkeley.

1964   Life-sized prehistoric creatures appear at the New York World's Fair in Flushing Meadows, Long Island: Sinclair Dinoland, presented by the Sinclair Refining Co., offers nine different kinds of dinosaurs made by sculptor Louis Paul Jonas in his Churchtown, New York, studio under the direction of paleontologists Barnum Brown and John H. Ostrom. Three Jonas creatures — *Tyrannosaurus, Triceratops* and *Apatosaurus* — are equipped to move. On the Magic Skyway ride inside the Ford Motor Company Pavilion, passengers in new-model convertibles are conveyed past scenes depicting different time eras. Some of these feature dinosaurs, prehistoric mammals and cave people, which, through the marvels of "Audio-Animatronics" created by technicians at WED (Walter Elias Disney) Enterprises, engage in various activities. The Jonas figures, both the originals and copies, will find homes at museums, zoos, schools, parks and other places of interest for years to come. Disney's more animated moving dinosaurs will take up residence at the Disneyland Park in Anaheim, California. They will later be seen in the park's Primeval World via the Disneyland Railroad.

is Paul Jonas' full-sized APATOSAURUS as it appeared at Sinclair's Dinoland exhibit, New York World's Fair (1964– Courtesy Sinclair Refining Company.

1996   "Our Weakening Web: The Story of Evolution" exhibition starts its tour at the Cincinnati Museum of Natural History, Cincinnati, Ohio. The exhibition, which focuses upon extinctions, is made available in three sizes, depending upon the budgets and space available to the institutions booking it. Included are fossils, dioramas, computer displays and other visuals treats.

~ 23 ~

1947   Everett Claire Olson publishes his study of the Diadectidae (a family of primitive reptiles of the Permian period) and its bearing on the classification of reptiles.

~ 24 ~

1944   Allied aircraft bomb the Institut für Paläontologie und Historische Geologie in Munich, Germany. Among the World War II casualties, lost to science forever, are the type specimens of the dinosaurs *Carcharodontosaurus*, *Bahariasaurus*, *Spinosaurus* and *Aegyptosaurus*.

1955   *Gojira no Gyakushu* ("Godzilla's Counterattack"), the first sequel to *Gojira*, is released in Japan. This is the first entry in the series to bring in a second Godzilla (again portrayed by Haruo Nakajima) and the last to be shot in black and white. The movie introduces another monster, the spiny-backed "ankylosaur" Angilas (played by Hiroshi Sekida and called "Angurus" in the American version), which will occasionally turn up in future sequels. The picture does not open in the United States until May 21, 1959, its title misleadingly changed to *Gigantis the Fire Monster*.

1997   An international team of paleontologists — including John H. Ostrom, the group's leader; pterosaur and fossil bird expert Peter Wellnhofer of the University of Munich; David Buber of the Academy of Natural Sciences of Philadelphia; fossil bird specialist Larry D. Martin of the University of Kansas; and Alan Brush of the University of Connecticut — make an exciting announcement at a press conference held at the Academy after returning from a two-week expedition to China earlier this month. A spectacular trove of dinosaur fossils of Late Jurassic or Early Cretaceous age has recently been discovered in a remote area near the village of Beipiao, Liaoning province, in northeastern China. Among the hundreds of treasures collected by a Chinese excavation team at this site are the first dinosaur internal organs ever seen and the first dinosaur fossil containing a mammal the animal had eaten — but not entirely digested — before it died. A small birdlike theropod (to be named

Sinosauropteryx) skeleton possesses a fiber-like dorsal crest that may be the remains of some kind of primitive feathers or fur. An entire ecosystem has been preserved at the locality including mammals, birds, dinosaurs, insects, plants, possibly even bacteria. Apparently this fauna had been suddenly wiped out, perhaps by some short yet deadly catastrophe such as an enormous volcanic eruption. As Dr. Ji Qiang, Director of the National Geological Museum of China, states: "I look forward to a wonderful cooperative project with American and other international paleontologists. This locality we have just begun to look at is not only a Chinese treasure, it is a global treasure."

~ 25 ~

1922 The exploratory party of the first Central Asiatic Expedition of the American Museum of Natural History establishes a camp at what will be known as the Iren Dabasu dinosaur locality in Inner Mongolia.

1923 Fossil collector George Olsen, assistant to chief paleontologist Walter Granger, discovers the first remains of a new theropod dinosaur in the Iren Dabasu Formation during the third Central Asiatic Expedition of the American Museum of Natural History. The specimen includes a nearly complete right hind limb. In 1933 Charles Whitney Gilmore will name the new dinosaur *Alectrosaurus olseni* ("Olsen's mateless lizard").

1924 Charles L. Camp finds an important series of small fossil vertebrates at the Blue Hills site in the Petrified Forest. Among specimens collected are numerous lungfishes (*Arganodus* sp.), armor plates of a new aetosaur (*Acaenasuchus geoffreyi*), bones of a small metoposaur (*Apachesaurus gregorii*) and remains of other small reptiles.

1933 Paleontologist Baron Franz Nopcsa, after murdering his Albanian secretary and lover Bajazid, fatally shoots himself, leaving this note: "The reason for my suicide is a complete breakdown of my nervous system. My old friend and secretary I shot in his sleep without his having the slightest idea of my deed. I did not want to leave him ill, miserable and poor, for further suffering in this world. My last request is that my body be cremated."

~ 26 ~

1910 Tomoyuki Tanaka is born. Tanaka will become a producer of more than 220 Japanese motion pictures. However, he will be best remembered among prehistoric-monster movie fans as the creator of Godzilla and producer or executive producer of all 22 entries in that monster's popular film series made by the Toho Co. Tanaka will also be responsible for the creation of various other Toho monsters. (Dies April 2, 1997.)

1940 The movie *One Million B.C.*, a "Stone Age" melodrama featuring cave people co-existing with dinosaurs and other anachronistic creatures, debuts at the Roxy in New York City. A *Tyrannosaurus* is portrayed by stuntman Paul Stader wearing a rubber costume, but most of the creatures are live animals (alligators, lizards, elephants, armadillos, pigs, etc.) dressed up with various accoutrements. The movie is a hit, not only for its entertainment value, but also for what it can supply — stock

Behind-the-scenes photo taken during production of ONE MILLION B.C. (1940): at the far left is special-effects man Fred Knoth, at the far right is actor Victor Mature, and in the center is stuntman Paul Stader as the world's shortest adult TYRANNOSAURUS REX.

footage and outtakes that will turn up in countless other movies (and also television shows and commercials) for more than half a century, among them: *Two Lost Worlds, Tarzan's Desert Mystery, Untamed Women, Devil Goddess, Valley of the Dragons, King Dinosaur, Robot Monster, Teenage Caveman, Journey to the Center of Time, Jungle Manhunt, Los Fantasmas Burlones, One Million AC/DC, Terrorvision, Attack of the B-Movie Monster, She Demons, Aventura al Centro de la Tierra, Horror of the Blood Monster, Isla de los Dinosaurios, Smoky Canyon, Lost Volcano, Voodoo Tiger*, the serials *Superman, Atom Man vs. Superman* and *The Lost Planet*, and short subject *Space Ship Sappy*.

1985 Bureau of Land Management area manager Frosty Littrell and the Museum of Western Colorado's Michael L. Perry sign a Cooperative Management Agreement for the Rabbit Valley Research Natural Area in the Morrison Formation (Upper Jurassic) of Colorado. The agreement will allow the new Dinosaur Valley exhibit's reopening of Rabbit Valley fossil quarries. This event marks the first Bureau of Land Management cooperative agreement ever signed and will serve as the model for future such agreements.

1989 Charles Shabica reports at the Geological Society of America Conference, held at Western Illinois University in Macomb, Illinois, on the discovery of 8,000-year-old petrified wood specimens — later determined to be oak — found beneath the waters of Lake Michigan off Calmulet Harbor. The fossil tree stumps, which confirm the existence of an erstwhile forest, were discovered by divers Al Olson, Keith Pearson and Taras Lyssenko, who had been alerted to the site by unusual readings on an underwater sonar device. The place where the ancient trees were found is dubbed the "Olson site" in honor of one of its discoverers.

1991 The half-hour situation-comedy series *Dinosaurs*, made by Disney Studios after an idea by Muppets creator Jim Henson, debuts on ABC television. The show is a satire of familiar sit-coms, albeit one populated by dinosaurs, paralleling various aspects of modern life. The dinosaur characters are costumes (worn by human performers) made by the Henson Creature Shop, enhanced with animatronics. The father of the Sinclair Family is a "mighty *Megalosaurus*" named Earl. His wife Ethel is of a different genus and species. However, this does not seem to be a problem as the Sinclairs have a healthy multi-generic family dominated by the demanding Baby Sinclair. After the show is canceled it will become popular in reruns, maybe for eons.

1993 A picture of *Mononykus olecrans*, an odd-looking, dinosaur-like Mesozoic flightless bird from Mongolia having only one finger on each "hand," is cover-featured on *Time* magazine.

~ 27 ~

1923 Charles L. Camp and Eustace L. Furlong, the former's field assistant and preparator, discover a fossil field near Billings Gap, Arizona. Here they will find the skull and jaws of a narrow-snouted phytosaur which Camp names *Machaeroproscopus tenuis*. Later, this specimen is referred to the phytosaur species *Pseudopalatus pristinus*.

1957 Paleontologist Richard Swann Lull, a pioneer in the study of some of the oldest dinosaurs, dies.

1960 The CBS television series *Men into Space* runs "From Another World," an episode in which astronaut Col. Edward McCauley (William Lundigan), while studying the geophysical composition of an asteroid, finds the fossil skeleton of a pterosaur-like prehistoric animal.

~ 28 ~

1953 Berislav V. Krzic is born in Zagreb, Croatia. The Czechoslovakian *Journey to the Beginning of Time* and American *Journey to the Center of the Earth* movies, as well as Rudolph F. Zallinger's "Age of Reptiles" painting, among other influences, will inspire Krzic to become an artist of prehistoric life.

1982 In response to requests by schoolchildren, headed by students from McElwain Elementary Schools in Adams County, Colorado, Governor Richard D. Lamm decrees *Stegosaurus* (whose mounted skeleton is displayed in the Denver Museum of Natural History) to be the state fossil. Children have nicknamed the dinosaur "Stegie."

~ 29 ~

1905 Emil Kuhn-Schnyder is born (as simply Emil Kuhn) in Zürich, Switzerland. Though one of his main interests will be Pleistocene mammals, the future paleontologist's work will mostly focus upon the Middle Triassic vertebrate fauna of Monte San Giorgio in Tessin, Switzerland, which, under his guidance, will become one of the world's best known fossil sites. In 1955, after becoming Professor of Paleontology at the Zoological Institute of the University of Zürich, Kuhn-Schnyder will succeed in funding the Paleontological Institute which will house the Monte San Giorgio specimens. Here he will develop new techniques in the preparation of vertebrate fossils. Many monographs about the Monte San Giorgio fauna will be published under Kuhn-Schnyder's supervision. (Dies July 30, 1994.)

1932 Charles L. Camp returns to the Blue Forest area of the Petrified Forest where he had prospected for specimens two years earlier. Here he finds a new fossiliferous zone that will lead into a hill containing much material pertaining to ancient crocodiles.

1938 Edwin Carter Galbreath publishes a paper about post-glacial age fossil vertebrates from east-central Illinois.

1965 David Jay Simmons names and describes *Tatisaurus oehleri*, what is interpreted as a primitive, possibly armored dinosaur from the Lufeng Basin (Lower Jurassic) of China. (Decades later, this dinosaur will be referred to the previously named armored dinosaur *Scelidosaurus*.)

1988 The "Readasaurus" egg is delivered by the United States Postal Service to the National Museum of Natural History in Washington, D.C., to be exhibited in its Hall of Dinosaurs.

1994 *Dinosaur Talks: Edwin H. Colbert*, the first in a series of audio-cassettes, is released by Fossil Records of Burbank, California. Professor Colbert talks about his life both personal and professional. Similar tapes featuring Elmer S. Riggs (1994) and Charles M. Sternberg (1997) will follow.

~ 30 ~

1996 Paleontologist Paul C. Sereno announces the new 90 million-year-old theropod *Deltadromeus* (meaning "delta runner") and newly found remains of *Carcharodontosaurus* ("shark tooth lizard"), both from Morocco, at the University of Chicago. *Deltadromeus*, the more slender and agile of the two, is based on a skeleton missing only the skull discovered the previous summer by American writer (and Paul's future bride) Gabrielle Lyon during a joint U.S.-Moroccan expedition led by Sereno. The original specimen of the more massive *Carcharodontosaurus* was first described in 1927. A reconstruction of this dinosaur's skull accompanies the announcement.

Family portrait of the Sinclairs, featured on the TV sit-com Dinosaurs. *© Disney Enterprises, Inc.*

MAY

~ 1 ~

1822   Gideon Mantell completes the dedication for his monograph *The Fossils of the South Down; or Illustrated Geology of Sussex*. The tome, partially illustrated by his wife Mary Ann, deals mostly with invertebrates. He will, however, also depict some teeth, allegedly discovered by his wife, which in three years he will name *Iguanodon*. This 1822 publication will be historically significant as constituting the earliest published figures of dinosaurian remains that can still be referred to or studied.

1870   William Marcey "Boss" Tweed takes office in New York and is immediately opposed to the Paleozoic Museum, apparently for financial (no profits for the Tweed Ring), religious ("animals *alleged* to be of the pre-Adamite period") and chauvinistic (Benjamin Waterhouse Hawkins, who is making the animals, is an Englishman, after all) reasons.

1893   The World's Columbian Exposition, the Chicago World's Fair of 1893, opens in Jackson Park. Geology and paleontology related exhibits are featured in the rather hastily constructed anthropology building including Benjamin Waterhouse Hawkins's skeletal cast of *Hadrosaurus foulkii*, originally displayed at the Smithsonian Institution; also a shaggy, bigger-than-life-sized replica of "The Great Mastodon" — one of a line of such figures advertised as the "The Siberian Mammoth" and sold in London as models for art students. Some of these exhibits will eventually find their ways into the Field Columbian Museum, to be located in what was originally the Exposition's Fine Arts Building. In the Woman's Building "Primitive Woman," a 15 by 72 feet mural by Mary Fairchild MacMonnies, portrays cavewomen as subservient to their cavemen mates.

1916 Borrowing $20 million from New York Bankers, Kansas entrepreneur Harry F. Sinclair establishes the Sinclair Oil and Refining Company which will become world famous for using dinosaurs in its advertising. Dinosaurs — particularly the *Apatosaurus* (popularly known as *Brontosaurus*), which will eventually become the company's symbol — are used to convey the message that the crude oils utilized by Sinclair are very old, having mellowed underground long before the advent of the earliest dinosaurs. Sinclair's dinosaur imagery will appear in myriad advertisements. Sinclair books, stamps, World's Fair exhibits, toys, souvenirs and service-station displays also make use of dinosaurs. Much of the company's dinosaur-related output will become highly collectible memorabilia in the coming years.

1988 "Dinosaurs!," the biggest exhibition of robotic creatures ever produced by Dinamation International Corporation, opens at Science World in the "golf ball" Expo Center building, on the former Expo site in Vancouver, Canada. The exhibition, sponsored by the provincial government, also features fossils, hands-on computer simulations and special live presentations.

"The Great Mastodon" (aka "The Siberian Mammoth"), following its appearance at the World's Columbian Exposition of 1893, at its new home, the Field Columbian Museum. Courtesy The Field Museum (neg. #8786).

Painting by artist James E. Allen of the crested hadrosaur Corythosaurus Casuarius *for* The Sinclair Dinosaur Book *(1934), one of many free promotional items put out by the oil company. © Sinclair Refining Company.*

1997 The United States Postal Services issues "The World of Dinosaurs," a series of interconnecting stamps featuring dinosaurs, illustrated by James Gurney, author and artist of the popular book *Dinotopia* (1992) and its sequel *Dinotopia: The World Beneath* (1996). An event commemorating the release is held outside the Two Rivers Events Center (originally scheduled for the Dinosaur Valley Museum, rescheduled because the museum is too small) in Grand Junction, Colorado. Paleontologist Robert T. Bakker is one of the speakers.

~ 2 ~

Benjamin Waterhouse Hawkins' ambitious Paleozoic Museum — planned but never realized for Central Park. From the Twelfth Annual Report (1868) of the Board of Commissioners of Central Park.

1868 Benjamin Waterhouse Hawkins is invited by park comptroller Andrew H. Green to come to the United States to create life-sized extinct animals, similar to those he made for Crystal Palace, for the "Paleozoic Museum" planned for Central Park in New York. Hawkins responds with a long letter stating, among other things, "The interest in the remains of ancient animal life which Geology has revealed within the last century is world wide, and almost romantic in its influence upon the imagination, and I quite agree with you that there can hardly be a question as to the advantage of representing these remains, clothed in the forms which science now ventures to define." Hawkins accepts.

1921 The Field Museum of Natural History (eventually shortened to The Field Museum) in Chicago, Illinois, opens to the public. Hall 38, or the Ernest R. Graham Hall of fossils, animals and plants, presents exhibits arranged according to their geological sequence. Displayed are numerous skeletons, a few of them, like the mammoth (the first and largest mounted in the United States), having been acquired from the nearby Chicago Academy of Sciences. Prominent in the center of the hall is the huge partial skeleton of *Apatosaurus* which Elmer S. Riggs described in 1903. In five years Charles R. Knight will begin painting his magnificent series of murals that will remain a part of Hall 38 until it is dismantled in the 1990s. In 1939 the Ward company's long displayed plaster cast of the skeleton of the giant ground sloth *Megatherium* will be replaced by a real one (a composite mounted by preparator Phil C. Orr), the bones having been collected by Riggs during the Second Marshall Field Paleontological Expedition to Argentina and Bolivia in 1927.

Hall 38 at the Field Museum of Natural History as it looked in 1921. In the foreground is a mammoth skeleton formerly exhibited at the Chicago Academy of Sciences. Courtesy The Field Museum (neg. #GEO58913).

1954   Movie producer Tomoyuki Tanaka hires noted Japanese science fiction author Shigeru Kayama to write the original screenplay for a movie that will eventually be titled *Gojira* in Japan and (dubbed in English) *Godzilla, King of the Monsters!* in the United States.

1996   Sculptor David A. Thomas personally delivers his full-scale (17 feet long) *Utahraptor ostrommaysi* model to Vernal's Utah Field House of Natural History.

~ 3 ~

1870 Boss Tweed's men barge into Benjamin Waterhouse Hawkins' studio and smash his prehistoric-animal models and molds, which become landfill at Central Park's 59th Street entrance. Hawkins manages to save his model of the Irish deer *Megaloceros* and mold of the skeleton of *Hadrosaurus foulkii* (both at the Smithsonian). In 1875 Hawkins will do a series of Paleozoic paintings for Princeton University.

1877 Francz Nopcsa (aka Ferencz or Francis, also von Felsö-Szilvás) is born in Deva, Transylvania. Baron Nopcsa will become one of the most colorful personalities in the history of paleontology, writing authoritatively on numerous subjects relating to this science, also living the life of a baronial lord, becoming a military leader and trying (but not succeeding) at having himself made king of Albania, among other activities. Not a field paleontologist, Nopcsa will write extensively on the dinosaurs of his homeland, introducing a number of new dinosaurian taxa, and also proposing the interesting but incorrect idea that the sometimes spectacular bony crests of hadrosaurs was a sexually dimorphic feature (only the males supposedly having them). Toward his latter years the Baron will be attacked by resentful peasants, suffering a head injury that will, at least in part, lead to a state of mind eventually resulting in his suicide on April 25, 1933.

1988 With much ceremony, the "Readasaurus" egg hatches at the National Zoo in Washington, D. C. The event is covered by television's *Good Morning America* show. The hatchling dinosaur then begins a nationwide tour sponsored by the U. S. Postal Service to promote reading.

1997 Filming officially begins in Manhattan of TriStar's new and revamped American movie version of *Godzilla* as the gigantic mutated (and much changed from the original) monster attacks North America.

~ 4 ~

1887 In the *American Naturalist*, Edward D. Cope publishes the first description of fossils obtained from collector and mountain man David Baldwin. The specimens, recovered about 25 miles away from Ghost Ranch, New Mexico, include bones of a small carnivorous dinosaur that Cope refers to the *Coelurus*, a genus named by his rival O. C. Marsh. Cope later refers this material to its own new genus *Coelophysis*.

1901 An expedition of the Imperial Academy of Sciences, in Russia, leaves Petrograd to retrieve a satisfactorily preserved mammoth carcass frozen into a cliff of the River Beresovka, a tributary of the River Kolyma, west of the Behring Strait in Siberia. The specimen had been discovered by Lamut S. Tarabykin at the end of August 1900 while he was chasing a deer. On the recovery expedition are staff zoologist Otto F. Hertz, taxidermist M. E. V. Pfizenmeyer and geologist M. D. P. Sevastianov of Yurievsk University.

1923 George Olsen finds a second specimen which he believes belongs to *Alectrosaurus*, although future research will show that this new material actually belongs to a therizinosaur, a very different kind of theropod possessing a manus or hands with very large claws.

1931 Walter William Bishop, born in England, will be known for his work on early man sites in East Africa and as Head of the Geology Department at Queen Mary College. About to be Director of the Peabody Museum of Natural History at Yale, he dies on February 20, 1977.

1955 The television series *Science Fiction Theatre* runs the episode "When a Camera Fails," about a geophysicist (Gene Lockhart) who invents a camera that takes pictures of past events that have been recorded on rocks and fossils. The pictures include dinosaurs and extinct mammals.

~ 5 ~

1988 "Australia: An Overview of Down Under" starts at L.A. County's Natural History Museum. The class on the evolving landscape since Paleozoic times coincides with the museum's "Fossils of the Australian Dreamtime: Kadimakara" exhibition.

~ 6 ~

1956 Rene Hernández-Rivera is born in Mexico City. Inspired by the relative lack of paleontological work done in Mexico, particularly that focusing on dinosaurs, Hernández will become a vertebrate paleontologist specializing in this group of animals. Eventually his will be one of his country's most prominent names in this field, with the discovery of the most complete hadrosaur specimen yet found in Mexico numbering among his accomplishments.

1970 The United States Postal Service issues its first dinosaur stamp. It reproduces part of the small preliminary painting made by Rudolph F.

Zallinger for his "Age of Reptiles" mural at the Yale Peabody Museum. The stamp includes *Apatosaurus* and *Stegosaurus*.

1994 Paleontologists William Hammer and William Hickerson, both of Augustana College in Rock Island, Illinois, announce new dinosaurs and other extinct reptiles of Late Triassic or Early Jurassic age found in an Antarctic riverbank deposit. One of these, a 25-foot-long theropod, is to be named *Cryolophosaurus*, meaning "frozen crested lizard," referring named both to the area in which it was found and the unusual thin crest atop its head. Other discoveries include remains of non-theropod dinosaurs, one of them probably a prosauropod, and a pterosaur and large tritylodont. These animals are similar to those found on other continents. The find indicates that the climate was more temperate during the Late Triassic or Early Jurassic.

~ 7 ~

1888 Sidney Henry Haughton is born in Bethnal Green, London, England. Influenced by paleontologist Robert Broom, Haughton's early work in this profession will focus on the fossil fauna of the Karoo sequence. In later years Haughton will author seven books (several of which, including *Geological History of Africa South of the Sahara*, will become standard texts), 218 scientific papers, 321 abstracts and 13 geological maps. He will enjoy memberships in the Royal Society of London, Royal Society of South Africa, Geological Societies of London, Belgium, America and South Africa (honorary member), African Geological Society and Associated Scientific and Technical Societies of South Africa. (Dies May 24, 1982.)

1911 Ishiro Honda is born. Honda-san will become a director of Japanese motion pictures. He will be best known for directing numerous films for the Toho Co. featuring giant monsters, including the first Godzilla movie (*Gojira*, released in Japan in 1954), which he co-wrote with Takeo Murata. Among Honda's credits will be the following movies which feature prehistoric creatures (original English-language titles and release dates): *Godzilla, King of the Monsters!* (1956), *Rodan the Flying Monster* (1957), *Varan the Unbelievable* (1962), *King Kong vs. Godzilla* (1963), *Godzilla vs. the Thing* (1964), *Ghidrah the Three Headed Monster* (1965), *Frankenstein Conquers the World* (1966), *Monster Zero* (1970), *Destroy All Monsters* (1970), *Godzilla's Revenge* (1971) and *The Terror of Godzilla* (1978). (Dies February 1993.)

1995   The blockbuster movie *Jurassic Park* premieres on network (NBC) television in a three-hour (including commercials) time slot. *TV Guide* magazine rates the film "three stars." The first of many reruns will soon follow.

~ 8 ~

1923   Charles L. Camp and Eustace L. Furlong discover remains of a new extinct reptile *Parrishia* at "Phytosaur Basin" (so named by Camp) south of Crocodile Hill in the Petrified Forest.

~ 9 ~

1932   Richard Estes is born in San Rafael, California. After becoming a paleoherpetologist, Estes will do extensive work on fossil and modern vertebrates including fishes, frogs, salamanders and lizards (including mosasaurs). Estes will be internationally known for his work, writing more than 100 published scholarly papers, authoring or editing four books and, finally, editing the *Journal of Vertebrate Paleontology*. In 1990 Estes will receive the Romer-Simpson Medal at the 50th Annual Meeting of the Society of Vertebrate Paleontology at the University of Kansas, this being the SVP's most prestigious award. (Dies December 28, 1990.)

1948   Remains of a giant theropod dinosaur are found by the Palaeontological Institute of the Academy of Sciences, Union of Soviet Socialist Republics, in the Nemegt Formation, Nemegt, Mongolia. It will be named *Tyrannosaurus bataar* in 1955, then renamed that same year *Tarbosaurus bataar*, finally returning to its original name in 1992.

~ 10 ~

1876   A. Leith Adams, Professor of Zoology at the Royal College of Science for Ireland, reads a paper before the Royal Irish Academy naming and describing the new genus and species *Arctosaurus osborni*. Adams believes the type specimen, a single vertebra found by Admiral Sherard Osborn in the Arctic, to be dinosaurian. In later years most paleontologists will disagree with his assessment.

1901   Cartoonist and writer V. (Vincent) T. Hamlin is born in Perry, Iowa. In 1930 Hamlin will become a newspaper man (reporter, staff artist and press photographer) with frustrations to write and draw his own comic strip. Believing the futuristic "Buck Rogers" type setting to be already tapped, Hamlin then goes in the opposite direction for subject matter, creating the classic strip *Alley Oop* which debuts in 1933. Interested in prehistoric life, Hamlin will interject a degree of authenticity into his drawings of dinosaurs and other ancient animals despite making them funny. An "extra" will be "Dinny's Family Album," an insert that (although the pictures are rather cartoony) gives factual information. (Dies June 14, 1993.)

~ 11 ~

1977   Charles E. ("Chuck") Finsley, Curator of Paleontology at the Dallas Museum of Natural History, and a museum crew begin collecting vertebrate fossils for the museum on the Miller Ranch, near Garzon County, Texas.

~ 12 ~

1905   Andrew Carnegie formally presents a cast of the skeleton of *Diplodocus carnegeii* (species named after him) to the Trustees of the British Museum (Natural History), thereby instigating an early dinosaur fad in England. Record audiences will visit the museum to view the mounted cast. There are also a score of political cartoons featuring the dinosaur, advertisements and even a series of "*Diplodocus* vases" bearing the animal's image on their sides in high relief, this being one of the earliest examples of dinosaur merchandising.

1987   Paleontologists from the Natural History Museum of Los Angeles County announce the discovery in Sherman Oaks, California, of a 10 million-year-old sperm whale, the first such animal ever found in the county. The specimen, consisting of pieces of the skull and jawbone, was found by Alison Epstein, who had been planting flowers for her backyard wedding. As there are two rows of large teeth as opposed to the single lower row of relatively small teeth possessed by modern sperm whales, the find helps fill a gap in sperm whale evolution. According to fossil whale authority Lawrence Barnes, Chairman of the Department of Vertebrate Paleontology, "This is a very significant find. We just don't have animals like this from other places on the coast, except for one dinky tooth fossil from Palos Verdes." Epstein says, "The big joke from people at the wedding was that it was going to start spouting."

1991   The "World of Dinosaurs" exhibit, a temporary display of large dinosaur models, opens at the Boston Museum of Science. As a promotion, newspapers the day before run a photograph of project coordinator Harry Shannon "wearing" the legs and feet of a *Tyrannosaurus.*

~ 13 ~

1832   Baron Georges Cuvier, regarded as the "Father of Paleontology," dies in France.

1903   Ellis Burman is born in Toledo, Ohio. Burman will become a make-up and property man for motion pictures, working for Howard A. Anderson and later establishing his own studio. *Unknown Island* (1948) will feature a menagerie of beasties made by Burman and staff including a *Dimetrodon* (a mechanical prop, which, minus its dorsal fin, will get recycled that same year for *Jungle Jim*), a pair of *Diplodocus* (wire-operated miniatures) and several *Ceratosaurus* (actors in costumes). Burman will provide another dinosaur suit for *Jungle Manhunt*, a 1951 "Jungle Jim" entry, but its scenes will only appear in the coming-attractions trailer. He will also dress up an elephant named Emma as a mammoth for the movie *Prehistoric Women* (1950) and for various personal appearances. (Dies 1977.)

Special-effects man and prop maker Ellis Burman with Emma, the Indian elephant he has transformed into a woolly mammoth, here apparently for a promotional stunt. Courtesy The Burman Studio.

1985   "Dinosaur Days" begins at the Denver Museum of Natural History in Colorado. Lectures, movies, a display of metal sculptures made by guest Jim Gary and other activities will fill out the eight-day festival.

~ 14 ~

1992   Thirty Federal Bureau of Investigation agents appear at the Black Hills Institute of Geologic Research, Inc., in South Dakota and confiscate the fossil bones of "Sue," the biggest and most complete *Tyrannosaurus rex* skeleton yet found. The prize specimen had been collected inside the Cheyenne River Sioux Reservation and may belong to the tribe. Black

Hills Institute president Peter Larson states that he paid $5,000 for the rights to recover the specimen from Sioux landowner Maurice Williams, though Williams replies that the Institute only had permission to look for — not collect — fossils. A *Newsweek* caption will sum up the situation: "Will the Sioux sue for Sue?" The specimen is summarily locked away in storage at the Museum of Geology at the South Dakota School of Mines and Technology, in Rapid City, inaccessible for study.

~ 15 ~

1904 Another of Frederick Burr Opper's comic strips satirizing modern life through prehistoric imagery is published. "How the Dinosaurs Went to the Show," subtitled "A Thrilling Tale of Antedeluvian Days," involves a "Dinosaurus" that tries to eat a mammoth, only to get kicked for its trouble.

1935 Sharat Kumar Roy publishes three papers on fossil invertebrates, including one naming and describing a new phyllopodous crustacean from the Silurian period.

Same day: Bryan Patterson publishes a paper describing a new specimen of *Argyrohippus*, a toxodont found in the Deseado Beds (Upper Oligocene) of Patagonia.

1995 The Dinosaur Depot officially opens in Cañon City, Colorado, emphasizing Late Jurassic fossil discoveries made in the Garden Park area. The facility has a viewable laboratory where visitors can watch fossil bones being prepared, a full-scale *Allosaurus* sculpture by David A. Thomas and tours and special presentations. The Dinosaur Depot was created through volunteer work by members of the Garden Park Paleontology Society (formed in 1990) and is the result of a unique public/private partnership comprising the GPPS, BLM (Bureau of Land Management), Denver Museum of Natural History, National Park Service, United States Forest Service, city of Cañon City, Fremont County and other parties. The facility allows Cañon City and Fremont County to share their wealth of fossil resources with the public. It is planned to be a companion project of the Dinosaur Discovery Center, a proposed world-class facility to be built in the future in the Garden Park Fossil Area.

~ 16 ~

1986 The flying *Quetzalcoatlus* is test-launched at Andrews Air Force Base, Maryland with no complications. Next, the Smithsonian...

1994 "Life Through Time," a renovated and permanent exhibit, opens at the Houston Museum of Natural Science in Texas. The exhibit, organized according to the passage of time and displaying more than 450 specimens, is intended to show the evolution of life before the emergence of man.

~ 17 ~

1847 The American Medical Association (AMA) is formed amid fossil skeletons at the Academy of Natural Sciences of Philadelphia. Some 250 physicians attend from 22 states, representing 28 colleges and 40 medical societies. The Parke-Davis company later commissions an oil painting of this historic event to use in its advertising.

1964 "Disneyland Goes to the World's Fair" airs on the *Disneyland* television series (now on NBC). Genial host Walt Disney takes viewers on a tour through his new "Audio-Animatronics" shop showing how its latest technologies bring dinosaurs, mammoths and cavemen (also not quite so old President Abe Lincoln) to mechanical life for the New York World's Fair (1964). In future years Disney's designers and technicians will bring this technology to even higher levels of realism.

1986 The flying *Quetzalcoatlus* model, the opening act at the annual Armed Forces open house, takes off from Andrews Air Force Base, Maryland rising majestically 600 feet. Seconds later, before hundreds of spectators, it crashes (a "Pterrible Ptragedy," according to a *Los Angeles Times* headline) after its tail rudder assembly prematurely falls off. The plunge is too rapid for its built-in parachute to be of use. Flight-designer Paul Mac-Cready quips, "Now we know why pterosaurs are extinct."

1996 *Science*, the weekly journal of the American Association for the Advancement of Science, announces the discovery of the new theropod *Deltadromeus* and newly found remains of *Carcharodontosaurus* in an article co-written by Paul C. Sereno and his international (United States and France) team. In the article *Deltadromeus* is officially named and described by the authors.

~ 18 ~

1866 Benjamin Waterhouse Hawkins is formally employed by the Commissioners of the Central Park of New York to build prehistoric animals for the Paleozoic Museum. Rather than have Hawkins repeat the animals he had portrayed in England at Crystal Palace, his employers decide that he should only recreate North American species like *Hadrosaurus* and *Laelaps* (later renamed *Dryptosaurus*). Hawkins establishes his studio on the Central Park grounds.

1930   Charles L. Camp starts collecting reptile fossils at what will later be called the *Placerias* Quarry in northeastern Arizona. The quarry becomes so named because of numerous specimens of the dicynodont *Placerias* that Camp and former student Samuel P. Welles find there and then describe.

~ 19 ~

1930   Charles L. Camp returns to what he mistakenly believes is the Shreve Quarry (named for local cobbler Roy Shreve) in the Petrified Forest where he collects fragmentary fossils of extinct reptiles. Eventually Camp will uncover 200 square feet of quarry floor and 200 pounds of fossil bones.

~ 20 ~

1920   Karl F. Hirsch is born in Germany. Although he will have the status of an amateur paleontologist with no formal training, Hirsch will specialize in fossil eggs and be recognized as one of the field's most prominent workers in the study of the microstructure of fossil eggshells. Among his published accomplishments will be co-editing, with Kenneth Carpenter and John R. Horner, the technical book *Dinosaur Eggs and Babies* (1994). When he dies on June 1, 1996, he will leave behind much unfinished work, some of which will be completed by his former assistants, among the most prominent of them being Emily S. Bray.

1996   The second cast of Paul C. Sereno's reconstructed skull of the giant theropod *Carcharodontosaurus* goes on display at the Crerar Library, University of Chicago, in Illinois.

1998   The mega-budget American *Godzilla* attacks motion-picture screens nationwide. Produced by Dean Devlin for TriStar and boasting state-of-the-art computer-graphics special effects, the movie features a brand new interpretation of the huge monster. Among the "improvements": Godzilla has lost his famous radioactive breath and he no longer has historical ties with Japan. The film's success is big but brief.

~ 21 ~

1799   Mary Anning is born in Lyme Regis, Dorset, England, the daughter of local fossil merchant Richard Anning. She will be regarded as a supposedly dull child who, after surviving a lightning bolt strike at the age of one, will develop talents that include finding fossils. Mary will become an amateur collecter, credited (erroneously, it seems) with discovering the first ichthyosaur specimen in 1812. In 1824 she will collect the first complete pterosaur specimen (of the genus *Dimorphodon*) found in Great Britain. Anning will die in 1847, then be buried in the churchyard at Lyme Regis near the fossil shop, a stained glass window with Mary's name overlooking her grave.

1916   John Franklin Lance is born in Vaughn, New Mexico. Lance will become a paleontologist whose main interest is fossil horses from the Late Cenozoic rocks of Chihuahua, Mexico. In 1950 he will publish a major study that will remain one of the most comprehensive analyses of the ancestry of modern horses. Starting in 1963 much of Lance's professional work will be with the National Science Foundation where he will serve in various administrative capacities, and from which, upon retirement in 1986, he will receive the Distinguished Service Award. (Dies May 27, 1991.)

1955   Mike Fredericks is born. Fredericks will found, publish and edit *Prehistoric Times*, a fan magazine that covers everything prehistoric, including memorabilia, movies, art, toys, museums and assembly kits. Debuting in 1993 as a humble black and white mail-order item, it will rapidly evolve and improve both in content and in look, also going on sale in many major bookstores.

1975   Former policeman turned paleontologist Stephen Hutt discovers the first bone belonging to a diplodocid — a giant but relatively slender and very long sauropod dinosaur — on the Isle of Wight, England.

1988   The San Diego Natural History Museum opens a special dinosaur exhibit highlighted by 10 mechanical creatures from Dinamation International Corporation.

~ 22 ~

1859   Arthur Conan Doyle is born in Edinburgh, Scotland. Though this future author, physician and fossil collector will be most famous for creating consulting detective Sherlock Holmes, he is also well known for his series of novels starring the bombastic Professor George Edward Challenger, especially the first *The Lost World* (1912). In the 1970s authors John Hathaway Winslow and Alfred Meyer will make a case linking "Sir Arthur" and details described in *The Lost World* to the infamous Piltdown Man hoax, implying his participation as a kind of revenge against the scientific community for its criticism of his beliefs in spiritualism. (Dies July 7, 1930.)

1903 Andrew Carnegie authorizes the Carnegie Museum of Natural History to acquire the famous Bayet fossil collection. Gathered over a 40-year span by Baron Ernst de Bayet of Brussels, Belgium, this is one of the largest private collections in the world, requiring a British Museum (Natural History) official five days to inventory, costing Carnegie $20,500 and filling 259 shipping cases. It includes everything from plants to vertebrates, some specimens being exquisitely preserved.

1953 Brontosaur Hall (aka the Hall of Early Dinosaurs) reopens at the American Museum of Natural History. It was renovated during the early 1950s under the direction of Curator Edwin H. Colbert. Included in the newly designed hall are the museum's classic Jurassic and Triassic dinosaur skeletons, also new specimens such as skeletons of the small Triassic theropod *Coelophysis*. Displayed for the first time — behind the *Apatosaurus* and near the *Allosaurus* — is the series of dinosaur tracks collected almost two decades earlier by Roland T. Bird from a bed of the Paluxy River, Texas. Another innovation is a series of chalk drawings on the blue perimeter walls above the display cases. Originally intended as only temporary, these pictures of extinct animals will remain until the hall again undergoes major renovations in the 1990s.

1985 Touchstone Pictures' *Baby ... Secret of the Lost Legend*, a movie inspired by claims that a live dinosaur known locally as Mokele-Mbembe exists in the Congo, opens nationwide. It is the story of an *Apatosaurus* family, including a hatchling called Baby, found in jungles of Africa, and a young couple's efforts to save the dinosaurs from an unscrupulous paleontologist. Special effects by Ron Tantin and Isidoro Raponi include animatronic dinosaurs that can interact directly with human actors.

1986 The First International Symposium on Dinosaur Tracks and Traces begins in Albuquerque, New Mexico, co-hosted by the New Mexico Museum of Natural History, Museum of Northern Arizona and University of Colorado, Denver. The subject is ichnology, or the study of trace fossils (mostly footprints) that give important information about living rather than dead animals. The event triggers a new interest in dinosaur tracks and traces, an aspect of ancient life that, in previous years, had largely been ignored.

1997 Paleontologists Fernando E. Novas and Pablo F. Puerta announce *Unenlagia comahuensis*, a "theropod" (later reclassified as a bird) from Patagonia that seems to be an intermediate form partially filling the morphological gap between the dinosaur *Deinonychus* and bird *Archaeopteryx*.

SAME DAY Bruce M. Rothschild, Darren Tanke and Kenneth Carpenter report the first evidence — spheroidal erosions in bone — that *Tyrannosaurus rex* suffered from the gout.

~ 23 ~

1707 Carolus Linnaeus (also known as Carl — or Karl — von Linné) is born in Rashult, Sweden. Linnaeus will earn his place in history as the "Father of Biological Classification," hailed as the greatest botanist of his day and one of the founders of modern botany. Since plant classification had been so chaotic as to be worthless, Linnaeus will introduce his own system based on the number of stamens and pistils in a plant. According to his system different organisms are grouped together into a hierarchical system of taxa, each taxon characterized by specific characters or sets of characters. What will be the so-called Linnaean system remains in use; it is also applied to extinct organisms until the second half of the 20th century when it is replaced by the cladistic method of classification. (Dies 1778.)

1927 Charles L. Camp starts digging for fossils in the Devil's Playground in the Petrified Forest.

1931 C. L. Camp returns to the original (and authentic) Shreve Quarry in the Petrified Forest. Here he will collect fragmentary remains of *Placerias*. Tomorrow, digging operations proceed on a much larger scale.

1946 Robert A. Long is born in Whittier, California. Long will become a research associate at the Museum of Paleontology at the University of California at Berkeley. Though Long will start his career as a paleontologist specializing in dinosaurs, his main expertise will evolve to the fauna of the Late Triassic, particularly that of the Chinle Formation of Arizona and New Mexico. With co-author Phillip K. Murry he will name numerous new taxa from these regions, including the very primitive dinosaur *Chindesaurus*. Long co-authors (with Rose Houk) the book *Dawn of the Dinosaurs: The Triassic in Petrified Forest* (1988) and (with microvertebrate specialist Murry) the monograph "Late Triassic (Carnian and Norian) Tetrapods from the Southwestern United States" (1995).

TYRANNOSAURUS REX and TRICERATOPS HORRIDUS, two of the 21 mechanical prehistoric creatures featured in Knott's Berry Farm's "Kingdom of the Dinosaurs" attraction. Courtesy Knott's Berry Farm, Buena Park, CA.

1988 The Kingdom of the Dinosaurs indoor ride opens at Knott's Berry Farm, Buena Park, California. Visitors in cars are whisked via a mad scientist's time machine back to different prehistoric eras. Creatures encountered during the seven-minute experience include cave people, extinct mammals and the dinosaurs promised by the ride's name. Extra ambience is the chill of the Ice Age and heat of an active volcano. The attraction includes 21 fully animated figures, 13 of which are dinosaurs, and has cost Knott's $7 million. The prehistoric visual effects were created by Bill Novey and Joe Garlington ("This was by far our most challenging and most rewarding project," according to Garlington) of Art Technology of Sun Valley, California. Kevin Nadeau and a team of sound designers provided vocal tracks. Background scenes were created by Montana artists Tom and Laurie Gilleon.

1997 *The Lost World: Jurassic Park*, director Steven Spielberg's more spectacular and realistic sequel to his *Jurassic Park*, opens nationwide on 3,024 screens amid a new blitz of promotion and merchandising. The same day sets from the movie are opened to the public at Universal Studios Hollywood. From the start the new movie will outdo the original, grossing almost $93 million the first weekend in domestic box office receipts and $100 million the first week, thereby more than making back its $74 million cost within just a few days. Already there are rumors of a third film to be made, perhaps, several years hence.

~ 24 ~

1911   United States president William Howard Taft signs a proclamation designating a vast canyon country in western Colorado as Colorado National Monument. The Monument, located in the Morrison Formation with majestic cliffs and canyons, is rich in fossils including those of plants, invertebrates and some of the best known Late Jurassic dinosaurs (e.g., *Allosaurus, Apatosaurus, Brachiosaurus* and *Stegosaurus*).

1931   Charles L. Camp initiates full-scale excavation at the original Shreve Quarry, now renamed the *Placerias* Quarry for the abundant remains of that genus found at this site.

1973   J. D. Stewart discovers the oldest known nodosaurid, a kind of armored dinosaur, from the Niobrara Chalk Formation, in Rooks County, Kansas. Nodosaurids belong to one of two families of the larger group Ankylosauria, usually possessing large laterally projecting spikes and a clubless tail.

1997   "The Dinosaurs of Jurassic Park" exhibit continues its successful tour, opening at the San Diego Natural History Museum in California to coincide with the opening of *The Lost World: Jurassic Park*, a movie in which the city of San Diego is victimized by a rampaging *Tyrannosaurus rex*.
Same day: "Dinosaur Families," a new traveling exhibit sponsored by the Museum of the Rockies in Bozeman, Montana, opens at The Field Museum. The exhibit includes fossils and casts of fossil skulls, skeletons and eggs of some of the dinosaurs collected in Montana by paleontologist John R. Horner. Featured are the duckbilled *Maiasaura*— represented by embryos to adults — and also the theropod *Troodon* and ornithopod *Orodromeus*. The Kokoro company provides the various mechanical dinosaurs.

~ 25 ~

1964   Ricardo Delgado is born in Los Angeles, California. As a child Delgado will develop a love for prehistoric animals through the paleontology exhibits at the Natural History Museum of Los Angeles County and creatures (sculpted by Marcel Delgado, no relation to Ricardo) in the movie *King Kong*. In the 1990s Delgado will create, write and illustrate *The Age of Reptiles* comic-book series featuring dinosaurs as characters. The series will prove popular enough for publisher Dark Horse Comics to reprint the collected stories in trade-paperback format, and in 1997 it will win the prestigious Eisner Award, given at the San Diego Comic-Con International annually for excellence in comic books. Also in the '90s Delgado will do character design work on Disney Studios' upcoming dinosaur-movie project.

1983 The British Museum (Natural History) begins collecting the holotype of the theropod dinosaur *Baryonyx walkeri* in Surrey, England.

~ 26 ~

1913 Peter Cushing is born in Kenley, Surrey, England. As a future character actor he will be best known for roles in British horror movies, but Cushing will also star in films with prehistoric themes. In *The Abominable Snowman of the Himalayas* (1957) he will play a paleontologist-type scientist searching for the legendary Yeti; in *Horror Express* (1972) he will deal with the remains of a prehistoric monster that revives and creates havoc on a train; in *The Creeping Flesh* (1973) he will be involved with an ancient skeleton that returns to life; in *At the Earth's Core* (1976), based on Edgar Rice Burroughs' stories, he will portray absent-minded Professor Abner Perry; and in the made-for-TV movie *The Great Houdinis* (1976) he will do a cameo as Sir Arthur Conan Doyle, author of *The Lost World*. (Dies August 11, 1994.)

1937 Elmer S. Riggs publishes a paper in which he describes the mounted skeleton of the Miocene toxodon *Homalodotherium* displayed at the Field Museum of Natural History.

1970 Paleontologist Craig C. Black names and describes *Pareumys*, a cylindrodontid rodent from the Duchesne River Formation of Utah.

1989 Paleontologists Phillip A. Murry, Kent Newman and Richard Wolfe begin digging at new microvertebrate fossil sites in the Rainbow Forest, Devil's Playground and Painted Desert, Arizona.

~ 27 ~

1854 Benjamin Waterhouse Hawkins lectures to the Society of Arts about the extinct-animal models he has made for the Crystal Palace and which will be unveiled in just two weeks. The figures — made of brick, cement and iron — constitute the first marriage of science and art in the recreation of Mesozoic reptiles. The full menagerie includes the dinosaurs *Iguanodon*, *Megalosaurus* and *Hylaeosaurus*; flying reptile *Pterodactylus*;

crocodile *Teleosaurus*; mammal-like reptile *Dicynodont*; amphibian *Labyrinthodont*; marine reptiles *Mosasaurus*, *Ichthyosaurus* and *Plesiosaurus*; and extinct mammals *Palaeotherium*, *Megaloceros*, *Anoplotherium* and *Megatherium*. The lecture, titled "On Visual Education as Applied to Geology," describes how Hawkins created this prehistoric bestiary. The full text will later be reprinted in the Society's journal, then published again as a leaflet by entrepreneur James Tennant.

Labyrinthodonts, giant amphibians recreated by Benjamin Waterhouse Hawkins for the Crystal Palace grounds and described in his talk. Photo by Bill Warren.

1922   The first Central Asiatic Expedition of the American Museum of Natural History expedition to Inner Mongolia ends, having primarily been a season of reconnaissance. Rather than the expected remains of early man, the group has collected bones of Late Cretaceous mammals and dinosaurs and also fossil eggshells presumed to be those of extinct birds. Paleontological history will be made when the expedition returns next year.

1933   The Chicago World's Fair, also known as A Century of Progress, opens around the Grant Park area. A number of attractions and exhibits featuring dinosaurs and other prehistoric creatures can be seen at the Fair. Century Dioramas Studios exhibits miniature dinosaur scenes based on Charles R. Knight's murals painted from 1926 to 1931 for the Field Museum of Natural History, just walking distance away. Tatterman's Marionettes, at the Kelvinator exhibit, perform a puppet play about cavemen preserving food. On a much grander scale, however, are the Sinclair Dinosaur Exhibit and "The World A Million Years Ago." The former, a free outdoor exhibit presented by the Sinclair Refining Company (a division of Sinclair Oil Corporation), features six full-scale dinosaurs (including a 70-foot-long *Apatosaurus*, which will be revamped for the 1934 season) designed by former movie special-effects man P. G. Alen. Some of them — including the *Apatosaurus*, *Tyrannosaurus*, *Triceratops* and *Corythosaurus*— move realistically, powered by hidden motors. "The World A Million Years Ago" is an indoor attraction created by Messmore and Damon, a company that makes props and mechanical figures, and is located directly across the midway from Sinclair's exhibit. Ticket-buying visitors enter a large, globe-shaped building and are conveyed by moving walkways "through time," passing dramatic tableaus presenting a wide variety of mechanical prehistoric reptiles, mammals and even cave people — also, to capitalize on the current hit movie *King Kong*, a giant "prehistoric gorilla." Some of the figures, including the *Apatosaurus*, mammoths and prehistoric people, were originally built during the 1920s for earlier exhibitions. For the second year of the Fair this attraction will be relocated and renamed "Down the Lost River: The World A Million Years Ago." Both the Sinclair and Messmore and Damon attractions will later move on to other fairs and locations, "The World A Million Years Ago" playing as late as 1972 in Old Town, Chicago, Illinois.

Full-sized mechanical APATOSAURUS, *the largest inhabitant of the Sinclair Dinosaur Exhibit at the 1933 Chicago World's Fair. The figure was slightly revamped for the 1934 season. Courtesy Chicago Historical Society.*

1994   *The Flintstones*, a major live-action motion picture based on the television cartoon series and produced by Steven Spielberg, is released by Universal Pictures. John Goodman stars as Fred, Elizabeth Perkins as Wilma, Rick Moranis as Barney and Rosie O'Donnell as Betty. State-of-the-art computer-graphics effects bring Dino and other Bedrock pets to life.

~ 28 ~

1930   Charles L. Camp collects fragmentary remains of a phytosaur at Point Bluff, southwest of the Blue Forest. This ends the paleontologist's work in the Petrified Forest. A half century later, the University of California at Berkeley will launch another series of fossil-collecting expeditions to this area.

1940   John R. Bolt is born in Grand Rapids, Michigan. Bolt will become a paleontologist specializing in primitive tetrapods. For several years he will be director of the geology department at The Field Museum and will later serve as Treasurer of the Society of Vertebrate Paleontology. In the latter 1990s Bolt will undergo a major study of the earliest known amphibians and redefine that major tetrapod group.

~ 29 ~ .

1946   Diane Gabriel is born in Brooklyn, New York. Gabriel will become a paleoanthropologist and a spokesperson for public understanding of science, particularly in the area of vertebrate paleontology. She will co-lead, with Rolf Johnson and Mac West, the Milwaukee Public Museum's "Dig-A-Dinosaur" program, resulting both in the recovery of important fossils from the Hell Creek Formation and also setting a standard for the involvement of volunteers with museum workers in performing paleontologic field work. (Dies September 14, 1994.)

~ 30 ~

1765   George Croghan, Irish trader recently appointed a deputy of Indian Affairs, writes in his log, while traveling down the Ohio River to attempt peace talks with Native Americans, about fossil bones he observes at the Big Bone Lick salt marshes between Covington and Louisville, Kentucky: "It appears that there are vast quantities of these bones lying five or six feet underground, which we discovered in the bank at the edge of the Lick. We found here two tusks about six feet long. We carried one, with some other bones to our boats and set off." A week later Croghan's party will be ambushed by Native Americans with Croghan being captured, then ransomed. Despite the dangers, he will return over a year later to collect fossils.

1891   Elmer S. Riggs, in Grand Junction, Colorado, investigating reports of dinosaur bones found in the Grand Valley, reads an article in the

Grand Junction News. It purports that, not only have agatized mastodon bones been found in the area, but also "8 mummified bodies of the genus *Homo,* 11 feet in height, and further." Not a gullible man, Riggs will check out the dinosaur bones instead.

1919   Dirk Albert Hooijer is born in Medan (Sumatra's Oostkust, a province of the former Dutch East Indies). He will become a paleontologist who, in 1971, will be awarded the Akzo Award for his work on Pleistocene mammals. One of his specialties will be the extinct rhinoceros. (Dies November 26, 1993.)

1988   "They're back!" proclaim advertisements for an appearance of a suite of Dinamation International Corporation's robotic full-sized dinosaurs at the Houston Museum of Natural Science in Texas. A lecture series accompanies the exhibition.

1997   Scientists announce the discovery in northern Spain of a new species of *Homo,* apparently a cross between Neandertal and modern human beings but not directly related to either. The fossils, dating back some 800,000 years, are the oldest hominid remains yet found in Europe.

Same day: Radio news programs report that a man has been sentenced to four years in prison for using *The Flinstones* theme music to jam airport radio signals, thereby delaying flights for some six hours.

~ 31 ~

1725   Professor Johannes Bartolomaeus Adam Beringer of Würzburg, Germany, makes a "discovery" that involves him in one of the earliest fossil frauds. According to the often repeated "fable," enhanced over the years by a various new details, Beringer's students, as a prank, had manufactured various "fossils" and buried them for their gullible professor to find. He finds them, believes them to be authentic, then later describes them in a beautifully illustrated portfolio. Eventually digging up a specimen bearing his name, he more than suspects the truth. Disgraced, Beringer will subsequently die of grief. The facts: In 1714, Beringer, a natural history professor and also a collector of natural curiosities, was guided by three local peasant boys from the village of Eibelstadt to "discover" numerous odd yet realistic-looking figures in shell limestone deposits near Würzburg. The figures ranged from flowers to animals (invertebrates, fishes, amphibians and reptiles, some in the acts of eating or copulating) to moons, suns, stars and even Hebrew symbols including the name Jehovah. Beringer regarded the "specimens," not as true fossils, but freaks or miracles of nature, created, he will write, as "mute but eloquent witnesses to God's perfection." Beringer will publish his report on the items in the volume *Lithographiae Wirceburgensis*, but not offering an opinion as to their origins, leaving their identity to others. The inevitable exposure of the hoax leads neither to disgrace nor death.

1927 Charles L. Camp and his assistant, geology student James P. Fox, begin geological reconnaissance at Blue Hills in the Petrified Forest. Here Camp will collect the first specimen ever found in Arizona of the spiked aetosaur *Desmatosuchus haplocerus*.

1972 The Republic of Maldives, an independent country south of Ceylon, issues a half dozen postage stamps of Paleozoic and Mesozoic reptiles. The stamps show the carnivorous pelycosaur *Dimetrodon*, a pair of flying *Pteranodon*, the plated dinosaur *Stegosaurus*, sauropod *Diplodocus*, ceratopsian *Triceratops* and theropod *Tyrannosaurus*. Although the *Tyrannosaurus* image had been based on Rudolf F. Zallinger's Peabody Museum painting, the other pictures were copied from Frederick E. Seyfarth's illustrations originally appearing in author Bertha Morris Parker's children's books *Life Through the Ages* (1947) and *Animals of Yesterday* (1952).

1996 Two movie-related exhibitions featuring dinosaurs open at the Museum of Science and Industry, Chicago, Illinois: "The Dinosaurs of Jurassic Park" and "Special Effects 2." In the latter attendees can ride the prop Monica the Dinosaur in front of a blank "green screen," while a monitor shows them composited with a background scene of Southern California's Venice Beach.

1997 Horton Plaza, in San Diego, California, begins three months of dinosaur-related activities including sand sculpting, displays and contests.

JUNE

~ 1 ~

1897 Yang Zhungjian (originally spelled Young Chung-Chien) is born in Shensi, China. Yang will become one of the most well-known and accomplished paleontologists of China. From the late 1920s into the 1930s, he will focus upon fossil mammals and the Cenozoic geology of northern China. In the late thirties Yang's attention will switch to Mesozoic reptiles (mammal-like reptiles and dinosaurs) and related stratigraphical problems. He will collect numerous fossil specimens including holotypes and write myriad scientific papers. Yang's most significant work will be done during the 1950s and 1960s when he describes a number of new taxa, including the prosauropod dinosaur *Lufengosaurus* and the incredibly long-necked sauropod *Mamenchisaurus*. Yang will become a professor at Peking University, Peking Normal University and University of Chungking; Chancellor of Northwestern University (Sian); a member of Academia Sinica (as Director of the Bureau of Compilation and Publication, Vice Chairman of the Committee of Quarternary Studies of China); Director of the Institute of Vertebrate Paleontology and Paleoanthropology (IVPP) and (concurrently) Director of the Peking Natural History Museum; a founder and President of the Paleontological Society of China and President of the Geological Society. In 1957 Yang will found *Vertebrata PalAsiatica* (the first periodical devoted exclusively to vertebrate paleontology papers) and in 1973 *Fossils* (a popular journal edited at IVPP). (Dies January 15, 1979.)

1903 Elmer S. Riggs publishes his osteology of *Nyctosaurus*, a medium-sized pterosaur from the Lower Cretaceous of Kansas. Riggs notes that the fine specimen described "is of unusual importance, as throwing much light upon the structure, not only of the American pterodactyls, but also upon certain characters of the European ones. It is, I believe, for purposes of study the most complete specimen of this order of reptiles now known, comprising as it does nearly every bone in the skeleton, for the most part associated in their natural relations."

1917 Elbert H. Porter is born in Orderville, Utah. Porter will become a sculptor probably best known for making, at his studio in the town of Draper, a series of life-sized dinosaurs and other extinct animals that will eventually find a permanent home outside the Utah Field House of Natural History in Vernal, Utah. According to Porter, he and his wife, after delivering an Indian figure to Vernal, visited Dinosaur National Monument. "If I can make an Indian 18 feet tall," he remarked, "surely I can make a dinosaur!"

Sculptor Elbert H. Porter in Orderville, Utah, with his life-sized EDAPHOSAURUS, one of a group of figures originally displayed as a tourist attraction in his hometown of Orderville, Utah. Courtesy State of Utah Division of Parks and Recreation.

1934　The MGM movie *Hollywood Party* opens wherein a group of scientists mistake Ted Healey's Stooges (Moe Howard, Jerry "Curly" Howard and Larry Fine) for prehistoric men.

1940　George Callison is born in Blue Rapids, Kansas. Callison will become a paleontologist who specializes in small dinosaurs. Eventually he will leave his teaching post at the University of California, Long Beach, to work full time for Dinamation International Corporation, becoming a board member and its senior scientist.

1958　A permanent museum highlighted by the vast, tilted sandstone wall — dubbed the "Dinosaur Ledge" or "Great Wall" — of the Dinosaur Quarry opens to the public at Dinosaur National Monument in northeastern Utah. The display shows more than 2,000 bones of Morrison Formation dinosaurs *in situ*. From 1953 through 1955 former Smithsonian Institution paleontologist Theodore ("Ted") E. White directed work in the quarry to expose the specimens contained therein and prepare them in bas-relief. Assisting "Doc" White were Tobe Wilkins and Frank MacKnight (replaced in 1958 by Jim Adams), members of the Monument's maintenance staff. Construction of the museum building, designed to enclose the quarry face (the first of this design ever attempted), began in 1957. Visitors can now watch preparators Wilkins and Adams work on the "Great Wall," further exposing its fossil treasures, among them the bones of such classic Late Jurassic dinosaurs as *Allosaurus, Stegosaurus, Camptosaurus, Apatosaurus* and *Camarasaurus*.

1985　The Museum of Western Colorado puts on a formal "Dinosaur Ball" at the Grand Junction Hilton Hotel. The gala celebration heralds the opening of Dinosaur Valley, the Museum's new Main Street facility.

~ 2 ~

1874　United States president Ulysses S. Grant lays the cornerstone of the American Museum of Natural History in New York where its Seventy-ninth Street entrance will be.

1894　The Columbian Museum is dedicated and opens its doors to the public in Jackson Park, Chicago, Illinois, in the former Fine Arts Building that was originally part of the World's Columbian Exposition of 1893. Hall numbers 59, 35 and 36, each designated a "Hall of Paleontology," contain real fossils and plaster casts of specimens purchased from Professor Henry

Ward's *Catalogue of Casts of Fossils from the Principal Museums of Europe and America* (1866), the famous Rochester, New York–based supplier of scientific materials. From the latter the giant carapaced mammal *Glyptodon* has been bought for a total price of $150, including mountings. Among the displays, some left over from the Exposition, are casts of the giant ground sloth *Megatherium* and Benjamin Waterhouse Hawkins' reconstructed dinosaur *Hadrosaurus*, while standing majestically in the main hall (the building's former Palace of Fine Arts) is a full-sized model woolly mammoth figure. Next year the museum will be renamed the Field Columbian Museum to commemorate its benefactor Marshall Field. In the early 1900s the partial real skeleton of the giant dinosaur *Apatosaurus* excelsus will be mounted. By 1921 the building, which was never meant to be permanent, will fall into such disrepair that the museum relocates to the relatively nearby Grant Park as the Field Museum of Natural History. The original building, rebuilt in stone, then becomes the Museum of Science and Industry, opening in 1933.

Photo (possibly taken opening day) of Hall 35 at the Columbian Museum. Among the exhibits are Ward's plaster casts of the armored GLYPTODON and giant ground sloth MEGATHERIUM. Courtesy The Field Museum (neg. #2975).

Ellis Burman with the dinosaur costume he made for the Johnny Weissmuller movie JUNGLE MANHUNT *(Columbia 1951), its scenes appearing only in the movie's trailer. Courtesy The Burman Studio.*

1904 Johnny Weissmuller is born in Windber, Pennsylvania. First gaining fame as an Olympic swimming champion, Weissmuller will achieve new notoriety as a motion picture star, best known for playing Edgar Rice Burroughs' jungle hero Tarzan. In *Tarzan's Desert Mystery* (1943) the Apeman, as played by Weissmuller, will visit an oasis populated by prehistoric reptiles (*One Million B.C.* footage). *Tarzan and the Leopard Woman* (1946) will have him opposing a murderous cult that worships a "Leopard God" idol in the image of a giant sabertoothed cat. After retiring as Tarzan, Weissmuller will play Alex Raymond's comic-strip hero Jungle Jim in a series of films, several of which will feature prehistoric creatures. In *Jungle Jim* (1948), the first, Jim will fight a strange swimming reptile (Ellis Burman's mechanical *Dimetrodon*, sans dorsal "sail," from the 1948 film *Unknown Island*). *Jungle Manhunt* (1951) will pit Jim against more *One Million B.C.* scenes; filmed, though shown only in the preview trailer, are scenes of Jim fighting a man-sized dinosaur (an actor wearing a Burman costume). *Jungle Jim in the Forbidden Land* (1952) will feature shaggy "missing links" called the Giant People, while *Killer Ape* (1953) will be about a giant prehistoric-type apeman. Weissmuller will also encounter prehistoric animals in the "Land of Terror" episode of his *Jungle Jim* (1955) television series, again footage from *One Million B.C.* (Dies January 20, 1984.)

1955 *Stone Age Romeos*, a Columbia comedy short in which the Three Stooges (Moe Howard, Larry Fine and Shemp Howard) masquerade as cavemen, opens. The prehistoric "flashback" scenes have been "lifted" from an earlier (1948) Stooges film entitled *I'm a Monkey's Uncle*.

1995 The American Museum opens its renovated Hall of Saurischian Dinosaurs and Hall of Ornithischian Dinosaurs, reorganized to reflect the modern cladistic method of classification. Renovations were done under the direction of geological paleontologist Lowell Dingus, who had overseen the development of the Museum's vertebrate paleontology exhibitions since 1987. Some of the dinosaur skeletons (e.g., *Tyrannosaurus* and *Apatosaurus*) have been remounted in more dynamic poses, their tails now correctly off the ground. The saurischian hall boldly proclaims that "birds are dinosaurs," which many vertebrate paleontologists now believe according to cladistic analysis. The new halls also feature more recently collected specimens like the Mongolian Cretaceous bird *Mononykus olecrans* and casts of important specimens housed in other museums. An attractive book, *Next of Kin*, written by Dingus, will be published the next year to celebrate the renovations.

~ 3 ~

1902   Ray E. Lemley is born in Rapid City, South Dakota. Although he will become a doctor of medicine, in 1960 he will pursue a boyhood interest of fossil collecting. In the Badlands of South Dakota Lemley will collect numerous specimens which, two decades later, he will donate to the Science Museum of Minnesota ("the most important collection ever received as a gift by the paleontology department"). One of Lemley's major accomplishments will be to help establish an exchange program for marsupial fossils between the United States and Australia. (Dies March 18, 1983.)

1908   Henry Anson Wylde is born in Belvidere, Illinois. Wylde's professions will be art and paleontology. While working at the Natural History Museum of Los Angeles County, sorting and cataloguing mammal fossils from Rancho La Brea, he will meet fossil-bird expert Hildegard Howard whom he will marry in 1930. Wylde will do much field work for the museum and initiate hundreds of new exhibits, utilizing new design and display techniques. Among the exhibitions Wylde will design for the museum are the Hall of Evolving Life (in 1953) and Cenozoic Hall (1960s) which remain unchanged for decades. (Dies October 8, 1984.)

1931   Siegfried Henkel is born in Dresden, Saxony. The future Professor Doctor Henkel will develop new techniques for efficiently retrieving small amounts of fossil material from large amounts of sediment. His "Henkel process" for obtaining small teeth will eventually become standard practice for other paleontologists. Among his accomplishments will be a ten-year involvement in the opening of the Guimaotra coal mine near Leira, Portugal, a site that will yield numerous remains of Late Jurassic mammals. (Dies 1984.)

1955 *Science Fiction Theatre* shows the episode "Spider, Inc.," in which a scientist (played by Gene Barry) deduces nature's secret for making petroleum from a piece of fossil amber preserving a dead spider.

1961 The Prehistoric Museum, College of Eastern Utah in Price, opens to the public. The museum displays original fossil material from the Morrison Formation including an *Allosaurus* skeleton and dinosaur footprints.

1986 The first Dinosaur Systematics Symposium begins at the Royal Tyrrell Museum of Paleontology in Drumheller, Alberta, Canada. Paleontologists from across the globe attend to discuss the ever-changing topic of dinosaurian classification.

~ 4 ~

1943 Universal Pictures opens *Captive Wild Woman*, the first in its new series of "programmers" about "Ape Woman" Paula Dupree. Paula starts life as a gorilla named Cheela (played by Ray "Crash" Corrigan), which is rapidly evolved into a beautiful woman (Aquanetta) by mad Dr. Sigmund Walters (John Carradine). Between these two rather extreme states Paula also reverts to a combination ape/human form. Though killed at the climax of the movie, Paula will return and undergo her transformations in two sequels, *Jungle Woman* (1944) and *Jungle Captive* (1945), the latter with Vicky Lane replacing Aquanetta in the title role.

1983 Avon Wildlife Trust places a scaled-down model of *Tyrannosaurus* in the shopping center at Broadmead, Bristol, England. The striking figure is intended to encourage people's support of Avon's Threatened Habitats Appeal. The dinosaur is supposed to convey the message that present-day wildlife must not go extinct.

1990 *Dinosaur Tracks*, the first album of paleontology-related music performed by the Iridium Band and featuring a dozen songs, is released on a stereo cassette by Fossil Records of Burbank, California. It will spawn the followups *More Dinosaur Tracks* (1991) and *Dinosaur Tracks Again* (1994), as well as a *Dinosaur Tracks* (1994) videocassette of six "Jurassic classics."

1993 The relatively low-budget ($1 million or less) movie *Carnosaur* premieres in theatres, promoted with the catchline, "It's no walk in the park." Its theme — live dinosaurs cloned via DNA engineering — is similar to that of another, much costlier film which will open just one week later. The source material, a novel by Harry Adam Knight, predates Michael Crichton's *Jurassic Park*, but producer Roger Corman graciously states that no plagiarism by Crichton was involved in their similarities. Reportedly *Carnosaur* will make back approximately 10 times its cost in its first week of home video release. It will hatch at least two sequels. Its full-scale mechanical *Tyrannosaurus*, made by John Carl Buechler's Magical Media Industries, will also cameo in Corman's *Dinosaur Island* (1994).

~ 5 ~

1998   The first JurassiCon is held at the Howard Johnson Midtown Hotel in Atlanta, Georgia, created and organized by William Bevil and Lewis Murphy. The three-day event is geared more toward the popular arts and dinosaur-memorabilia collecting, but also features science-oriented activities. Guests at the non-profit event include paleontologist David R. Schwimmer and "dinosaur artists" Rick Spears and Craig Hamilton.

~ 6 ~

1947   Artist Rudolph F. Zallinger completes painting his mural "The Age of Reptiles" (started in 1943) at the Peabody Museum of Natural History, Yale University. The painting depicts the evolution of reptilian life from Paleozoic through Mesozoic time. Two years later this mural will win the artist a Pulitzer Prize.

1949   Eugene S. Richardson names and describes *Dalmanites oklahomae*, a new genus and species of Silurian trilobite.

1980   *Science* magazine publishes the article "Extraterrestrial Cause for the Cretaceous-Tertiary Extinction," written by University of California at Berkeley geologist Luis Alvarez, co-authored with his son Walter Alvarez, Frank Asaro and Helen Michel. The piece suggests that the presence of iridium — number 77 on the periodic table of elements — at various sites at the Cretaceous-Tertiary boundary is evidence of the possible impact, some 65 million years ago, of a giant meteorite (meteors being known to contain this element) or asteroid. The authors hypothesize that the impact of some huge celestial body measuring some six miles across threw a dust cloud around the Earth that darkened the sky for years, thereby interrupting the food chain and, consequently, causing the extinction of all dinosaurs, as well as various other Late Cretaceous groups of animals and plants. Though speculation, this so-called "asteroid theory" will have another kind of impact, attracting seemingly unending media coverage, rapidly finding acceptance with much of the public as the definitive answer to the question of the dinosaurs' extinction. Many paleontologists, however, will remain skeptical.

1985 The skeleton of the dinosaur *Chindesaurus bryansmalli* is airlifted by helicopter from the Painted Desert in southeastern Arizona and flown to the Museum of Paleontology at the University of California, Berkeley. Footage of the event will be incorporated into the television documentary *A Whopping Small Dinosaur.*

~ 7 ~

1873 Franz Weidenreich is born. In 1934 Dr. Weidenreich, anatomist and physician, will become successor to Davidson Black, discoverer of Peking Man (now called *Homo erectus*). During the next 10 years Weidenreich will be responsible for the collection of 14 skulls, 14 lower jaws and almost 150 teeth representing 45 individuals, from juvenile to adult, belonging to this hominid species that he believes is ancestral to modern man. According to Weidenreich, "In its general form and size (*Homo erectus*) skull agrees with the Java skull to such an extent that it identifies Pithecanthropus too as a true man, and a creature far above the stage of an ape." In his popular book *Apes, Giants, and Man* (1946) Weidenreich will announce the anthropoid *Gigantopithecus* which he incorrectly interprets as a giant "missing link" between ape and man, towering some 8 feet tall and weighing over 400 pounds (this genus now known to have no role in human evolution). (Dies July 11, 1947.)

1944 "Stairway to the Sun," a lost-world adventure serial inspired by Arthur Conan Doyle's *Lost World* novel, bows on writer Carlton E. Morse's *I Love a Mystery* radio show (NBC). Its action, involving dinosaurs and other threats, is set atop a lost plateau.

~ 8 ~

1927 Working in badlands southeast of the Round Rock Trading Post in the Petrified Forest, Charles L. Camp and James P. Fox find a slightly crushed yet excellently preserved skull of the rutiodont reptile now called *Smilosuchus gregorii.* In the same general area, near the Lukachukai Trading Post, Camp will soon find the skull of another large rutiodont.

1956   Catherine A. Forster is born. Forster will become a paleontologist specializing in dinosaurs and publishing major studies on such animals as *Tenontosaurus* and *Triceratops*. Much of her field work will be in Africa where she will be a member of teams responsible for the discovery and collection of new and important dinosaur material.

1962   Fairway International's low-budget movie *Eegah!* is released. Richard Kiel, an actor towering 7 feet 2 inches tall, plays the titled character, a giant prehistoric caveman surviving in today's world. Eegah will nobly shed his beard for the love of a modern girl. And the film will deservedly achieve future fame as one of the worst movies of all time.

1985   Gala opening ceremonies are held at Dinosaur Valley in Grand Junction, Colorado. The museum, a new facility of the Museum of Western Colorado, features real dinosaur fossils, casts of skeletons (including "Lazarus" the *Allosaurus* and a *Stegosaurus* mounted rearing up on its hind legs) and several permanent displays of robotic dinosaurs purchased from Dinamation International Corporation.

~ 9 ~

1993   Chinese scientists find a fossil dinosaur rib approximately 100 million years old in Beijing, about 12 miles from the site of the original Peking Man discovery. This constitutes the first dinosaur fossil ever found in China's capital city. According to Zhao Xijin, a professor at the Institute of Vertebrate Paleontology and Anthropology in Beijing, in a statement released by the New China news agency on July 8, the size of the specimen indicates that it is the left rib of a sauropod having a total length of more than 33 feet.

~ 10 ~

1854   The Crystal Palace (site of the Great Exhibition of the Works and Industry of All Nations, which closed October 11, 1851) and its grounds, new and improved thanks to sculptor Benjamin Waterhouse Hawkins' models of extinct animals — created in brick, cement and plaster over iron frameworks — reopens in Sydenham, London. Queen Victoria takes part in the ceremonies. Among the 40,000 attendees are Hawkins and Richard Owen who are formally presented to Her Majesty by Samuel Laing, Chairman of the Crystal Palace Company: "May it please your Majesty, the restoration from a single fossil fragment of complete skeletons of creatures long since extinct, first effected by the

IGUANODON "life sized" model made by artist Benjamin Waterhouse Hawkins as displayed on the Crystal Palace grounds in Sydenham, London. This dinosaur was later found to be primarily bipedal, the nose "horn" actually a spiked thumb. Photo by Bill Warren.

Sculptor Marcel Deldago's stop-motion TYRANNOSAURUS as it appeared in the popular movie DINOSAURUS! (1960). © Jack H. Harris and Universal Pictures.

genius of Cuvier, as always being considered one of the most striking achievements of modern science. Our British Cuvier, Professor Owen, has lent his assistance in carrying these scientific triumphs a step further, and bringing them down to popular apprehension. Aided by the zealous and indefatigable exertions of Mr. Waterhouse Hawkins, who with his own hand moulded the gigantic Iguanodon, the ichthyosaurus, and other monsters of the antediluvian world, will now present themselves to the eye as they once disported themselves and pursued their prey amid the forests and morasses of the secondary and tertiary periods."

1960 *Dinosaurus!* (Universal-International), a science-fiction movie conceived and produced by Jack H. Harris, opens. A young boy (played by Alan Roberts) befriends a "Neanderthal" caveman (Gregg Martell) and a friendly *Apatosaurus*, all three of which are menaced by a nasty *Tyrannosaurus*. The dinosaurs are revived from suspended animation on screen by lightning, but are actually given life by Tim Baar, Wah Chang and Gene Warren working stop-motion and mechanical models made by Marcel Delgado.

1983   The British Museum (Natural History) completes its recovery of the holotype of the big-clawed dinosaur *Baryonyx walkeri*.

1985   "Frozen in Time," a special dinosaur exhibition including robotic dinosaurs from Dinamation International Corporation, opens at the San Diego Natural History Museum.

~ 11 ~

1961   A five and a half foot long worm, recently caught by Marté Latham in the Andes of Colombia, South America, and dubbed "Gertrude" by the press, arrives in London for study by the London Zoological Society. According to accounts, some scientists believe the creature is a prehistoric species. Gertrude will die, unfortunately, on July 21 before studies can begin.

1988   "Dino-Rama," an exhibition of a dozen robotic prehistoric animals from Dinamation International Corporation, opens at the Chicago Academy of Sciences. The display is presented outside the building within a specially constructed, enclosed outdoor habitat amid plants similar to those existing in the Mesozoic.

1993   Director Steven Spielberg's mega-budget motion picture *Jurassic Park*, based on Michael Crichton's best-selling novel and co-scripted by Crichton, opens to long lines of theatre patrons, quickly becoming the highest-grossing movie in history ($913 million in box office receipts). Produced through Spielberg's company Amblin Entertainment, the movie stars Sam Neill, Laura Dern, Jeff

A TYRANNOSAURUS REX (state-of-the-art full-sized animatronic figure by Stan Winston) menaces Dr. Alan Grant (Sam Neill) and Lex Hammond (Ariana Richards) in Steven Spielberg's blockbuster movie JURASSIC PARK (1992). © & ™ Universal City Studios & MCA, all rights reserved.

Goldblum and Sir Richard Attenborough, though its real stars are the dinosaurs. At first considering stop motion, Spielberg had gambled on the newer and experimental technique of Computer Graphics Imagery (CGI), thereby changing the look of movie dinosaurs forever. Through a combination of these groundbreaking, state-of-the-art computer effects (by Dennis Muren of Industrial Light and Magic, working from original stop-motion animation created by Phil Tippett), full-sized mechanical figures (by Stan Winston) and, in a minimum of scenes, actors in costumes, the dinosaurs on screen seem real and alive. Audiences are suitably impressed and *Jurassic Park*, within just a week or so, will become to date the most profitable motion picture in the history of the industry. Words from the script like "Jurassic" and the misused suffix "raptor" instantly become part of our common lexicon. The film industry will also be impressed, the movie winning three Academy Awards (for Visual Effects, Sound and Sound Effects Editing). Preceding, accompanying and following the film's release is a seemingly unending stream of merchandise including comic books, trading cards, toys, model kits, music albums, magazines, masks, costumes, games and countless other items. There will also be several different touring exhibits based on the movie and, at Universal Studios in California, the inevitable "Jurassic Park — The Ride." *Jurassic Park* becomes the most powerful force driving the dinosaur craze of the 1990s. Spielberg will channel some of the movie's profits into serious dinosaur research. The storyline, not surprisingly, is left open-ended for at least one sequel.

All seven Geology Department curators gathered on May 4, 1994, in the soon-to-open "DNA to Dinosaurs" exhibit in The Field Museum's Hall 29, skeleton of APATOSAURUS EXCELSUS *in background. From left to right: Lance Grande (Curator, Fossil Fishes), John J. Flynn (Curator, Fossil Mammals and Chair), Olivier C. Reippel (Curator, Fossil Amphibians and Reptiles), Peter R. Crane (Curator, Fossil Plants), John R. Bolt (Curator, Fossil Amphibians and Reptiles), Scott Lidgard (Associate Curator, Fossil Invertebrates) and Matthew H. Nitecki (Curator, Fossil Invertebrates). Courtesy The Field Museum (neg. #GEO858891).*

1994   The Field Museum in Chicago, Illinois, officially opens its new "DNA to Dinosaurs" (later renamed "Life Through Time") exhibit. The exhibit, arranged according to geological time, is on the opposite side of the second floor from the old Hall 38. Included are most of the fossil specimens previously displayed in the old hall, though some of them — including skeletons of *"Gorgosaurus"* and *Apatosaurus excelsus*— have been remounted under the direction of William F. Simpson in more dynamic poses to reflect modern paleontological ideas. Most of the excellent, though somewhat dated, Charles R. Knight murals have been relocated to the new halls, though not in the sequence the artist originally intended. Some specimens, including the partial skeleton of the duck-billed dinosaur *Parasaurolophus crytocristatus* (in storage since it was first collected back in 1923), are on exhibit for the first time.

~ 12 ~

1898 Paleontologist Jacob Wortman, former medical doctor, research assistant of E. D. Cope and now leader of one of the first major field projects by the American Museum of Natural History's new Department of Vertebrate Paleontology at Como Bluff, Wyoming, spots a hilltop cabin a mile or two away. Wortman decides the cabin will be the benchmark for the next day's fossil prospecting. As his exploratory team nears the cabin, they see that it is constructed of giant dinosaur bones cemented together with adobe and sod! The fossil site, to be established as Bone Cabin Quarry by O. C. Marsh, will become one of the richest in North America. The cabin had been built by a shepherd needing a winter shelter. The site itself may have been discovered by Frank Williston, brother of Samuel Wendell Williston.

1921 Charles L. Camp arrives from New York in Adamana, Arizona, and begins the first systematic collection of vertebrate fossils at Petrified Forest National Monument. He will spend the rest of the month digging for and finding specimens belonging to Triassic amphibians and reptiles.

1923 Leading a field party from the Royal Ontario Museum of Paleontology, Toronto, G. E. Lindbald collects the partial skeleton of a medium-sized dinosaur in the Horseshoe River Formation (Late Cretaceous), along the Red Deer River in southern Alberta, Canada. Not until 1988 will this specimen be examined by paleontologist Hans Dieter-Sues, who will identify it as belonging to *Chirostenotes pergracilis*, a species of bird-like theropod.

1946 George Olshevsky is born in Buffalo, New York. Olshevsky will be mostly noticed by paleontologists in the 1970s when he starts publishing computer print-outs of dinosaurian taxa. During the 1980s he will be hired by Dinamation International Corporation to edit a planned *Dinosauria* magazine. Though several issues will be planned, the periodical does not see print. Olshevsky will later form his own publishing company, Publications Requiring Research, specializing in serious dinosaur-related material. Among the titles he will produce are *Mesozoic Meanderings* and *Archosaurian Articulations*. In the former, "Dinosaur (or simply Dino) George" will propose his own revised classification of the Dinosauria and introduce a few new names for some old taxa.

1969 Pit 91 at Rancho La Brea in Los Angeles is reopened — having been originally opened in 1914, the exposed Pleistocene-age fossil bones left in place as an exhibit until asphalt and debris covered them again. New state-of-the-art diggings redress the bias of early paleontologists who tended to collect only large remains (or macrofossils). Next year workers will discover here a densely packed amassment of bones. Starting in 1984 volunteers will regularly work this pit, extracting from it a treasure trove of Ice Age fossils excellently preserved by asphalt, including smaller items (microfossils).

THE BEAST FROM 20,000 FATHOMS (1953), a monster movie based in part on a short story written by Ray Bradbury, with stop-motion special effects by Ray Harryhausen. © Warner Bros.

~ 13 ~

1953 *The Beast from 20,000 Fathoms,* inspired by fantasy author Ray Bradbury's short story of the same title and with stop-motion special effects by Ray Harryhausen, opens. The story is about an impossibly big fictitious Mesozoic reptile called a "Rhedosaurus" that, awakened from suspended animation during an atomic-bomb test in the Arctic, attacks New York City. Inspired by the previous year's re-release of *King Kong*, the movie will launch the "giant-monster" craze of the 1950s and, with the former film, inspire Japan's successful *Godzilla, King of the Monsters!*

1991 *Hadrosaurus foulkii*, a duckbilled dinosaur discovered in Haddonfield, is named the official state fossil of New Jersey.

~ 14 ~

1852 Gideon Mantell concludes writing the diary he has been faithfully keeping for almost 30 years.

1931 Roy Shreve informs Charles L. Camp that he is not digging at Shreve Quarry—but two miles away. Because of this error, Shreve's name gets removed (unfortunately for him) from what will become one of the highest-yielding sites of Late Triassic terrestrial vertebrates.

~ 15 ~

1850 Charles H. (Hazelius) Sternberg is born in Oswego, New York. "CH" Sternberg will be inspired to collect fossils by the beauty of fossil leaves. As he will write in his autobiography *The Life of a Fossil Hunter* (1909), "At the age of seventeen, therefore, I made up my mind what part I should play in life, and determined that whatever it might cost me in privation, danger, and solitude, I would make it my business to collect facts from the crust of the earth." Sternberg will professionally begin his beloved career in 1876 working for Edward D. Cope in the Judith River beds of Montana. His three sons George, the oldest, Charles M. and Levi, the youngest, will work with him in the field, each one of them going on to become paleontologists in their own right. During their expeditions they will make such significant finds as the famous *Edmontosaurus* "mummy" in 1908. Sternberg will also author the book *Hunting Dinosaurs in the Bad Lands of the Red Deer River, Alberta, Canada* published in 1917. (Dies July 20, 1943.)

1886 Alexander Wetmore is born in North Freedom, Wisconsin, the son of a doctor. A future ornithologist and paleontologist, his primary interest will be modern birds, followed by a fascination with fossil birds.

Wetmore's studies of fossil bird bones will constitute the groundwork upon which subsequent paleontologists will build their studies. In 1945 he will be appointed the sixth secretary of the Smithsonian Institution. (Dies December 7, 1978.)

1891　Jacob L. Wortman is made assistant curator and leader of field work at the American Museum of Natural History. Wortman's career in paleontology is relatively brief, his allegiance to any one institution never long. Atypically for one of his profession, he will soon grow weary of fossils. In 1908, Wortman will move to Brownsville, Texas, opening a drugstore at which he will work until his death almost 20 years later.

1933　Bryan Patterson, Assistant in Paleontology in the Field Museum of Natural History's Department of Geology, having been granted a leave of absence, departs for Colorado where he will spend most of the summer. Patterson will do field work, continuing the collection of fossil mammals and other geologic specimens he began there in 1932.

1946　John R. Horner is born in Shelby, Montana. "Jack" Horner will find his first dinosaur fossil when only eight years old. He will become a Green Beret who looks for fossils while mapping enemy territory and ducking bullets in Vietnam. Horner will become a leading paleontologist specializing in hadrosaurs or duckbilled dinosaurs and also in dinosaur behavior. He will publish data from which he derives new ideas that will saliently affect modern conceptions about dinosaurs. While curator of paleontology at the Museum of the Rockies in Bozeman, Montana, Horner will make discoveries that soon revolutionize earlier ideas about dinosaur behavior, including discovering the first dinosaur eggs in the Western Hemisphere and first dinosaur embryos. Skeletons representing embryos to adults belonging to the Montana hadrosaur *Maiasaura* (which he will name and describe with Robert Makela in 1979) subsequently yield information suggesting that at least this kind of dinosaur may have had a social structure that included parental care. Work on *Maiasaura* will become instrumental in Horner's being awarded, in 1986, an honorary doctorate of science and a MacArthur Fellowship award. Horner's accomplishments will also influence the popular arts: He will be the real-life model for the paleontologist character Alan Grant in the novel and movie *Jurassic Park* (Horner also serving as dinosaur consultant in the film and its sequel *The Lost World: Jurassic Park*) and, through numerous television appearances, become one of the relatively few celebrity paleontologists. In 1997 Jack will become the third acting President of The Dinosaur Society.

~ 16 ~

1902 George Gaylord Simpson is born in Chicago, Illinois. Simpson's knowledge as a future paleontologist will be expansive, including descriptive paleontology, taxonomic practice and the mechanics of evolution. He will author numerous papers, some technical, others popular, on such subjects as biogeography, faunal history and the fossil record. Among the books he will author are *Tempo and Mode in Evolution* (1944), *The Meaning of Evolution* (1949) and *The Major Features of Evolution* (1953). Simpson will become a member of the National Academy of Sciences, the highest scientific body of the United States, and a founder of the Society of Vertebrate Paleontology. Before his death on October 6, 1984, he will be regarded as one of the top paleontologists and evolutionists of his generation.

1992 The tabloid newspaper *Weekly World News* proclaims in a headline that "SPACE PROBE FINDS DINOSAURS ON MARS." According to the story, written by Kenneth Lee, the *Viking I* probe discovered live dinosaurs on the red planet 16 years ago but did not release the information. The "proof" of this new government cover-up is "a mind-boggling NASA photograph." However, the creatures posing in this group shot look suspiciously like modern marine iguanas.

~ 17 ~

1888 Thomas C. Weston, official fossil collector for the Geological Survey of Canada, starts exploring formations above Big Valley — territory previously explored by young geologist Joseph Burr Tyrrell — eventually continuing to the mouth of the Rosebud River in the badlands of Alberta, Canada. Weston remains in this area for the rest of the month. By the first of next month he will move on to new territory where significant fossil finds will be made.

1955 Lippert Pictures' *King Dinosaur*, a low-budget movie about the discovery and exploration of a prehistoric planet, opens — produced, written and directed by Bert I. Gordon. Gordon has also tackled the "B.I.G." special effects scenes using the old "live reptiles" technique. The titled monster, supposedly a *Tyrannosaurus rex*, is actually a green iguana propped up, at least for its opening scenes, by wires. The best scenes, not surprisingly, consist of stock footage from 1940's *One Million B.C.*

Retouched and pasted-up publicity photo from producer/director Bert I. Gordon's first movie KING DINOSAUR (1955), another movie in which lizards "portrayed" prehistoric reptiles. © Lippert Pictures.

1988 "Dinamation Exhibit" opens at the Utah Museum of Natural History, University of Utah Campus, Salt Lake City. In addition to Dinamation International Corporation's robotic dinosaurs the museum offers special dinosaur-related programming for the event.

1990 Baby dinosaurs (i.e., little moving *Apatosaurus* and *Triceratops* models) appear for the benefit of young dinosaur fans on Level 3 of the 900 shopping mall on Michigan Avenue in Chicago, Illinois. The "Prehistoric Storyteller" tells prehistoric stories and Professor Rives Collins of Northwestern University informs children about dinosaurs. According to advertisements, "There are great hands-on educational exhibits, too. Dino Puzzles. Even a Fossil Touch Chart." The event, which will last for a week, is sponsored by The Chicago Academy of the Sciences.

~ 18 ~

1911   Theodore Galusha is born near Central City in Hamilton County, Nebraska. Finding fossils along Antelope Creek near his family's farm in Dawes County will inspire the young Ted toward a future career as a paleontologist specializing in field work and collecting. His published writings will include a stratigraphy of the Santa Fe Group and Zia Sand of New Mexico and the Box Butte Formation of Nebraska. (Dies August 2, 1979.)

1952   John Carl Buechler is born in Belleville, Illinois. Buechler will become a make-up and special effects artist specializing in movie monsters. In 1993 Buechler and his company Magical Media Industries will create the full-sized and miniature dinosaurs for the movie *Carnosaur*, continuing the work into two sequels. More prehistoric creatures, both animal and humanoid, will be made by Buechler's shop for the 1997 television series *Tarzan: The Epic Adventures*. In addition to effects work, Buechler will also direct, helming various episodes of the 1991 version of television's *Land of the Lost* series.

~ 19 ~

1931   Ermin C. Case, a paleontologist at the University of Michigan in Ann Arbor, obtains permission to excavate Upper Triassic fossils on the Fuller Ranch in Scurry County, Texas, this site having been discovered earlier by geologist A. N. Huddleston. A university field party will briefly work this site, during which time the holotype of the reptile "*Buettneria*" (*Metoposaurus*) *bakeri* is recovered. Eventually the site yields numerous skeletons of *M. bakeri*.

1947   Excavations officially begin at the Ghost Ranch quarry in New Mexico, led by Edwin H. Colbert of the American Museum of Natural History. George O. Whitaker, a young fossil preparator at the museum and Colbert's working companion, finds an excellently-preserved skull of a phytosaur, a long-snouted reptile resembling a crocodile. The specimen will require three days of preparation. Its discovery will inspire Colbert, who had stopped at Ghost Ranch en route to Petrified Forest National Monument where he had planned to spend the season collecting, to continue digging at this site. A major discovery will be made here, the group never making it to the Petrified Forest.

1951   *The Neanderthal Man*, a low-budget science-fiction movie released by United Artists, debuts. A scientist, played by actor Robert Shayne, takes a drug that "de-volves" him to a primitive state. The scientist also manages to regress a kitty into a vicious "sabretoothed tiger" which, unfortunately, only possesses its characteristic fangs in freeze-frame shots.

~ 20 ~

1952   David B. (Bruce) Norman is born in Ilfracombre, North Devon, England. Norman will become a paleontologist specializing in the relationships between dinosaurs. He will work as a lecturer in zoology at Brasenose College, Oxford; be a research fellow of the University Museum, Oxford, and hold a Royal Society Fellowship in Brussels. His accomplishments will include publishing numerous scientific papers, many of them devoted to *Iguanodon*, a dinosaur about which Norman will become a leading authority, and also authoring the semi-popular book *The Illustrated Encyclopedia of Dinosaurs*.

1986   *On the Wing*, the IMAX film featuring Paul MacCready's successfully flying *Quetzalcoatlus* model, debuts at the Air and Space Museum in Washington, D.C. The actual prop used in the film is exhibited at the opening.

1996   Paleontologists Eric Buffetaut, Varavudh Suteethorn and Haiyan Tong publish their joint paper naming and describing *Siamotyrannus isanensis*, a theropod dinosaur founded upon a partial skeleton from the Lower Cretaceous Sao Khua Formation of Khon Kaen Province in northeastern Thailand. The large animal (measuring about 23 feet in length) has been interpreted by the authors as the earliest known member of the family Tyrannosauridae.

~ 21 ~

1821   Gideon Mantell displays fossil bones of *Iguanodon* at the Geological Society of London.

1876   Harry Govier Seeley names and describes the new titanosaurid sauropod *Macrurosaurus* before the Geological Society of London, the dinosaur known only from vertebrae found on the Isle of Wight, England.

1931   Ermin C. Case and Theodore E. White resume the slow work of fossil collection in the hard clay conglomerate at Fuller Ranch in Texas. Not even dynamite can loosen the rock layers.

1977   Workmen find a rare, 13,300-year-old woolly mammoth skeleton under five feet of clay in the Blackwell Forest Preserve, DuPage County, Warrenville, Illinois. About three-fourths complete, the specimen is missing the skull, parts of the shoulders and most of the forelegs. Promptly causing a sensation and drawing crowds of spectators during excavation, the bones will be put on display in 1986 at the Fullersburg Woods Environmental Education Center in Oak Brook, Illinois.

1988   The Forbes Marketing Firm of the Year award goes to The DinoStore ("Gifts of Extinction"), located in a small shopping mall in Birmingham, Alabama. The store, owned and managed by Rick Halbrooks, sells mostly items relating to dinosaurs and other prehistoric animals. It also boasts its own adjoining Dinosaur Museum displaying real fossils, a mounted skeletal cast of a *Stegosaurus* obtained from DINOLAB in Salt Lake City, some hands-on exhibits and various dinosaur-related memorabilia. Ahead of its time, The DinoStore will become extinct before the big dinosaur craze of the 1990s.

1996   "Jurassic Park — The Ride" opens to record-breaking attendance at the Universal Studios Hollywood theme park in southern California. The ride had been seriously considered shortly after publication of Michael Crichton's novel *Jurassic Park* and was in development three years before the release of the movie version. Occupying six and one half acres, the attraction carries people on a 25-person boat through a tropical environment inhabited by life-sized mechanical dinosaurs, some of them patterned on those in the movie *Jurassic Park*. The creatures, made by Sarcos, a Salt Lake City–based company whose work is mostly contracted for the Department of Defense, include the movie's popular *Tyrannosaurus*, *Dilophosaurus* and *Velociraptor*. The ride climaxes with a plunge down a steep, 84 feet high water slide that soaks usually delighted passengers. A counterpart to the popular ride will soon go into production at Universal Studios' Islands of Adventure theme park in Orlando, Florida.

~ 22 ~

1947   George O. Whitaker, after he and Edwin H. Colbert's team prospect for more fossils at Ghost Ranch, finds the first of myriad theropod specimens in the quarry that will later be named after him. Colbert identifies the remains as those of *Coelophysis*, a small meat-eating dinosaur described by Edward Drinker Cope late in the 19th century.

~ 23 ~

1930 Ralph Hornell finds remains of the duckbilled dinosaur *Tetragonosaurus* in Alberta, Canada. (Today, this genus is regarded as a juvenile *Lambeosaurus*, a crested hadrosaur, although some specimens referred to it belong to another crested form, *Corythosaurus*.)

1997 The reconstructed skull of *Giganotosaurus carolinii*, a gigantic carnivorous dinosaur from Argentina, apparently bigger than the famous *Tyrannosaurus rex*, is placed on display at the Academy of Natural Sciences of Philadelphia.

~ 24 ~

1944 The Monogram horror movie *Return of the Ape Man* is released. Bela Lugosi and John Carradine portray scientists who find a prehistoric caveman (Frank Moran) frozen in an Arctic iceberg and successfully revive him from his long bout of suspended animation. Not content with this pseudoscientific triumph, Lugosi's character transplants into the "Ape Man's" head part of the Carradine character's brain. The horrific results are not surprising.

1947 Fossil collector Joseph T. Gregory starts measuring a strategic section of Upper Triassic fossil localities in east-central New Mexico.

1955 *Science Fiction Theatre* airs the episode "Marked Danger," in which mice rocketed into the ionosphere return to Earth where they transform into higher life forms, thereby validating Darwin's theory of evolution.

1987 On this last day of a three-month dig along the Milk River, south of Calgary in Alberta, Canada, technician Kevin Aulenback discovers seven Late Cretaceous dinosaur nests, each nest containing as many as 20 eggs, some of them containing fetuses. Aulenback states, "And somehow there's something in the water that keeps [the eggs] from decaying. Like creosote it smells." The eggs were probably laid by duckbilled dinosaurs.

~ 25 ~

1901 George C. Page is born in Fremont, Nebraska. A farm boy, Page will move to California at the age of 16 with $2.30 in his pocket, a sum which the young entrepreneur will gradually, through various profitable enterprises, turn into millions. In 1973 Page, distressed that the fossil treasures recovered from the "tar pits" at Los Angeles' Rancho La Brea were housed and displayed at the Natural History Museum of Los Angeles County, some driving distance away, rather than where they were found, will offer to build a new kind of museum on the site. The innovative museum, which is to open four years later, will be named after him — the George C. Page Museum of La Brea Discoveries.

1946 Edwin H. Colbert, having obtained a collecting permit from the United States Department of the Interior, returns to the Petrified Forest for a second visit (he had been here the previous year) looking for Late Triassic fossils, particularly amphibians and reptiles.

1953 Astor Pictures' *Robot Monster*, among the worst and most ludicrous movies ever made, premieres. Ro-Man, the titled alien villain, is played by George Barrows wearing a gorilla costume topped off with a space helmet. Though shot in three dimensions, the picture includes stock footage and outtakes from the older 2-D films *One Million B.C.* and *Lost Continent*— but not nearly enough to enhance the movie's production value.

~ 26 ~

1955 Steveville-Dinosaur Provincial Park is created in Alberta, Canada, by the Alberta government. The Park, established in order to protect the area's dinosaur fossils, has come about through the efforts of local doctor W. G. Anderson and a few other citizens. Through their efforts, the government had sought paleontologist Charles M. Sternberg to help decide upon a location for the Park. Sternberg suggested an area between Steveville and Little Sandhill Creek, an area of badlands particularly rich in dinosaur remains. The name Steveville will be dropped in 1961.

1983 The Witte Museum in San Antonio opens its new and permanent exhibit "Dinosaurs: Vanished Texans." The display focuses upon the Late Cretaceous and includes fossils and casts of dinosaurs, pterosaurs and other animals from that period.

~ 27 ~

1829 Lonely nobleman and scientist James Smithson, the founder of the Smithsonian Institution, dies in Italy, having, for reasons unknown, willed the British equivalent of $508,318.46 "to the United States of America, to found at Washington, under the name of the Smithsonian Institution, an Establishment for the increase and diffusion of knowledge among men," thereby achieving his own kind of immortality. Later his remains will be transferred to the United States to be interred in the original Smithsonian building, which, because of its architectural design, comes to be known as "the Castle."

1905 Wesley L. Bliss is born on a farm near Greeley, Colorado. Bliss will begin his career in science as a day laborer at the Los Angeles Museum of History, Science and Art (now Natural History Museum of Los Angeles County) digging for fossils at the Rancho La Brea "tar pits" site. From 1929 to 1930 Bliss will become the first worker to collect microfossils from these deposits, the so-called "Bliss 29" sites yielding thousands of plant and animal specimens. In 1931 Bliss will work for Chester Stock collecting vertebrate fossils and mapping sediments in southern California. His main professional interests would focus upon anthropology and archaeology. Among Bliss' accomplishments will be the discovery of some major fossil and early-man sites. (Dies 1996.)

1907 Robert Broom announces to the Geological Society of South Africa the new prosauropod *Gryponyx*, founded on a partial postcranial skeleton discovered in Fouriesburg. About three-quarters of a century later paleontologist Michael R. Cooper will synonymize this genus with the better known prosauropod *Massospondylus*.

1915 Jesse Marsh is born in Florence, Alabama. Marsh will become a comic-book artist for Western Publishing Company in the late 1940s through Dell Comics and, in the 1960s, through Western's own subsidiary company Gold Key Comics. With a simple style influenced by adventure-strip artists like Milton Caniff, Marsh will draw the most commercially successful and long-lasting *Tarzan* comic-book series ever published. Frequently he will bring Edgar Rice Burroughs' hero into contact with the dinosaurs and other prehistoric inhabitants of Pal-ul-Don, sometimes in a more exclusive part of that lost land called the "Valley of Monsters." A familiar Marsh image will be that of Tarzan riding a "gryf," the animal drawn in the artist's distinctive style as a basic *Triceratops* without the extra accoutrements Burroughs had given it. (Dies April 29, 1966.)

1927 Charles L. Camp concludes excavations at the *Placerias* Quarry. The same day he finds two vertebrate fossils near Blue Mesa. In his field diary for today, Camp writes: "Noted a couple of what appears to be amphibian 'sexual combs' perhaps from the inside of the limbs of males." Later these specimens will be correctly identified as the first evidence (toothplates) of lungfishes in the Petrified Forest.

~ 28 ~

1947 Edwin H. Colbert reports the discovery of the *Coelophysis* quarry to the American Museum of Natural History paleontologist and colleague George Gaylord Simpson, currently staying at the Collins Ranch near Lindreath, New Mexico. Excited, Simpson agrees to go to Ghost Ranch to see the find for himself.

~ 29 ~

1895 Thomas H. (Henry) Huxley, one of the foremost vertebrate paleontologists of England, dies. Born in 1825 in Ealing, near London, Huxley was also a doctor of medicine. He authored many papers on biology and paleontology, books on biology and physiology, received many honors for his work and, in 1881, became President of the Royal Society of London. Huxley supported Charles Darwin's theory of evolution, proudly referring to himself as "Darwin's bulldog." His major work in paleontology includes research into the evolution of birds and horses.

1920 Ray Harryhausen is born in Los Angeles, California. Harryhausen, a dinosaur buff since childhood, will be inspired to go into the profession of stop-motion, or dimensional, animation after seeing the movie *King Kong* at the impressionable age of 13. Early in his career Harryhausen will meet his idol and future mentor Willis O'Brien who had created the special effects for *King Kong*. Eventually the two will work together on projects like the dinosaur sequence of *The Animal World* (1956). In 1953 Harryhausen will create the striking visual effects for *The Beast from 20,000 Fathoms*, loosely based on a short story written by his friend, fantasy author Ray Bradbury, about a prehistoric reptile Harryhausen names "Rhedosaurus." Other Harryhausen movies featuring prehistoric creatures will be *Mysterious Island* (1961); *One Million Years B.C.* (1967, a remake of *One Million B.C.*); *The Valley of Gwangi* (1969, a reworking of an unfilmed 1940s O'Brien project about dinosaurs vs. cowboys) and *Sinbad and the Eye of the Tiger* (1977), with a sabertoothed cat.

Ray Harryhausen with ALLOSAURUS model, sculpted by Arthur Hayward of the British Museum (Natural History) and animated by Harryhausen, for THE VALLEY OF GWANGI (1969). © Warner Bros. Courtesy Ray Harryhausen.

1940   Karl P. Schmidt publishes a paper describing a new specimen of *Podocnemis*, a genus of turtle from the Cretaceous of Arkansas.

1994   Metropolitan Transit Authority workers make a discovery while digging out a tunnel underneath Hollywood Boulevard for a new subway system — Ice Age (about 10,000 years old) fossils including the leg and toe bones of an extinct species of horse, molars from a camel, the left forefoot of a bison and the incomplete lower molar of a mastodon. Work on the subway will be temporarily put on hold while the specimens are collected.

~ 30 ~

1841   Richard Owen officially names the sauropod dinosaur *Cetiosaurus* ("whale-like lizard"), founded upon various massive bones found on the Isle of Wight, in Sussex, Buckingham, and Oxford, England. He believes these remains are those of some huge aquatic crocodile.

1860   Thomas H. Huxley, scientist, and Samuel Wilberforce (nicknamed "Soapy Sam"), Bishop of Oxford, debate over Charles Darwin's theory of evolution at a meeting of the British Association for the Advancement of Science held at the University Museum, Oxford. Huxley argues on behalf of debate-shy Darwin while Wilberforce has been coached by Darwin opponent Richard Owen, also present. Wilberforce, beginning to lose the debate, says to Huxley, "If you truly believe that you are descended from an ape, it would interest me to know whether the ape in question was on your grandfather's or your grandmother's side." Huxley replies, "If you ask me whether I would prefer to have a wretched ape for my grandfather or a brilliant man of great importance and influence who uses his gifts to make mock of a serious scientific discussion, then I unhesitatingly declare that I prefer the ape," thereby gaining the upper hand and alienating himself from Owen.

1941   Paleontologist Samuel P. Welles collects, near Cameron, Arizona, a skeleton of the rauisuchian reptile *Postosuchus kirkpatricki*, one of the largest and most dangerous of the Petrified Forest fauna. The find constitutes the western-most occurrence of this species.

1947   George Gaylord Simpson and field worker Bill Fish arrive at Ghost Ranch, Simpson declaring the quarry to be the greatest discovery ever made in the Triassic of North America. As a result, he and Edwin H. Colbert decide to remain at the site rather than continue to the Petrified Forest and collect the myriad *Coelophysis* specimens.

1989   The five-day, dinosaur-themed science-fiction convention "Conosaurus" (aka Westercon 42) begins at the Anaheim Marriott Hotel in Anaheim, California. Dinosaurs are the subject of panel discussions and other programming.

1993   Naturhistorisches Museum in Vienna, Austria, opens its "Dinosaurier — Faszination & Wissenschaft" exhibit. Included among the displays are fossil specimens from Mongolia, computerized exhibits and mechanical dinosaur figures.

JULY

~ 1 ~

1822   James Parkinson publishes the name *Megalosaurus* in a paper titled "An Introduction to the Study of Fossil Remains" two years before William Buckland announces the genus, thereby becoming part of the history of paleontology as author of the first published dinosaur name.

1858   Charles Darwin's and Alfred Russel Wallace's respective theories of evolution are both read before the Linnean Society, in London, by its secretary. Darwin's work, still only in short form, is titled "An Abstract of an Essay on the Origin of Species and Varieties through Natural Selection or the Preservation of Favoured Races in the Struggle for Life." He had labored on the project for over 20 years but procrastinated in assembling the data into final form when naturalist Wallace, unaware of Darwin's work, informed him of his own independent and virtually identical project. Neither Darwin nor Wallace attend the reading. Society members have come expecting a paper written by George Bentham confirming his contrary idea that species do *not* change. The papers read, there is stunned silence in the room and Bentham withdraws his paper. After 13 months and 10 days, Darwin will have expanded his abstract to book-length in *The Origin of Species*.

1908   The main building of the Colorado Museum of Natural History opens to the public. New additions will be added over intervals of ten years. (The name will be changed to the Denver Museum of Natural History in 1948.) Among the paleontology exhibits displayed in two halls devoted to ancient vertebrates are skeletons of the dinosaurs *Stegosaurus*, *Edmontosaurus* and *Diplodocus*, the plesiosaur *Thalassomedon* and a good collection of fossil mammal skeletons including a large mammoth from Nebraska. The halls will remain virtually unchanged until 1995.

1927 Alan J. (Jack) Charig is born in England. Charig will become one of his country's best known and regarded paleontologists, most of his career to be based at the then named British Museum (Natural History). A master at explaining science to non-scientists, Charig will write the 10-part BBC television series *Before the Ark* (1974) and author the semipopular book *A New Look at the Dinosaurs* (1979). During the mid–1980s he will be a prime mover in refuting claims, championed by Sir Fred Hoyle, that the British Museum's *Archaeopteryx* skeleton was a forgery. In 1986 Charig will see the publication of his paper (co-authered with Angela Milner) naming and describing the unusual fish-eating dinosaur *Baryonyx*. After suffering a severe stroke, Charig will die on July 15, 1997, a month after his monograph (with Milner) on *Baryonyx* sees print. His planned description of the postcranial anatomy of the primitive armored dinosaur *Scelidosaurus* is left unfinished.

1931 Ermin C. Case and Theodore E. White continue to remove fossils at Fuller Ranch through July 4, extracting many specimens.

1933 Chicago's Museum of Science and Industry (incorporated as the Rosenwald Industrial Museum, after Julius Rosenwald, who conceived of the museum and became its driving force) opens to the public in the building reconstructed in limestone from the Palace of Fine Arts, a structure erected in staff-covered wooden lattice for the World's Columbian Exposition (1893).

Century Dioramas Studios Late Jurassic miniature scene exhibited at the 1933 Chicago World's Fair, combining images from three Charles R. Knight murals and featuring the dinosaurs APATOSAURUS, STEGOSAURUS *and* COMPSOGNATHUS, *the pterosaur* RHAMPHORYHCHUS *and the ancient bird* ARCHAEOPTERYX. *This diorama was subsequently displayed at the Museum of Science and Industry. Courtesy Chicago Historical Society.*

Although the interior will not be finished until 1940, the main attraction — a realistic "working" coal mine — is already open to the public. At the end of the mine exhibit are Century Diorama's miniature Mesozoic scenes made for the recent Chicago World's Fair (1933-34). Other paleontology-related exhibits will follow including, during the 1970s, a life-sized mechanical mammoth.

1947 Joseph T. Gregory collects Late Triassic fossils in Bull Canyon, New Mexico. Among the specimens recovered is the skull of a pseudopalatine reptile, a slender-snouted phytosaur.

1948 Karen Black is born. Black will star in many motion pictures, her acting credits to include *The Great Gatsby* (1974), for which she is nominated for an Academy Award, and *Dinosaur Valley Girls* (1996), in which she portrays cave-woman ruler Ro-Kell (and is not nominated for an Oscar).

1960 The first remake of *The Lost World* (20th Century–Fox) is released to theaters. Though Willis O'Brien has executed the visual effects, he was denied use of the stop-motion techniques he perfected for the 1925 silent movie version. Instead he had to use live lizards and alligators decked out with

The first of several inferior remakes of THE LOST WORLD, this one featuring blown-up, rubber enhanced lizards as dinosaurs and released in 1960. © 20th Century–Fox.

unconvincing rubber fins, horns and frills. Young children in the audience snicker when Professor Challenger (Claude Rains) refers to these overblown critters as "*Brontosaurus*" and "*Tyrannosaurus rex.*" Much of the film's effects footage, as well as outtakes, will later turn up in television shows produced by 20th Century–Fox.

1964 Thomas R. Dickens is born in Fort Lauderdale, Florida. A future artist, sculptor and conceptual designer, Dickens will, in the 1980s and 1990s, sculpt a series of accurate dinosaur models sold as assembly kits through companies like Saurian Studios, make and animate prehistoric animals for television commercials and for such motion pictures as *Stanley and the Dinosaurs*, *Rock-o-saurs* (both 1991, made for television), *Carnosaur* (1993) and *The Dinosaurs of Skull Island* (1994). Through his company, Integrity Productions, which is started in 1995, Dickens will create the dinosaur effects—sculpting the models, then animating, directing and photographing them—for the movie *Dinosaur Valley Girls* (1996).

1966 Primeval World—among the scenics encountered along the Santa Fe and Disneyland Railroad—opens at Disneyland Park in Anaheim, California, featuring animatronics models originally seen at the 1964-65 New York World's Fair. Train riders are taken through a cavern where they see a *Triceratops* family, a group of hungry *Apatosaurus* and an ongoing confrontation between a *Tyrannosaurus* and *Stegosaurus*.

1981 Zdenek Burian, among the most respected and influential artists of prehistoric life, dies in Prague, Czechoslovakia, soon after beginning a new canvas depicting an *Ichthyosaurus*. Born in 1904 (some sources give 1905), Burian was one of the few early successors to Charles R. Knight, giving to the world a new and, at the time, somewhat "modernized" look of extinct animals. In 1935 Burian met paleontologist Josef Augusta, Professor of Paleontology at the Charles University of Prague. After Augusta's death, Burian teamed with Augusta's successor, Professor Zdenek V. Spinar, and later with Dr. Mazak of the National Museum in Prague. With these men Burian created striking visuals for a number of illustrated books that have become classics, including *The Miracles of the Past* (1942), *Prehistoric Animals* and *Prehistoric Man* (both 1960), *The Age of Monsters* (1966), *Prehistoric Sea Monsters* (1964) and *Life Before Man* (1972). In addition to books about paleontology, Burian is also remembered for his artwork depicting the prehistoric worlds of author Edgar Rice Burroughs and for illustrating an edition of Arthur Conan Doyle's *Lost World*.

1987 Excavation of fossil remains of the horned dinosaur *Pachyrhinosaurus* starts at Pipestone Creek, Alberta, Canada, under the direction of paleontologist Darren Tanke. By the end of the digging on September 9, some 320 bones and the skulls of nine adult individuals will be collected at this site.

1996 The movie *Dinosaur Valley Girls* has its cast and crew screening at Tempest nightclub in Beverly Hills, California. When the movie ends, some attendees will be speaking to each other in cave ("tooka-tooka!") lingo.

~ 2 ~

1933 Dinosaurs, apparently those at the Sinclair Dinosaur Exhibit, are the theme of Betty Fisher's comic strip "Bill and Jean at the Fair," published in *Official World's Fair Weekly* magazine, a souvenir of A Century of Progress. The captions are written in rhyme.

1951 The *Lights Out* (NBC) television series broadcasts live the fantasy "And Adam Begot," starring actor Kent Smith. Set in modern-day France, the drama focuses upon three tourists who, following a car accident, fall from a cliff and are captured by a living Neandertal caveman (Kurt Katch as "the Man"). Most of the show's half hour is taken up detailing the threesome's attempts to escape the caveman before the characters realize they have been hurled through time back to the Stone Age.

~ 3 ~

1899 A Carnegie Museum field crew dispatched by director William J. Holland, led by preparator Arthur S. Coggeshall and recruited American Museum of Natural History Curator of Paleontology Jacob L. Wortman, arrive at the Morrison Formation locality of Sheep Creek, Wyoming. They are here to find more of what the *New York World* has called the "Most Colossal Animal Ever on Earth Just Found Out West!" which Andrew Carnegie wants to display in his museum. Thus far the coveted dinosaur is known only from a single bone found by American Museum collector William H. Reed. Promptly they start searching for more remains of the elusive fossilized critter.

1946 Still working in the Petrified Forest, Edwin H. Colbert finds a phytosaur skull and partial rutiodontine skeleton on the John Jones Ranch, south of Devil's Playground.

1990   Bill McKamey drives an almost 90 percent complete skeleton of *Tyrannosaurus rex* to its new home, the Museum of the Rockies in Bozeman, Montana. The skeleton, found in September 1988 by Kathy Wankel in McCone County and collected in June of the next year, will be subsequently prepared and exhibited at the museum.

~ 4 ~

1834   Gideon Mantell writes in his diary about leaving London and visiting the quarry at Maidstone, in Kent, England, where a partial skeleton of *Iguanodon*— the best specimen to date — has been found. Until now *Iguanodon* is known only from scrappy fossil remains. Mantell wants to purchase this so-called "Maidstone *Iguanodon*" from the quarry's owner and operator W. H. Bensted.

1866   Bernhard Hauff is born in the village of Holzmaden, Germany. Hauff will become a quarryman working in the Posidonian shale at the quarry owned by his chemist father in Holzmaden where many beautifully preserved skeletons of ichthyosaurs have been found. At 17 years of age he will exhibit a strong interest in science and is taken as an apprentice by famous German paleontologist Eberhard Fraas. Hauff will soon become a paleontologist himself, returning home to collect and carefully prepare ichthyosaurs and other fossils taken from his father's quarry, the sale of some specimens saving his family from financial problems. Many of the best ichthyosaur specimens, to be housed in museums around the world, will be purchased from Hauff. Among his more important future finds is a specimen amazingly preserved in the act of giving live birth and with embryonic skeletons still inside the body, this proving the reptiles were oviparous. In 1921 Hauff will be recognized for his work by being made doctor honoris causa of Tübingen University (Dies July 10, 1950.)

1899   Fossil preparator Arthur S. Coggeshall finds the toe bone of a hind foot of a giant dinosaur at Sheep Creek, Wyoming. Digging begins and by noon the Carnegie Museum crew exposes the left pelvis from the matrix. Remembering what day it is, the patriotic Coggeshall suggests that the find be called the "Star Spangled Dinosaur." The site is designated Camp Carnegie and the dinosaur will be named *Diplodocus carnegii*.

1900   On this good day for sauropod discoveries Field Columbian Museum fossil collector H. [Harold] W. Menke finds what will be known as quarry number 13 and makes a fine discovery in the Grand Valley, near Grand Junction, Colorado — a great reason to shoot off Fourth of July fireworks. "Menke took his pick and canteen, and went prospecting alone," Elmer S. Riggs will recall in 1939. "At dusk he returned, announcing he had found 'the biggest thing yet!' It proved to be the skeleton of *Brachiosaurus*, indeed, and by far, 'the largest known dinosaur.'" Riggs named and described this dinosaur, Brachiosaurus altithorax, in 1903.

1998 The Dinosaur Discovery Museum, sponsored by Dinamation International Society and the City of Grants, intends to celebrate Independence Day by opening in Grants, New Mexico. The museum focuses on educating families in entertaining ways. Featured are Dinamation International's mechanical dinosaurs, plus exhibits about dinosaurs and the local (volcanic) geology. Alas, opening day is delayed until summer 1999.

~ 5 ~

1888 Thomas C. Weston's Geological Survey of Canada field party reaches Dead Lodge Canyon in the Alberta badlands. Here they discover what turns out to be the richest lode of fossil beds of the Red Deer River Valley. Although most of the specimens collected will crumble away before Weston's eyes, he comprehends the significance of the beds themselves, the oldest dinosaur-bearing beds in the valley. In the years following, a treasury of dinosaur specimens will be extracted here.

1931 As of today, 3,850 square feet of quarry and three tons of fossils have been removed from Arizona's *Placerias* Quarry.

1954 Tomoyuki Tanaka officially announces that his movie *Gojira* is going into production. Two years later the film will be known in the United States as *Godzilla, King of the Monsters!*

1989 After a brief hiatus, digging resumes at Pit 91 at Rancho La Brea.

~ 6 ~

1934 Paleontologists Ermin C. Case, Floyd V. Studer, Theodore E. White and William H. Buettner begin prospecting for fossils in the Upper Triassic strata around San Juan, New Mexico.

~ 7 ~

1901   Eiji Tsuburaya is born. Tsuburaya-san will become a master of special effects for motion pictures made by the Toho Co. in Japan. Strongly influenced by Willis O'Brien's *King Kong*, he will be best known for his work for the Toho Co. wherein giant monsters, usually actors in rubber costumes, destroy highly detailed miniature cities. Among Tsuburaya's credits will be many films (original English-language release titles and dates) featuring prehistoric creatures, like *Godzilla, King of the Monsters!* (1956) and *Rodan the Flying Monster* (1957). Tsuburaya also creates the popular *Ultra Q* and *Ultraman* television series, both premiering in 1966 and including prehistoric monsters in a number of their episodes, and provides the special effects for the 1977 television movie *The Last Dinosaur*. (Dies January 10, 1970.)

1931   Ermine C. Case and William H. Buettner start digging for Late Triassic fossils along breaks of the Sierrita de la Cruz Creek in western Texas. Among the specimens found is the fragmentary skull of an amphibian which will later be designated *Buettneria perfecta*, named for one of its discoverers.

1934   E. C. Case and his prospecting team of Floyd V. Studer, Theodore E. White and William H. Buettner find a fossiliferous horizon near the Porter Ranch south of San Juan, New Mexico. The site yields a wealth of fossil fishes and phytosaur material.

1940   Ringo Starr is born (Richard Starkey) in Liverpool, England. While enjoying a career as a drummer, Ringo will also become an actor who stars as the bumbling caveman hero in the appropriately titled movie *Caveman* (1981).

1985   A major exhibition of *Iguanodon bernissartensis* skeletons, on loan from the Institut Royal des Sciences Naturelles de Belgique, bows at the National Science Museum in Tokyo, Japan.

~ 8 ~

1923   The Central Asiatic Expedition of the American Museum of Natural History returns to the fossil-rich Flaming Cliffs in Mongolia. Before the expedition ends, more than 100 specimens of *Protoceratops* will be collected, displaying a complete range of growth and age from hatchling to adult, with some skeletons complete and articulated.

1933 Edwin H. Colbert marries Margaret Matthew, daughter of William Diller Matthew and a staff artist at the American Museum of Natural History, at a ceremony in Newark, New Jersey. The Colberts will become a professional team, Margaret providing drawings, paintings and sculptures for some of "Ned's" projects, including illustrations for his book *The Year of the Dinosaur* (1977). In 1940 Margaret will design a logo (vertebrae of the Permian amphibian *Eryops* in front of a "Marsh pick," the most frequently used tool of paleontologists, behind which is a unifying circle) that will become that of the Society of Vertebrate Paleontology.

1947 American Museum of Natural History fossil preparator and good field man Carl Sorensen joins the Colbert field party at Ghost Ranch. Shortly after arriving, he collapses, not accustomed to the hot sun and higher altitude. By tomorrow, fully recovered, he will be happily back on the job.

~ 9 ~

1946 Edwin H. Colbert finds another phytosaur skull with lower jaws, probably belonging to the common Carnian-age genus *Leptosuchus*, near Devil's Playground in the Petrified Forest.

~ 10 ~

1925 The gavel sounds through history as the famous Scopes "Monkey Trial" begins. John Thomas Scopes, a science teacher at Rhea County High School in Dayton, Tennessee, has been arrested for violating a state law by teaching Darwin's theory of evolution. Arguing for the prosecution is William Jennings Bryan, secretary of state in President Woodrow Wilson's cabinet, three-time presidential candidate and an advocate for a literal interpretation of the account of creation as related in the book of Genesis. Defending Scopes is liberal attorney Clarence Darrow. In the days that follow Darrow will put his opponent Bryan on the witness stand where Bryan foolishly tries to rationalize some of the more unexplainable incidents related in the Bible, and show that both the Earth and mankind are only thousands of years old.

1929 William H. Buettner finds the lower jaws of the phytosaur *Angistorhinus megalodon* in Upper Triassic rocks of Howard County, Texas. Two years later this area will be further excavated by University of Oklahoma field teams under the direction of paleontologist J. Willis Stovall.

1931   Ermine C. Case arrives at Rotten Hill (Upper Triassic), Texas, and discovers a bone bed containing both well- and poorly-preserved phytosaur and metoposaur remains.

1934   Collector Robert Abercrombie and E. C. Case begin recovering Triassic reptile footprints (or ichnites) on the northeast corner of Mesa Redonda, Quay County, New Mexico. Four slabs containing such tracks will be collected.

~ 11 ~

1918   Roy G. Krenkel, Jr., is born in New York City. Krenkel will become one of the leading fantasy artists of the 1960s, known especially for his cover paintings and black and white interior illustrations for Edgar Rice Burroughs' stories reprinted in paperback format by Ace Books. Among the Ace/Burroughs titles featuring prehistoric themes illustrated by Krenkel will be: *At the Earth's Core, Pellucidar, Tanar of Pellucidar, The Land That Time Forgot, The People That Time Forgot, Out of Time's Abyss* and *The Eternal Savage*. (Dies February 24, 1983.)

Life restoration of the stegosaur Kentrosaurus aethiopicus *by artist Roy Krenkel, done for the book* The Dinosaur Dictionary *(1972).*

1947 Members of Edwin H. Colbert's field team at Ghost Ranch begin erecting wooden supports, consisting of two-by-fours and cross beams and a tarpaulin-covered plank roof, at the *Coelopysis* quarry. This structure will protect the *in situ* specimens — and also the men working at the site — against the severe winds and rains of the summer months.

1960 The rock 'n' roll song "Alley Oop" by the Hollywood Argyles, having been recently issued on a 45 rpm single and inspired by V. T. Hamlin's comic strip, reaches the Number 1 position on *Billboard* magazine's weekly hit list. The record, like the comic feature it was based upon, will become a classic, eventually being reissued and finding continued longevity over the decades on numerous novelty and other collections.

1986 *Man About Town*, a television pilot for an unsold situation comedy, is aired. The plot involves a tour to a museum and a mounted dinosaur skeleton that falls apart.

~ 12 ~

1922 The third Central Asiatic Expedition of the American Museum of Natural History finds the skull of a relatively small and primitive horned dinosaur in the Gobi Desert, Mongolia. The next year, paleontologists William King Gregory and Charles L. Mook will describe this dinosaur, naming it *Protoceratops andrewsi*.

1979 "Egg Mountain" is discovered by Fred Tannenbaum on the Teton River, west of Choteay, in Teton County, Montana. The site, to be worked by John R. Horner and Robert Makeala, will yield countless specimens of bone and eggshell (some with embryos) belonging to a new kind of hypsilophodontid dinosaur, a small swift-running herbivore to be named *Orodromeus makelai* by Horner and Johns Hopkins University paleontologist David B. Weishampel. Also to be found at the "Egg Mountain" site are mammal and lizard fossils.

1987 Sculptor David A. Thomas' life-sized bronze *Gorgosaurus libratus* is installed outside the New Mexico Museum of Natural History. The 30-foot-long carnivore, perfectly balanced on one foot, is set across the walkway facing its enemy "Spike," the *Pentaceratops sternbergii*. Details on the *Gorgosaurus* include healed wounds as if from some previous violent encounter.

1996 The 900-seat Imperial Cinema in Montreal, Canada, starts its FantAsia Festival. Among the prehistoric-monster films screened are *Destroy All Monsters, Godzilla vs. the Smog Monster* and *The Terror of Godzilla* (as well as various *Ultraman* television episodes). The festival will be a success, continuing through August 11.

~ 13 ~

1902 Paleoanthropologist Gustav Heinrchich Ralph von Koenigswald is born. He will be best known for his work on fossils of early man and his ancestors, including naming new genera and species. (Dies July 10, 1982.)

1923 George Olsen makes paleontological history when he finds three fossil eggs in the Gobi Desert of Mongolia. The eggs, unlike those of birds, are elongate and shaped somewhat like those of modern lizards. More such eggs will be subsequently found, some of them having been laid in circles somewhat in the fashion of modern marine turtles. They will finally be identified as the first verifiable eggs of dinosaurs. Though these eggs are presumed to be those of *Protoceratops*, in the 1980s they will be identified as theropod.

1940 Jim Danforth is born in Chicago, Illinois, where he will become inspired by visits to the Field Museum of Natural History. Danforth will create stop-motion animation effects and matte painting for motion pictures. He will be nominated for an Academy Award for his stop-motion effects for the movie *When Dinosaurs Ruled the Earth* (1971) and become one of the most admired artists in this field.

1977 W. Amaral of Harvard University finds the second specimen (a partial skeleton) of a small, primitive armored dinosaur in Lower Jurassic sediments of the Kayenta Formation, northeast of Flagstaff, Arizona. The holotype, an almost complete skeleton, had been discovered in June 1971 by David Lawler, then a summer assistant at the Museum of Northern Arizona, in sediments north of Flagstaff. In 1981 Edwin H. Colbert will name this dinosaur *Scutellosaurus lawleri*.

~ 14 ~

1992 Dinamation International Society announces the discovery of a new dromaeosaurid that is similar to but twice the size of the famous

Paleontologist James I. Kirkland holding the giant foot claw of UTAHRAPTOR OSTROMMAYSI on the day of this fossil's discovery in 1992. Courtesy James I. Kirkland and Dinamation International Society.

dromaeosaurid *Deinonychus*, and several more times bigger than another dromaeosaurid *Velociraptor*. Next year the theropod will be named *Utahraptor ostrommaysi*. The announcement of the discovery comes at a good time for the makers of the movie *Jurassic Park*, which had recently been criticized for depicting sickle-clawed *Velociraptor* several times too large. The implication in the popular press will be that the movie had somehow predicted the real discovery. Actually *Utahraptor* and *Velociraptor* differ in more significant ways than simple size disparity.

1993   After more than a year's work, sculptor and former welder Joe Barrington completes his full-sized steel *Apatosaurus* model, done on commission to be displayed on the site of the Cimarron County Historical Society museum in Boise City, Oklahoma. The sculpture is 65 feet long, 35 feet tall at the raised head, weighs 9 tons and cost $12,000 to make. Its intended purpose is to help draw attention to the county's historic and archaeological attractions.

~ 15 ~

1931   Ermin C. Case finds teeth of a small carnivorous dinosaur and also from 35 to 36 vertebrae of the giant carnivorous reptile *Postosuchus kirkpatricki* at Rotten Hill, Texas.

~ 16 ~

1931 Always-busy Ermin C. Case finds a partial skeleton, including the vertebral column and some armor plates, part of the pelvis and numerous dermal plates, belonging to the aetosaurian reptile *Stagonolepis wellesi* at Rotten Hill, Texas. Case incorrectly believes he has found another phytosaur.

1937 Leonard B. Radinsky is born in Staten Island, New York. As a professor of anatomy at the University of Chicago, Radinsky will specialize in the evolution of the mammalian brain as revealed by endocasts of the brains of fossil and extinct mammals. He will amass a large collection of such casts (now housed at The Field Museum) and publish 25 papers on brain evolution. Radinsky will contend that the morphology of living animals must first be understood, especially the functional importance of structure, before fossil morphology can be understood. (Dies August 30, 1985.)

1947 A writer and a photographer from *Life* magazine arrive at the important, new Ghost Ranch *Coelophysis* quarry dinosaur dig to do an article.

~ 17 ~

1766 George Croghan returns with a team including Philadelphia trader George Morgan and military engineer Ensign Thomas Hutchins to the Big Bone Lick to collect fossils. They are to ship two loads of specimens to London, one to Lord Shelburne, the King's Minister for the Colonies, the other to Benjamin Franklin. If possible, another is to be sent to George's brother Dr. John Morgan of the College of Medicine in Philadelphia. The collecting will proceed, this time with Croghan evading any ambushes.

1959 Anthropologists Louis and Mary Leakey, also husband and wife, discover the 1.75-million-year-old remains of an early hominid in the Olduvai Gorge, a dry river gulch in northern Tanzania, a site they have been working for 28 years. The remains consist of part of the facial region of a hominid with large teeth, this fossil resembling the larger and more robust kinds of australopithecines being found in South Africa. (Earlier, the Leakeys had found perplexing primitive tools at this site and also an enormous number of animal fossils.) Louis, finding the Olduvai partial skull to be more robust than the South African skulls, will designate it the type of new genus and species *Zinjanthropus boisei*. Later this taxon will be regarded as another species of *Australopithecus*.

~ 18 ~

1786   The first advertisement for artist Charles Willson Peale's private museum, the Peale Museum in Philadelphia, is published in *The Pennsylvania Packet*: "Mr. Peale will make a part of his House a Repository for Natural Curiosities." The museum houses such great "curiosities" as mammoth remains from Big Bone Lick, formerly in the Philadelphia home of Dr. John Morgan.

~ 19 ~

1992   Families enjoy one of Dinamation International Society's Dinosaur Discovery Expeditions to Upper Jurassic country in western Colorado, led by a team of paleontologists.

~ 20 ~

19th century caricature of Sir Richard Owen (who coined the word "Dinosauria") riding a skeleton of MEGA-THERIUM, a giant ground sloth researched by Owen.

1804   The future Sir Richard Owen is born in Lancaster, England. Schooled as a physician at the University of Edinburgh, he will complete his education at St. Bartholomew's Hospital in London but will become more interested in natural history than medicine. A personal friend of Queen Victoria, he will spend much time at the palace instructing her and the Royal Family about the wonders of nature. Owen will become interested in the remains of the various huge and perplexing reptiles being discovered in Great Britain and, by 1841, name and describe some of them, including the sauropod *Cetiosaurus*. Arguably Owen's most significant contribution to the new field of paleontology will be his coining of the word "Dinosauria," which he will announce later that year. A rigid, yet calm, opinionated and religious man, Owen will not adapt to the rapid changes occurring in the scientific world, particularly those brought about by Darwin's theory of evolution, which he will oppose up to his death in 1892.

1985 While prospecting for unionid and snail fossil sites in Upper Triassic rocks near Lacey Point at Petrified Forest National Park, Steven Good of the University of Colorado, Boulder, finds a nice skeleton of the archosaur *Arribasuchus buceros* near a series of petroglyphs. The specimen will be prepared at the New Mexico Museum of Natural History.

~ 21 ~

1786 Charles Willson Peale, elected to the American Philosophical Society in Philadelphia, starts requesting fossils and other "oddities of Nature" for display in his Peale Museum.

1925 John Thomas Scopes is found guilty of teaching evolution in a public school and is fined $100. The trial and its decision will have an impact on a global basis, with repercussions felt throughout this century. As British anatomist Frederic Wood Jones will say in later years, the outcome of the trial provokes "a return to the age of dogmatism" by opponents of evolution. Among the more positive effects of the trial will be the play *Inherit the Wind*, the names changed probably to protect playwrights Jerome Lawrence and Robert E. Lee. Movie adaptations of the play will follow (1960 and 1988).

1994 Sunshine City shopping center in Tokyo hosts a major (and rather high-tech) display of Godzilla items — including original movie props, costumes, stationery and animatronic models, specially constructed displays, interactive video games and memorabilia — to celebrate the 50th anniversary of the first *Gojira* (aka *Godzilla, King of the Monsters!*) movie. Also included is a live stage presentation. Admission is 1100 yen for adult Godzilla fans and 700 for youngsters. The event will continue until August 31.

~ 22 ~

1822 Gregor Johann Mendel is born in Heinzendorf, a tiny village in Moravia. Although he will become a monk and then Abbott of the Augustinian monastery at Brünn, Mendel will be famous for discovering the laws of heredity. Working with peas grown in the garden beneath the walls of the Augustinian monastery at Altbrünn, Austria, Mendel will formulate three laws of inheritance: 1. Every living thing comprises a number of independent heritable units, each one independent of the others; 2. each pair of contrasted characters goes through its own hereditary separation, thereby allowing all possible combinations through hybridization; and 3. hereditary factors are unchanged and unaffected by their long association in an individual. Mendel will maintain his interests in science, including that of meteorology, but also become involved in Church vs. State politics until his death on January 6, 1884. Despite his achievement, Mendel will remain an unknown figure in the history of science, his work not generally known until being inadvertently rediscovered in 1900.

1839   Fossil collector James Hall writes to Yale University natural history instructor Benjamin Silliman, offering him "a valuable collection ... of Geological specimens, fossils, etc., which the State of New York will furnish...." Hall brags about the number of items and their excellent condition. Silliman, convinced of the collection's value and importance, makes Hall a sufficient offer and soon takes possession of the "New York geological specimens."

1988   "From the Land of Dragons," a traveling exhibit of Chinese dinosaur and other fossils, opens at the American Museum of Natural History.

1994   The Devil's Canyon Science and Learning Center has its grand opening in western Colorado, the result of a unique partnership between the City of Fruita and Dinamation International Society. The 22,000 square-foot facility includes over a dozen robotic prehistoric animals from Dinamation International Corporation, a working fossil preparation laboratory and hands-on educational exhibits.

~ 23 ~

1978   John R. Horner and Robert Makela spot dinosaur bones being sold at a rock shop in Bynum, Montana. The shop's owners reveal where the bones were found. This will lead directly to the discovery by Horner and Makela of nesting grounds, in the Upper Cretaceous Two Medicine Formation, of a new duckbilled dinosaur, which they will name *Maiasaura* the following year. The site will yield a wealth of fossil bones and eggs representing an ontogenetic series from embryo to adult.

1988   Dinosaur Days begins its week-long run at the Museum of Western Colorado, Grand Junction. To help celebrate the event the Best Western Horizon Inn erects a big prop dinosaur in its children's playground.

~ 24 ~

1865　Yale University announces its establishment of the country's first chair of paleontology, the professorship going to Othniel Charles Marsh. In truth Marsh himself had engineered this new position. While visiting England in the early 1860s he persuaded his wealthy uncle George Peabody to endow a museum at Yale. The museum will bear Peabody's name and provide a base of operations from which Marsh can enjoy his new title. Marsh will return to Yale later this year.

1898　A Geological Survey of Canada field party led by paleontologist Lawrence M. Lambe arrives at Berry Creek in the Alberta badlands. Within a month Lambe and his team will collect a dozen boxes of specimens calculated to have a combined weight of more than 1.5 tons.

1931　A new show with dinosaurs opens at the Roxy Theatre in New York, two of its features being titled "Fifty Million Years Ago" and "Holocaust." The dinosaurs are mechanical figures created by Messmore and Damon. Included in the cast is "Dolores, the last of the Dinosaurs," played by Messmore and Damon's giant mechanical "Brontosaurus" (*Apatosaurus*), who at one point scoops up one of the cavegirl dancers in its mouth and whisks her off into the wings. According to critic Henry Beckett: "In putting on such a show it was unnecessary to bother much about the accuracy of details, because no patron is in a position to prove them wrong; and still it is possible that the management was just a little reckless in having a dinosaur and a cave man on the stage at the same time. Moreover, the little girl, almost seven, who took us to the show insists that the prehistoric beast which rages there is a special kind of dinosaur known as the brontosaurus, and, therefore, unsuited to the role of eating a sacrificial virgin."

1975　The Valley of Dinosaurs, a permanent outdoor exhibition of life-sized dinosaur replicas, opens in the Silesian Park of Culture and Recreation in Chorzow, Poland. Created under the direction of paleontologist Zofia Kielan-Jaworowska of the Institute of Paleozoology of the Polish Academy of Sciences, Warsaw, the display features reconstructions of dinosaurs whose fossils were recovered in the Gobi Desert during the Polish-Mongolian Paleontological Expeditions launched from 1963 to 1971. Represented are such Mongolian dinosaurs as the sauropod *Nemegtosaurus*, theropod *Saurornithoides*, hadrosaur *Saurolophus* and ankylosaur *Saichania*.

Full-scale statue of the giant hadrosaur SAUROLOPHUS ANGUSTIROSTRIS *at the Valley of Dinosaurs, Silesian Park of Culture and Recreation, in Chorzow, Poland. Courtesy Zofia Kielan-Jaworowska.*

~ 25 ~

1806   William Clark, half of the famous Lewis and Clark Expedition to explore the upper Missouri River, writes in his journal about a probable dinosaur bone found at the south bank of Yellowstone River, near Billings, Montana (grammatical errors and misspellings his): "dureing the time the men were getting the two big horns [mountain sheep] which I had killed to the river I employed my self in getting pieces of the rib of a fish which was Semented within the face of the rock this rib is (about) inches in Secumpherence about the middle it is 3 feet in length tho a part of the end appears to have been broken off (the fallen rock is near the water — the face of the rock where rib is perpendr — 4 is lengthwise, a little barb projects I have several pieces of this rib the bone is neither decayed nor petrified but very rotten. the part which I could not get out may be seen, it is about 6 or 7 Miles below Pompys Tower in the face of the Lar [boar]d Clift about 20 feet above the water." This constitutes one of the earliest such accounts in North America.

1874   The Cope-Marsh feud is fueled as Edward Drinker Cope's ego is bruised once again. Cope, having arrived at Pueblo, Colorado, learns that he is not to be in charge of the United States Geological Survey team he has joined but will merely serve as its geologist of topographical exploration through the Sangre de Cristo Mountains toward Santa Fe. The boss will be a zoologist named Yarrow.

1884   Davidson Black is born in Toronto, Canada. Black will become a physician and professor of anatomy at Peking Union Medical College in China. His most important contribution to paleoanthropology will be made in the 1920s after he is shown a fossil tooth (a specimen that had escaped being ground up to be sold for medicines or magical potions) from Chou-koutien, China. Identifying the tooth as that of an ancient human being, Black will declare it to represent a new genus which will become known as Peking Man (officially *Homo erectus*). In 1927 work will begin to collect more specimens of Peking Man, though Black will never see this work completed; he will die of a heart attack in 1934.

1902   Max Pfannenstiel is born in Wanzeneau, near Strasbourg/Alsace. Pfannenstiel will become a paleontologist, working on both invertebrates and vertebrates, and specializing in the historical aspects of paleontology and geology. Among his major accomplishments will be research published in 1932 on the brain and sensory organs of fossil amphibians, especially the mastodonsaurs of the Triassic of southwestern Germany. In later years he will hold the honor of professor emeritus of geology and paleontology and director of the Geological and Paleontological Institute of the University of Freiburg, Breisgau, Germany. (Dies January 1, 1976.)

1956   The American Museum of Natural History's newly renovated Tyrannosaur Hall (also called the Cretaceous Hall and Hall of Late Dinosaurs) opens to the public. The mounted skeletons of *Tyrannosaurus*, *Triceratops* and two hadrosaurs called *Trachodon* (later renamed *Anatotitan*) are displayed on a center island. New additions include specimens of *Protoceratops* collected by the Central Asiatic Expeditions of the American Museum in the 1920s and a skeleton of the giant flying reptile *Pteranodon*.

~ 26 ~

1866   Othniel Charles Marsh is officially appointed America's first professor of paleontology at Yale. The position requires no teaching by Marsh and pays him no salary. The Great Hall of Yale's new Peabody Museum of

Natural History will become a monument to Marsh and his work that the paleontologist will enjoy for the rest of his life.

~ 27 ~

1933 Robert F. Thomas and Max Littlesalt discover bones of the carnivorous dinosaur *Segisaurus* in the Navajo sandstone (probably Lower Jurassic) on the north branch of Segi Canyon, Navajo Indian Reservation, Arizona. This find constitutes the first vertebrate fossil material found at this locality.

Full-scale model of the horned dinosaur TRICERATOPS HORRIDUS *made by Louis Paul Jonas for Sinclair Dinoland, New York World's Fair (1964-65). An exact copy of this model, named "Uncle Beazley," now resides outside the National Museum of Natural History. Courtesy Sinclair Refining Company.*

1967 "Uncle Beazley" arrives at the Smithsonian Institution, stopping at his new permanent home in the park across from the National Museum of Natural History. The 22-foot-long fiberglass *Triceratops* model, equipped with a moving head and neck, is an exact copy made by Louis

Paul Jonas of one of the dinosaurs his company created for the Sinclair Dinoland at the 1964-65 New York World's Fair. Recently "Uncle Beazley" had starred in "The Enormous Egg," based on a story by Oliver Butterworth, for the television anthology series *NBC Children's Theater.* In it a young boy hatched a *Triceratops* which rapidly grew to adult size, after which the boy walked the dinosaur to the Smithsonian.

1992 The movie *Prehysteria!* starts shooting in Los Angeles. Based on an idea by co-producer Pete Von Sholly, it shows what happens when a home is taken over by a group of miniature dinosaurs. Geared toward younger audiences, *Prehysteria!*, released in 1993, will spawn two sequels, each with the same title followed by a number.

Original clay model of the dinosaur CHASMOSAURUS BELLI *sculpted by Andrea Von Sholly for the motion picture* PREHYSTERIA! *Photo by Pete Von Sholly.*

~ 28 ~

1840 Edward Drinker Cope is born in Fairfield, near Philadelphia, Pennsylvania. At six years old the precocious Cope will study the exhibits at the Peale Museum, making keen observations of and taking notes on an ichthyosaur skeleton displayed at the Academy of Natural Sciences of Philadelphia. By eight he will be making accurate drawings of fossil plants and animals and at 18 have a paper ("The Primary Divisions of the Salamandridae with Descriptions of the New Species") accepted by Joseph Leidy and his associates for publication in the Academy's *Proceedings.* Educated in Europe and North America, the financially comfortable Cope will author some 1,400 scientific papers and monographs, name and describe myriad

*Paleontologist Edward Drinker Cope as a young man.
Courtesy Department Library Services, American Museum
of Natural History (negative #312408).*

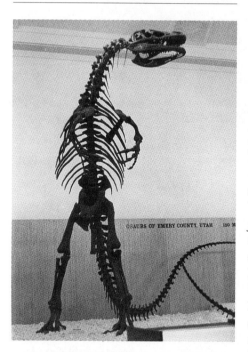

Skeleton of ALLOSAURUS FRAGILIS *comprising elements collected at the Cleveland-Lloyd Dinosaur Quarry, mounted
at the Utah Museum of Natural History under the direction of James H. Madsen, Jr. Courtesy James H. Madsen,
Jr., and University of Utah.*

new genera and species of dinosaurs
and other extinct animals, and generally accomplish considerably more
than would Othniel Charles Marsh
with whom Cope bitterly feuds for
nearly three decades. Two years before
his death Cope will be honored by
being elected President of the American Association for the Advancement
of Science. His final days will be spent
as a salaried professor at the University
of Pennsylvania. (Dies April 12, 1897.)

1932   James H. Madsen, Jr., is
born in Salt Lake City, Utah. Madsen
will specialize in dinosaurs of the
Morrison Formation, particularly the
theropod *Allosaurus* on which he will
become a leading authority. In the
1960s Madsen will become Chief
Curator and Research Paleontologist,
Department of Geology and Geo-
physics and Adjunct Curator of Paleontology at the Utah Museum of
Natural History, University of Utah.
During the 1970s Madsen will be
appointed State Paleontologist of
Utah. His monograph on *Allosaurus
fragilis* (1976), based largely on skeletons Madsen has collected, prepared
and studied from the Cleveland-Lloyd
Dinosaur Quarry in Utah during the
University of Utah Cooperative
Dinosaur Project, and including an
osteology, will be the definitive work
on this genus and species. After retiring from his State Paleontologist post
in the late 1980s, Madsen (with wife
Susan) will start DINOLAB, a company based in Salt Lake City that

makes and distributes casts of Cleveland-Lloyd dinosaurs including *Allosaurus*, these reproductions to be exhibited in museums and other institutions the world over.

~ 29 ~

1938   *Three Missing Links*, a Columbia Pictures comedy short starring the Three Stooges — Moe Howard, "Curly" (Jerry) Howard and Larry Fine — is released. The plot involves a movie being made about prehistoric people and a gorilla. When Curly, disguised as an ape, meets a real female gorilla (Ray "Crash" Corrigan in Simian drag), and Curly inadvertently eats some magic "love candy," then … well, you get the idea.

~ 30 ~

1871   Othniel C. Marsh discovers the skeleton of a new, medium-sized duckbilled dinosaur near Smoky Hill River, Kansas. Marsh names it *Claosaurus agilis*. However, as only fragments of the skull have been found, not much can be said about the animal other than it is a fairly primitive form.

1930   Davidson Black announces the discovery of a partial second Peking Man skull at a second special meeting of the Geological Society of China. The specimen comprises some small uncrushed fragments collected on the recently named Sinanthropus Hill in Choukoutien that fit together nicely, forming the vault and part of the base of the skull. According to the minutes of the meeting, "As the discovery of Sinanthropus had aroused general public interest, the meeting was attended by an unusually large audience to hear Dr. Black's report and to see the second skull." *Sinanthropus* will later be referred to *Homo erectus*.

~ 31 ~

1897   Lawrence M. Lambe and his Geological Survey of Canada field party begin their exploration of the Red Deer River of the Alberta badlands. This will be the first of three such missions that will inevitably establish this area as rich for collecting dinosaur fossils.

1931   The holotype of the aetosaur *Stagonolepis wellesi* is shipped from Amarillo, Texas, to the University of Michigan for preparation and study.

A CHASMOSAURUS sculpted by Jim Danforth and animated by David Allen for the movie WHEN DINOSAURS RULED THE EARTH (© Hammer Films/Warner Bros., 1971).

1963 John H. Ostrom names and describes a new species of the duckbilled dinosaur *Parasaurolophus*, *P. crytocristatus*, found in New Mexico. The tube-like crest of this species is shorter and more curved than that of the type species *P. walkeri*. In later years some paleontologists will regard the new species as valid, others will interpret it as a female of the type species.

1986 Sculptor Stephen A. Czerkas, holding a press conference at the Natural History Museum of Los Angeles County, announces his new interpretation regarding the arrangement of the back plates in *Stegosaurus*. In the past most paleontologists have accepted Charles W. Gilmore's arrangement of two rows of alternating plates. Czerkas has rearranged the plates into a single row with some small plates near the neck leaning in alternating directions and has also made a sculpture of the dinosaur to illustrate his idea. For a while Czerkas' arrangement will almost become the norm, some museums displaying their *Stegosaurus* skeletons with one row of plates. However, in less than a decade, with the discovery of additional articulated specimens showing two staggered rows, Gilmore's arrangement will be shown to be correct after all.

AUGUST

~ 1 ~

1872   Joseph Leidy mails out advance copies of his paper naming and describing *Uintatherium*, a newly discovered horned and tusked mammal from the Upper Eocene of the Uinta Basin in Utah. This is the first generic name given to a uintathere.

1903   Elmer S. Riggs, comparing the sauropods *Apatosaurus* and *Brontosaurus* (both named and described by O. C. Marsh at different times during the same year), finds their respective bones to be mostly the same, any differences between them attributed to degrees of maturity. Riggs concludes, "In view of these facts the two genera may be regarded as synonymous. As the term 'Apatosaurus' has priority, 'Brontosaurus' will be regarded as a

The partial skeleton of APATOSAURUS EXCELSUS, *which Elmer S. Riggs described in 1903, as originally exhibited at the Field Columbian Museum. Courtesy The Field Museum (neg. #26576).*

synonym." Thus the name for this most familiar of dinosaurs officially becomes *Apatosaurus* forever. The public, however, will generally use the name *Brontosaurus* at least until its correct skull is put on mounted skeletons 75 years later.

1940 The Works Progress Administration (WPA) starts a fossil-collecting operation in Upper Triassic rocks of the Herring Ranch area along the Sierrita de la Cruz near Rotten Hill, Texas.

1947 Edwin H. Colbert and his field team begin the work of channeling between the heavy blocks of matrix containing fossils, protected by reinforcing jackets of burlap and plaster, at the *Coelophysis* quarry, Ghost Ranch.

Same day: Joseph T. Gregory ships the fossil skull of *Arribasuchus buceros* from Blue Canyon, New Mexico, to the Peabody Museum. Then, with G. D. Guadagni and B. Mikula, Gregory starts digging in the Revuelto Creek area.

1948 Robert Broom discovers the almost perfect pelvis of a hominid in a stone slab in a cave at Sterkfontein, South Africa. This find will show that *Paranthropus crassidens* was a biped.

1984 Paleontologists J. Michael Parrish (University of Chicago), Robert A. Long and Steve Gatesy continue their field work in the Petrified Forest. They are soon joined by Bryan Small, a graduate student from Texas Tech University, and Michael T. Greenwald of the Museum of Paleontology at the University of California, Berkeley. Discovered on the northeast side of "The Flattops" will be a large concentration of remains of the wide-bodied aetosaur *Typothorax*. South of this area a skull of the phytosaur *Pseudopalatus pristinus* will be found.

1995 Artist Rudolph F. Zallinger, best known for his paintings depicting life through time for Yale University's Peabody Museum of Natural History, dies. Zallinger's son Peter and daughter Jean Day will continue his artistic tradition, creating their own life restorations of extinct animals which reveal the stylistic influence of their father.

~ 2 ~

1841 Richard Owen speaks before the British Association for the Advancement of Science at a meeting held at the Museum in Plymouth.

In his "Report on British Fossil Reptiles to the Geology Section," the main topics include three recently discovered giant fossil reptiles —*Megalosaurus, Iguanodon* and *Hylaeosaurus.* Owen proposes that these newly found fossils represent a group which, the following year in an Association's report he will officially name: "The combination of such characters, some, as the sacral ones, altogether peculiar among Reptiles, others borrowed, as it were, from groups now distinct from each other, and all manifested by creatures far surpassing in size the largest of existing reptiles, will, it is presumed, be deemed sufficient ground for establishing a distinct tribe or suborder of Saurian Reptiles, for which I would propose the name of *Dinosauria.*"

1968 A tiny jaw fragment, the first evidence of a fossil vertebrate found in Antarctica, is described by Edwin H. Colbert, Peter Barrett and Ralph Baille. The jaw, discovered by Ohio State University student Baille the previous field season about 400 miles away from the South Pole, is identified by Colbert as belonging to a labyrinthodont, a kind of amphibian known from other continents. This identification will constitute the key to confirming the existence of a supercontinent during the Triassic Period and the theory of continental drift.

1977 A large scale model (slightly bigger than human-sized) of a *Tyrannosaurus* makes a startling impression on a London street on its way back from a fair in Woburn, England.

~ 3 ~

1769 Spanish explorer Gaspar de Portola discovers "springs of pitch" in the Los Angeles area during the Portola California Expedition of 1769–1770. He records in his diary: "The 3rd, we proceeded for three hours on a good road; to the right of it were extensive swamps of bitumen which is called *chapapote.* We debated whether this substance, which flows melted from underneath the earth, could occasion so many earthquakes." The scientific excavation of this 23-acre site will begin in 1901, after which it becomes famous as the Rancho La Brea "tar pits." (Quakes will continue in L.A.)

1937 A field party from the United States National Museum starts collecting fossils in the Petrified Forest. A large skull of the phytosaur *Leptosuchus adamanensis* will be found near Twin Buttes southwest of Adamana.

Rancho La Brea, with its lake of asphalt (from which countless Ice Age fossils have been recovered), as it looked in 1914. Courtesy George C. Page Museum of La Brea Discoveries.

1960 An expedition of geologists, under the auspices of the Twenty-First International Congress of Geology and led by fossil-fish authority Professor Anatol Heintz of the University of Oslo, finds footprints of dinosaurs atop a sandstone cliff on the coast of Spitzbergen, Svalbard, Norway. The tracks were made by large ornithopod dinosaurs like *Iguanodon*. Apparently the trackmakers had no trouble surviving in colder climates and during extended periods of night.

1996 Japan America Theatre in Los Angeles' Little Tokyo (part of the city's Ninth District) puts on a Godzilla Film Festival as part of the Nisei Week Japanese Festival. Screened are three of the "Big G's" more popular movies — *Destroy All Monsters, Godzilla vs. Hedorah* (aka *Godzilla vs. the Smog Monster*) and *Terror of Mechagodzilla* (aka *The Terror of Godzilla*). Between today and August 11 Godzilla himself, in the form of an American stuntman wearing a Japanese promotional outfit, will make various personal appearances, including one before L.A. Mayor Richard Riordan. As the Godzilla suit will prove too hot to wear for more than five minutes, it will be mounted sans stuntman for the monster celebrity's truck ride in the festival's parade.

~ 4 ~

1918   Yoshibumi Tajima is born. Tajima-san will become a character actor best remembered by fans of Japanese prehistoric-monster movies in the role of entrepreneur Kumayama in *Godzilla vs. the Thing* (1964), army generals in *Destroy All Monsters* (1969) and *Monster Zero* (1970) and a police detective in *Godzilla's Revenge* (1971).

1940   Michael J. Williams is born in Ina, Illinois. Williams will become a paleontologist specializing in fossil fishes, most of his work done while directing the Cleveland Museum of Natural History. Among his accomplishments with dinosaurs will be co-authoring the paper naming the small tyrannosaurid theropod *Nanotyrannus lancensis* (now regarded as a juvenile Tyrannosaurus rex).

1994   Paleontologists Bernardo P. Pérez-Moreno, José Luis Sanz, Angela D. Buscalloni, José J. Moratalla, Francisco Ortega and Diego Rasskin-Gutman publish their joint paper naming and describing *Pelecanimimus polyodon*, an ornithomimosaur from the Lower Cretaceous lithographic limestones of Las Hoyas, province of Cuenca, Spain. The ostrich-like dinosaur is unique in possessing more than 200 teeth. Skin impressions are found with the type specimen, the front half of an articulated skeleton with skull.

~ 5 ~

1910   Arthur Conan Doyle, in a letter to his friend Sir Roger Casement, describes his plans for writing *The Lost World*. Casement is to be the model for the novel's explorer and sportsman Lord Roxton. Conan Doyle will complete the novel by December of next year.

1922   The first skull of the largest known land mammal, originally named *Baluchitherium* (now *Indricotherium*), is discovered in Tsagan Nor Basin, Mongolia, by Walter Granger during the Central Asiatic Expedition of the American Museum of Natural History to China and Mongolia. The skull, incomplete and broken into pieces, will be described by Henry Fairfield Osborn who estimates the animal's size as about 28 feet long and 17 feet tall.

1937   Charles W. Gilmore and assistants George Sternberg and G. B. Pierce collect a pseudopalatine skull and the first evidence of the aetosaur *Paratypothorax* from the southeast side of Billings Gap in the Petrified Forest.

~ 6 ~

Photo (taken circa 1910) of the full-sized IGUANODON model made by sculptor Josef Franz Pallenberg for Carl Hagenbeck's Tiergarten (aka the Hamburg Zoo) in Stellingen, Germany.

1882   Josef Franz Pallenberg is born in Germany. Circa 1909 the German sculptor will be commissioned to make a set of life-sized figures of dinosaurs and other extinct reptiles — the first made since those of Benjamin Waterhouse Hawkins, and the first to be done in a more accurate and modern style — for permanent display at Carl Hagenbeck's Tiergarten, the world's first zoo without bars, located in Stellingen, near Hamburg, Germany. The models (including *Iguanodon, Diplodocus, Stegosaurus* and *Pteranodon*) will be made of plaster and burlap and occupy their own section of the Hamburg Zoo. An especially interesting tableau will show a family of *Triceratops* with one of the adults half-submerged in water. (Dies 1946.)

1898   G. E. (Ernest) Untermann is born in Berlin, Germany, the son of Ernest Untermann, Sr. G. E. Untermann and his wife Billie R. (born in Vernal, Utah, July 29, 1906; dies 1972) will serve as a ranger team at Dinosaur National Monument, mapping the area's geology, after which he is designated Director of the Museum Project which will lead to the establishment of the Utah Field House of Natural History in Vernal. After the museum building's completion in 1948, the State of Utah will appoint G. E. Director and Billie Staff Scientist, both of them also to serve as curators. (Dies 1975.)

1988   The complete skeleton of a new troodontid theropod dinosaur is discovered during the Sino-Canadian Dinosaur Project in dark red sandstone west of Muhuaxiao Village, near the northern plain of the Ordos, Inner

Mongolia. The skeleton, which will be given the name *Sinornithoides* by paleontologists Dale A. Russel and Dong Zhiming in 1993, represents the most complete troodontid specimen yet known. It is found buried lying on its stomach, the skull resting on the left shoulder, tail curved to the left. Remains found with the fossil include bones of a turtle, pterosaur and other kinds of dinosaurs.

~ 7 ~

1933 *Alley Oop*, V. T. Hamlin's comic strip featuring cavemen and dinosaurs, bows in newspapers. It opens with caveman hero Alley Oop lost and alone in a swamp infested with menacing dinosaurs. Soon readers of the strip will be introduced to its cast of characters. This and subsequent story-lines will be collected and reprinted in 1987-88 by Dragon Lady Press.

1996 NASA holds a news conference, broadcast live on television and radio, announcing the discovery of a rock seemingly from Mars containing possible fossil evidence that bacteria-like invertebrate life may have once existed on that planet. The findings will be formally published nine days later.

~ 8 ~

1846 Alfred Giard is born in Valenciennes, France. Giard will become a zoologist, biologist and oceanographer. As Professor of Zoology at the University of Lille, Giard will become famous as the first scientist to teach evolution in that country. After Giard dies on August 8, 1908, he will be honored with the publication of his writings collected into a single volume bearing the dedication, "Aldred Giard — Works, collected and republished by a group of his students and friends."

1857 Henry Fairfield Osborn is born into a wealthy family in Fairfield, Connecticut. Osborn (sometimes referred to as HFO) will become a larger-than-life figure and true giant in the field of vertebrate paleontology. A future student of Edward D. Cope, Osborn's main interests in the field will focus on fossil mammals (particularly proboscideans and horses) and man and, to a lesser degree, fossil reptiles. In 1891 he will join the staff of the American Museum of Natural History, soon founding its Department of Vertebrate Paleontology and later becoming the museum's President. From here Osborn will launch major expeditions to Wyoming, Canada and Central

Paleontologist Henry Fairfield Osborn in the field during his later years. Courtesy Edwin H. Colbert.

Asia during which many of the institution's prized dinosaur specimens are collected. The museum's Osborn Hall of Early Mammals, opening in the early 20th century, will be a tribute to the man and his work. During Osborn's long career he will be made professor emeritus at Columbia University, President of the American Association for the Advancement of Science and recipient of myriad degrees and other honors. He authors numerous scientific papers (in one he names and describes the famous *Tyrannosaurus rex*), though many of them are largely researched by assistants and colleagues. Some of his writings will achieve classic status (e.g., the book *Men of the Old Stone Age*, published in 1916). (Dies November 6, 1935.)

1884 Joseph Burr Tyrrell finds a skull of the giant theropod dinosaur *Albertosaurus* in Alberta, Canada.

1968 Czechoslovakia issues four postage stamps of indigenous Paleozoic-age fossils and minerals to publicize the 23rd International Geological Congress, which had met in Prague in August of 1968. Images include the ammonite *Hypophylloceras*, trilobite *Selenopeltis*, bivalve *Chlamys* and frog *Paleobatrachus*.

1987 "Dinosaur Daze" begin at the Calgary Zoo in Alberta, Canada. Numerous activities — including dinosaur-related songs, tours, old movies, crafts and a guided walk through the badlands outside the Royal Tyrrell Museum of Palaeontology — will take place throughout the month.

~ 9 ~

1935 "Dinny the Dinosaur," last of North America's first group of dinosaur models made for permanent display, is unveiled at the Calgary Zoological Society's new Prehistoric Park at the Calgary Zoo. The concrete "Brontosaurus" (more correctly *Apatosaurus*) figure — sculpted in miniature by Charlie Beil, then scaled-up by engineer Aarne Koskelainen — is considerably larger than life, measuring 107 feet in length and 32 feet tall and weighing 120 tons. Reportedly at least one Model A Ford and much lumber salvaged from outhouses culled from a nearby campground have contributed to Dinny's insides. The figure will be promoted by the zoo as "Our *Brontosaurus*— the biggest thing in town." In 1959 Dinny will become the zoo's official mascot. And on August 9, 1987, the Provincial Government will officially declare Dinny an Alberta Historical site. Some of the other early models will later be removed, but not Dinny.

1936 Robert Broom arrives at Sterkfontein, South Africa, where he begins paleontological excavations and soon will find significant fossils pertaining to the evolution of early man.

~ 10 ~

1846 United States President James K. Polk signs a bill chartering the Smithsonian Institution in Washington, D.C., putting into operation the request set down by James Smithson in his will. The original Smithsonian Institution building, which will be referred to as "the Castle," is completed in 1855. Soon, however, its collections will outgrow the building.

1874 Edward Drinker Cope, a member of the United States Geological Survey team, discovers the tooth of an Eocene mammal at Rito, Colorado. Cope will subsequently name the tooth *Bathmodon*, though it will later prove to be synonymous with the previously named *Coryphodon*. Cope's discovery of this specimen will lead to a new major fossil find and new insights regarding this genus.

1914 Jean-Pierre Lehman is born at Caen in Normandy. Lehman will become a paleontologist specializing in Paleozoic and Triassic lower vertebrates. He will be honored many times, his personal favorite achievement being his election to the Academy of Sciences of the Institute of France. (Dies February 26, 1981.)

~ 11 ~

1923   Peter C. Kaisen discovers the first specimen, comprising a skull and finger with claw, of a new small carnivorous dinosaur in the Djadochta Formation at Shabarakh Usu, Outer Mongolia. In 1924 Henry Fairfield Osborn will name this theropod *Velociraptor*.

1940   Lower jaws of a Late Triassic phytosaur are collected by a Works Progress Administration project on the Herring Ranch. The jaws measure 1.07 meters in length.

1947   *Life* magazine publishes its article on the Ghost Ranch *Coelophysis* quarry. The piece is illustrated with posed photographs of Colbert's crew supposedly working at the quarry and also with a life restoration of this dinosaur drawn by Rudy Freund. According to Colbert (in *The Little Dinosaurs of Ghost Ranch*), though the fossil material is largely unprepared and unstudied, Freund's restoration is quite accurate, though "the neck is too short and the heel on the hind foot is too prominent."

~ 12 ~

1933   Dinny, Alley Oop's faithful dinosaur pet, debuts in the *Alley Oop* comic strip. Dinny is a fictional species invented by strip artist V. T. Hamlin, having a sauropod

Artist Rudy Freund's drawing of the small theropod dinosaur COELO-PHYSIS *based upon specimens found at Ghost Ranch, New Mexico.*

type body, large head and row of prominent dorsal spines along the neck, back and tail. Oop meets Dinny by plopping onto the dinosaur's tail while escaping from an angry cave bear.

1990   Susan Hendrickson, field collector for the Black Hills Institute of Geologic Research, finds a *Tyrannosaurus rex* skeleton in western South Dakota. The skeleton, the most complete (about 90%) and largest *T. rex* specimen yet found, will be excavated later this month. In Hendrickson's honor it is dubbed "Sue," a nickname which will take on new meanings in the coming months.

~ 13 ~

1912   Charles H. Sternberg finds remains of a hadrosaur, the first complete dinosaur skeleton to be recovered in Canada, in Upper Cretaceous rocks near Drumheller, Alberta. Sternberg, now Chief Collector and Preparator of the Geological Survey of Canada, has been working here with eldest son George under the direction of Lawrence Lambe, trying to compete with the American Barnum Brown who has been collecting Canadian specimens for New York's American Museum of Natural History.

1913   The new duckbilled dinosaur *Hypacrosaurus* is named by Barnum Brown. The high-spined, crested hadrosaur is established on a headless skeleton with tall back spines collected in 1910 by Brown in the Edmonton Formation above Red Deer River in Alberta, Canada.

1937   Charles Whitney Gilmore and his field party find the skull of the phytosaur *Leptosuchus adamenensis* near Twin Buttes in the Petrified Forest.

1986   Paleontologist Sankar Chatterjee of Texas Tech University announces what he interprets to be the earliest known bird, predating the famous *Archaeopteryx* by some 75 million years. Later named *Protoavis* by Chatterjee, the new animal's fossil remains were found in Texas mudstone dated as about 225 million years old. If Chatterjee's assessment is correct, then early birds were much more widely distributed globally than previously believed. However, some paleontologists will interpret *Protoavis* to be a non-avian theropod dinosaur.

1994   The Park Lane Hotel Antiques Fair is held in London. Antiques exhibitor Ingrid Nilson attends, selling fossil eggs laid by a huge sauropod dinosaur from Xinjiang, China.

~ 14 ~

1834   Gideon Mantell writes in his diary about failing to purchase the Maidstone *Iguanodon*. He offers the specimen's owner W. H. Bensted 10 pounds for it. Bensted will refuse, stating that someone else had offered him double that amount and that he will not part with his fossilized prize for less than 25 pounds. Mantell has nice friends who will come to his rescue, meeting Bensted's price. As a result of the fossil's discovery, *Iguanodon* will become part of the city of Maidstone's official civic coat of arms, while a commemorative verse about Mantell and the specimen will appear in the volume of the AMICI society of gentlemen (to which Bensted belongs).

1856   Dean William Buckland, the scientist who described *Megalosaurus*, dies.

1946   Edwin H. Colbert collects the skull with lower jaws of the phytosaur *Pseudopalatus pristinus* near Billings Gap, Arizona.

1983   Karen Murry, Phillip A. Murry, Roy Frosch and their crew begin fossil collecting at Joseph T. Gregory's New Mexico sites.

1985   Paleontologist William Clemens of the Museum of Paleontology at the University of California, Berkeley, announces that remains of at least three different kinds of dinosaurs have been found on the northern coast of Alaska. Professor Clemens tells reporters, "I think what has been discovered on the slope adds a new facet to our knowledge of the biology of these animals and raises some new biological questions about the degree of tolerance they had to periods of darkness and to different types of climates."

1992   The United States Army airlifts an articulated *Stegosaurus* skeleton, found *in situ* with dorsal plates in place and arranged in two alternating rows, from Garden Park, Colorado.

1993   The traveling "Great Russian Dinosaurs Exhibition" opens at the Monash Science Centre, Melbourne, Australia. Organized by paleontologist Patricia Vickers-Rich, the show includes 24 full skeletons, 50 skulls and numerous other specimens, many of them of dinosaurs, some of them important holotypes (e.g., the type skull of the theropod *Tyrannosaurus bataar*, sometimes called *Tarbosaurus*, and the skeleton of the giant duck-billed dinosaur *Saurolophus angustirostris*). The exhibition is sponsored by the Monash Science Centre, Queen Victoria Museum (Launceston), and Palaeontological Institute (Moscow). The exhibition had last been seen in Japan.

~ 15 ~

1820 According to the traditional though unconfirmed account, Mary Ann Mantell, wife of Dr. Gideon Algernon Mantell, while accompanying him on a house call, discovers large fossil teeth in a roadside gravel pit. The teeth will later be studied by her husband and named *Iguanodon* (the second dinosaur to be named) because of their resemblance to teeth of a modern iguana lizard.

1861 *Archaeopteryx* is named and described by Hermann von Meyer based primarily on a well-preserved skeleton with feather impressions, collected recently from a fine-grained lithographic limestone in the Solnhofen Limestone quarry at Franconia, Bavaria. As this specimen had been found only two years after publication of Darwin's *Origin of Species* and exhibits characteristics of both reptiles and birds, it is regarded as an all important intermediate form or "missing link" between two major groups of animals.

1994 Dino II, a green and gold, 90-foot-tall *Tyrannosaurus*, filled with hot air and dwarfing its real-life counterpart, looms high above the city of Bristol, England. The giant inflatable creature, made by local firm Cameron Balloons and carrying human riders in a basket suspended from its underside, has been created for a group of Calgary-based Canadian businessmen. Dino II is a replacement for its predecessor, the original Dino, which had served the same purpose for six years while also becoming the city's symbol for its Winter Olympics in 1988, then later doing brief promotional work for the movie *Jurassic Park*. Dino II required 3,000 yards of canvass-type fabric and three miles of stitching. The balloon cost 50,000 pounds to create.

1995 The first official G-Con, a convention devoted to Japanese movie monsters (particularly Godzilla), is held at the Radisson Hotel in Arlington Heights, Illinois. The event, which lasts for three days, is sponsored by the Godzilla Society of North America. Among its offerings are guest speakers, panel discussions, presentations, film screenings, an auction, contests and the buying and selling of Godzilla-related memorabilia.

~ 16 ~

1899　Glenn Strange is born in Carlsbad, New Mexico. Though future character actor Strange will mostly appear in movie Westerns, he will also play prehistoric creatures. In the 1936 serial *Flash Gordon* Strange will portray a giant dinosaur-like creature (based on the Gocko, an underground monster in Alex Raymond's comic strip). In the 1949 Monogram comedy *Master Minds* he will play Atlas, a hairy primitive man revived from suspended animation to menace the Bowery Boys. Also, he will be one of the actors in the early 1950s to be tested, because of his six-foot three-inch height, for the Gill Man role in *Creature from the Black Lagoon*. (Dies September 20, 1973.)

1945　Charles L. Camp visits Petrified Forest National Monument to show Edwin H. Colbert, Curator of Fossil Amphibians and Reptiles at the American Museum of Natural History, and Park Naturalist L. F. Keller the fossil sites he had worked during the 1920s. Colbert very much wants to acquire a Petrified Forest vertebrate collection for the American Museum.

1995　Paleontologist Robert M. Sullivan collects a nearly complete left tibia belonging to the "ostrich dinosaur" *Ornithomimus antiquus*, from the Kirtland Formation (Upper Cretaceous) of San Juan County, New Mexico. The specimen has preserved the distinctive cnemial crest, which Sullivan recognizes as distinctive for this genus.

1996　The journal *Science* announces the startling possibility that life may have once existed on Mars. A meteorite, apparently once a part of that planet, has been found in Antarctic ice bearing worm-like structures that some scientists interpret as possibly fossil invertebrate remains. Soon afterwards United States President Bill Clinton, in a press conference carried on radio and television, will announce this information to the world.

~ 17 ~

1909　After many days of searching, Carnegie Museum of Natural History paleontologist Earl Douglass writes in his diary regarding his discovery in a sandstone ledge in the Morrison Formation of northeastern Utah: "At last in the top of the ledge where the softer overlying beds for a divide … I saw eight of the tail bones of a *Brontosaurus* in exact position." In 1915, the site of this dinosaur (later called *Apatosaurus*) find will be named Dinosaur National Monument.

1936   G. W. Barlow, manager in charge of the quarries and caves at Sterkfontein, South Africa, where paleontologist Robert Broom is looking for early hominid fossils, finds two-thirds of a fossil brain cast. Broom later finds more of the skull, pieces it together and discovers that it represents a member of the same apeman group to which the Taung child belongs. Broom will name this new hominid *Australopithecus transvaalensis*, then later refer it to a new species of *Plesianthropus*, a genus of the same family.

1951   The black and white movie *Lost Continent* opens, about a group of military men tracking a runaway missile to a green-tinted plateau where Mesozoic Era reptiles still roam. The special effects are credited to Augie Lohman, though the true identity of the person apparently responsible for the stop-motion dinosaur and pterosaur scenes will remain a mystery.

1998   The Brickyard Mall in Chicago opens "Dinamation's Dinosaurs Alive and in Color," an exhibition of six robotic prehistoric creatures from Dinamation International oration The show — featuring an *Allosaurus*, *Stegosaurus*, *Apatosaurus*, *Pachycephalosaurus*, *Triceratops* and *Dimetrodon* — will continue to September 16. The event also includes various activities including videos, hands-on exhibits, a "dino dig" and souvenirs.

~ 18 ~

1947   Edwin H. Colbert's team at Ghost Ranch begins the work of undercutting the very heavy blocks of *Coelophysis* skeletons.

1988   Brian Versey and Cliff Miles find several sacral vertebrae and the right ilium of a sauropod dinosaur ("world's largest bone complex ever found") at the Dry Mesa Dinosaur Quarry in west-central Colorado.

~ 19 ~

1872   Edward Drinker Cope and Othniel Charles Marsh each publish their own new names for fossils of the same kind of uintathere recently collected in Upper Eocene rocks of the Uinta Basin of Eastern Utah. Cope names his genus *Loxolophodon* and Marsh his *Tinoceras*. Each collector believes his name to be the valid one, apparently forgetting that Joseph Leidy's name for the same beast *Uintatherium* has already been published, has been in distribution for 18 days and has, therefore, priority.

1970   Rainer Zangerl and Wann Langston, Jr., publish a joint paper describing the vertebrate fauna of the Selma Formation of Alabama. Among the new taxa is the ornithopod *Lophorothon atopus* which Langston describes as a hadrosaur.

1996   Frontline Entertainment's educational short *Before La Brea* is shot for the "Dinosaur Theater" at the George C. Page Museum of La Brea Discoveries. It explains to disappointed visitors why there are no dinosaurs to be found at Rancho La Brea while at the same time showing them some, including stop-motion dinosaur footage from the short *Prehistoric Beast*, shot more than a decade ago by *Jurassic Park*'s Phil Tippett.

~ 20 ~

1841   Charles Lyell and his wife, recently arrived in the United States from England, are escorted by fossil collector James Hall to the Hudson & Mohawk Railroad terminal to start a journey of exploration of "the succession of mineral groups" of the area. Lyell will write in his *Travels in North America*: "In the course of this short tour, I am convinced that we must turn to the *New World* if we wish to see in perfection the oldest monuments of earth's history, so far at least as it relates to its earliest inhabitants. Certainly in no other country are these ancient strata developed on a grander scale, or more plentifully charged with fossils...."

1946   Peter Dodson is born. Dodson will become a paleontologist specializing in dinosaurs, particularly ceratopsians. Work on this group will include naming and describing the small new genus *Avaceratops* in 1986 and authoring the book *The Horned Dinosaurs* (1996). Though a research associate at the Academy of Natural Sciences of Philadelphia, Dodson will be primarily based at the School of Veterinary Science at the University of Pennsylvania where he is Associate Professor of Anatomy. He will author and co-author numerous scientific papers about dinosaurs and, in 1991, be one of the founders of The Dinosaur Society.

1954   Allen A. Debus is born in Chicago, Illinois. Debus will become the regional expert chemist for the Environmental Protection Agency (EPA). His interest in prehistoric life will lead him to become a sculptor of dinosaurs and, with wife Diane, establish Hell Creek Creations. The company will make available dinosaur models made by Debus; the book *Dinosaur Sculpting* (1995, co-authored by Debus, sculptor Bob Morales and Diane) and (with Diane and also co-editor/publisher Gary Williams) the magazine *Dinosaur World*.

1993   "Dinosaurs: The Greatest Show Unearthed," a world-touring exposition of fossil specimens put on by the Ex Terra Foundation, opens at Ontario Place, Toronto, Canada. Advertisements proclaim, "See the real Jurassic giants." Included in the exhibition are mounted skeletons of new genera and species of dinosaurs discovered during the Sino-Canadian Dinosaur Project.

~ 21 ~

1866   Edward Drinker Cope describes poorly-preserved bones of the large carnivorous dinosaur he names *Laelaps* (later renamed *Dryptosaurus*) to 22 members of the Academy of Natural Sciences of Philadelphia, at the same time exhibiting the bones. The remains had been found by workmen of the West Jersey Marl Company in marl pits of Barsborough, Glouster County, New Jersey. This dinosaur is important in paleontological history as the first theropod described from North America and the only large one known from eastern North America. Cope envisions this animal as some giant, leaping kangaroo-like saurian.

Painting by Charles R. Knight of Dryptosaurus aquilunguis *done in 1897 under the direction of Edward Drinker Cope, who named and described this dinosaur over three decades earlier as* Laelaps aquilunguis. *Cope mistakenly placed the large manual claws on the dinosaurs' feet. Courtesy Department Library Services, American Museum of Natural History (neg. #335199).*

1872   K. W. Cooke makes a drawing of Gideon Mantell's original *Iguanodon* quarry near Cuckfield, England. The picture depicts a party from the British Association for the Advancement of Science visiting the site shortly before it was closed down and filled in. Almost a century later, details of Cooke's drawing will lead British paleontologist W. E. Swinton on an investigative journey that reveals the former quarry's precise location.

1895   Leslie E. Wilson is born in Rimini, Montana. Among Wilson's future accomplishments as a paleontologist will be describing the giant fossil whale *Macrodelphinus kellogg*, named in honor of his assistant Remington Kellogg. Following Kellogg's death, Wilson and his wife will establish the Kellogg Memorial Fund at the University of California, Berkeley, to support student research of marine mammals. (Dies 1969.)

1909   Earl Douglass writes to the Carnegie Museum of Natural History about the find he has recently made in Utah: "I have discovered a huge Dinosaur. And if the skeleton is as perfect as the portions we have exposed, the task of excavating will be enormous and will cost a lot of money, but the rock is the kind to get perfect bones." Douglass goes on to boast that this specimen will be "the best Jurassic Dinosaur in existence."

1988   Collecting begins in the Bayin Gobi Formation of Inner Mongolia of the most complete specimen of any known Asian theropod dinosaur, these remains found during an expedition of the Sino-Canadian Dinosaur Project. The excavation will continue until the second day of next month. In 1993 Dale A. Russell and Dong Zhiming will name this odd-looking animal *Alxasaurus*, envisioned by them as generally resembling a moderately large prosauropod with a small head, relatively long neck, long arms and short tail.

~ 22 ~

1836   Archibald M. Willard is born in Bedford, Ohio. Willard will start his artistic career decorating circus wagons, then move on to oil and watercolor paintings. Although destined to be best known for his patriotic "Spirit of '76" or "Yankee Doodle" painting done in 1876, he will create what may be the world's first painting depicting Mesozoic reptiles — including marine animals, dinosaurs and pterosaurs. The painting (possibly one of a series) was done on commission to accompany a lecture titled "Marvels of the Natural World," given in Cleveland by a visiting scientist in 1872. It has incorporated various imagery from earlier sources including John Martin's engravings of marine reptiles from *Geology for Beginners* (1842), Benjamin Waterhouse Hawkins' *Megalosaurus* statue from Crystal Palace and Edouard Riou's *Pterodactylus* engraving from *La Terre avant le Déluge* (1863). (Dies October 11, 1918.)

1920   Ray Bradbury is born in Waukegan, Illinois. A future professed lover of dinosaurs, Bradbury will author numerous science-fiction and fantasy stories about these creatures (e.g., "A Sound of Thunder" and "Tyrannosaurus Rex"), also poems, some of which will be reprinted many times over, some collected into the book *Dinosaur Tales* (1983). Bradbury's dinosaur stories will provide material for various movie, radio, television and comic-book adaptations. "The Beast from 20,000 Fathoms" (aka "The Fog Horn"), a short story about a huge prehistoric reptile attracted to a lighthouse believing it to be its mate, will inspire the motion picture *The Beast from 20,000 Fathoms* (1953), with special effects by Bradbury's good and long-time friend Ray Harryhausen.

1984   Paleontology graduate student Bryan Small discovers a primitive "Great Dane"–sized dinosaur skeleton in the Painted Desert, Arizona. "I was walking along one of the little canyons and the fossils had washed up out of the ground," Small later informs reporters. "I found them when I stepped on them." The skeleton, representing one of the oldest dinosaurs known, is quickly nicknamed "Gertie" after Winsor McCay's animated-cartoon character. Later the specimen will be officially named *Chindesaurus bryansmalli* in Small's honor.

1996   The "Mesozoic Vertebrate Faunas of Central Europe" symposium begins in Deva, Romania. At the event paleontologists David B. Weishampel and Coralia-Maria Jianu announce an as yet unnamed theropod dinosaur found in the Hateg Basin in Transylvania.

~ 23 ~

1769   Georges-Léopold-Chrêtien-Frédéric-Dagobert, Baron Cuvier is born in Montbeliard, France. Baron Cuvier will devote his life to the study of anatomy, first human and then animal. In the early 19th century he will propose his theory of comparative anatomy, according to which every bone has a specific relationship to all other bones; the purpose of one bone can be determined by its shape and size; and examination of a bone can give enough information about the organism's size and behavior so that the shape and size of other bones can be deduced without that bone having been seen. Cuvier will apply these principles to interpreting fossils, determining from a single skeletal element the genus and sometimes species to which it belongs, even imagining how that extinct animal may have appeared in life. Though he will maintain a belief in the biblical Deluge and deny the existence of prehistoric man, his techniques will become the foundation for the new science of paleontology. As the foremost French scientist of his day, Cuvier will be honored by Napoléon Bonaparte and kings Louis XVIII, Charles X and Louis Philippe. (Dies May 13, 1832.)

1877 Edward Drinker Cope names the new 55-foot-long, Late Jurassic sauropod *Camarasaurus*. Again competing with rival O. C. Marsh, Cope has quickly written and published his name and description of this dinosaur based on partial skeletal remains collected by Canyon City superintendent of schools O. W. Lucas in the Morrison Formation at Garden Park, Canyon City, Colorado. Subsequent discoveries will make *Camarasaurus* the most completely known North American sauropod genus and the most abundant Morrison dinosaur.

1947 The team led by Edwin H. Colbert succeeds in overturning the first block of *Coelophysis* material at Ghost Ranch.

1985 *Godzilla 1985*, the American version of Japan's *Gojira* (1984), is released in the United States. In this version (for both insurance and nostalgia), Raymond Burr is called back to reprise his reporter role from the original movie. The new film will prove successful enough to "jump start" a new series of sequels. As in previous color movies of the original series, Godzilla sports a black-colored (not green, the popular misconception) hide.

1997 During the first hour of this first day of Dinamation International Society's expedition to Bayan Zag (the so-called "Flaming Cliffs"), Mongolia, the exploratory team finds a partial *Velociraptor* skeleton with skull. By late afternoon the specimen is safely in camp in a protective plaster and burlap jacket.

~ 24 ~

1943 Arch Oboler's anthology radio series *Lights Out* (ABC) broadcasts the horror drama "Sub-Basement." A despondent husband brings the wife he plans to murder into the dark depths below a big department store. The appearance of a lizard-like dinosaur, blinded from so many years spent living in darkness, upsets his plans and alters his opinion of his wife. In the end he sacrifices his own life to the monster so that she can escape.

1954 James I. (Ian) Kirkland is born in Weysmouth, Massachusetts. Kirkland will become Senior Paleontologist of the Dinamation International Society, after which he will name and describe a number of new dinosaurian taxa including the armored *Mymoorapelta* and giant dromaeosaur *Utahraptor*. In 1999 he leaves Dinamation to become State Paleontologist of Utah.

1992 The movie *Jurassic Park* starts filming in a real tropical paradise — the Hawaiian island of Kauai. Three weeks later there will be trouble in paradise as Hurricane Iniki descends with the primeval force of its 120 miles per hour winds. Cast and crew will take shelter in the old ballroom of the Weston Hotel. The film company's generators will be utilized to aid island inhabitants and tourists. Also, the company will arrange for over 20,000 pounds of relief supplies to be brought in from Honolulu and Los Angeles for victims of the hurricane. Soon the production will move to the considerably safer sound-stage environments at Universal Studios, California.

1997 Jim Kirkland celebrates his birthday at Bayan Zag, Mongolia, as a 13-year-old Dinamation International Society expeditioner finds a skull in two separated parts. The boy believes these are two skulls of the horned dinosaur *Protoceratops*. Kirkland correctly identifies them as together comprising one skull of the armored dinosaur *Pinacosaurus*. Two more skulls will soon be found at this same locality and identified by Kirkland as possibly representing a male and two females.

~ 25 ~

1835 Andrew Carnegie is born in Dunfermline, Scotland. A future steel magnate and philanthropist, Carnegie will give large sums of money to the institution bearing his name, the Carnegie Museum of Natural History. In 1898, just three years after the museum's founding, Carnegie will develop a strong interest in dinosaurs. This interest will prompt Carnegie to dispatch museum collectors out West to recover a treasure trove of fossils comparable to that already housed at the American Museum of Natural History. The collectors will subsequently amass one of the world's finest collections of dinosaur and other fossils. (Dies 1919.)

1937 The new Natural History Park is opened by the Honorable R. B. Bennett at the Calgary Zoo, the dinosaurs in its Prehistoric Park area acclaimed as the most modern in the world. A number of new figures, including the duckbilled *Corythosaurus*, have been added to the park this year. This collection will be largely completed by 1957.

1948 John Thomas Jenkins, Jr., is born in St. Paul, Minnesota. A future geologist and paleontologist, Jenkins will serve as honorary Curator of Vertebrate Paleontology at the Houston Museum of Natural Science, excavate a Pleistocene ground sloth and be elected president of the Western Interior Paleontological Society. Dino Productions, his family-run company, will provide such services as his giving lectures to children's groups. (Dies April 25, 1993.)

1987 The Germain Collection of fossils is accessed by the Carnegie Museum of Natural History.

1992 Paleontologist Daniel Grigorescu hosts the first (10-day) dinosaur tour of Transylvania, Romania. The tour includes visiting fossil sites for Transylvanian dinosaurs and places of historic importance, such as those associated with colorful Hungarian paleontologist Baron Franz Nopcsa.

~ 26 ~

1940 The rest of the phytosaur skull belonging to the jaws discovered on August 11 is found near those jaws. Although both specimens are from the Herring Ranch, records will not indicate which quarry yielded them.

1990 The British Association for the Advancement of Science meets at the Museum in Plymouth, England, for five days, the program of the Geology Section commemorating the 150th anniversary of Richard Owen's coining of the word "Dinosauria." Festivities include the major exhibition "The Dawn of the Dinosaurs" and release by the British Office of a set of special dinosaur stamps.

~ 27 ~

1863 Lawrence M. Lambe is born. Beginning his paleontological career as an artist for the Geological Survey of Canada, Lambe will make three exploratory trips, between 1897 and 1901, to the Red Deer River badlands of Alberta, Canada. Lambe's explorations there will alert other workers to the importance of the fossil-bearing rocks along the Red Deer River, leading directly to a "golden age" of collecting in this region. With the encouragement of Henry F. Osborn, Lambe will become the first Canadian paleontologist to make scientific descriptions of the fossils collected from the Judith River Formation in Alberta, naming many new genera and species of dinosaurs in a monograph to be published in 1902. (Dies March 12, 1919.)

1909   Paul O. McGrew is born in Ottumwa, Iowa. Much of McGrew's early activity as a paleontologist will be in the field, collecting fossil mammals for the University of Nebraska at Tertiary-age sites in western Nebraska and eastern Wyoming. In 1938 he will be named Curator in Paleontology at the Field Museum of Natural History. Eight years later he will venture to Laramie where he will develop what becomes the museum at the University of Wyoming. Among McGrew's most important contributions to paleontology will be collecting an abundance of vertebrate fossils (particularly those of his favorites subjects, Tertiary mammals) and dating many sequences of Tertiary strata. His other accomplishments will include being a president of the Society of Vertebrate Paleontology. (Dies January 30, 1983.)

1954   The Falmouth *Enterprise* publishes "In Memoriam of Charles R. Knight," a poem written by Rhoda (Knight) Steel, the artist's granddaughter.

1982   A hominid jaw bone is discovered at Baragoi, in the Samburu hills of western Kenya, some 325 miles away from Nairobi. The discovery and its implications will be announced in four days.

~ 28 ~

1898   Rachel H. Nichols (*née* Husband) is born in Eugene, Oregon. Among her future accomplishments as a paleontologist, she will spend 35 years in the Department of Vertebrate Paleontology of the American Museum of Natural History in New York City. There she will be the guardian of the fossil vertebrate collections and, in her later years, custodian of the Osborn Library. (Dies April 18, 1985.)

1917   Jack Kirby is born (as Jacob Kurtzberg) in New York, New York, where he will eventually become a highly prolific and influential comic-book

artist. During his long career Kirby will work in all genres of the medium, drawing countless stories, many of which will feature dinosaurs and other creatures out of prehistory. Most fondly remembered of Kirby's dinosaur-related output will be *Devil Dinosaur* which he will create, write and draw for Marvel Comics. *Devil Dinosaur*, first issue dated April 1980, will present the continuing saga of young hominid Moon-Boy and his pet — a huge *Tyrannosaurus*-like dinosaur he nurses back to health after it is burned red by volcanic fire. This will be regarded as Kirby's version of "a boy and his dog" with a dash of *Androcles and the Lion*, though set in the prehistoric past. (Dies February 6, 1994.)

1937 The Calgary Zoo's Prehistoric Park is officially opened. The origins of the park date back to 1931 when zoo director Lars Willumsen visited the Hamburg Zoo in Germany. Inspired by the German park's concrete dinosaurs, Willumsen then proceeded to design a similar park — the first such permanent display in North America — at Calgary. The models, the first to undergo construction being *Chasmosaurus belli*, were sculpted by Charlie Beil, later assisted by zoo worker John Kanerva, and scaled up by engineer Arne Koskeleinen. All models were done under the supervision of paleontologists Charles M. Sternberg, Barnum Brown and W. E. Swinton, the latter describing them as the most accurate dinosaur figures yet sculpted. In 1956 all of the prehistoric creatures will be refurbished. Ground will be broken in 1978 for a new Prehistoric Park project at the zoo. In 1983 the new east section of this Prehistoric Park will be opened, followed by the new west section in 1984. New additions to the display will include some full-scale dinosaur figures made by the Jonas Studios.

1964   John S. Ostrom discovers the amazing dromaeosaurid *Deinonychus* (meaning "terrible claw," after the large sickle claw of its hind foot) in the Lower Cretaceous Cloverly Formation of Montana, naming and describing it five years later. The find will drastically alter old conceptions of dinosaurs. The skeleton of this theropod is clearly that of an active animal, not a slow and sluggish creature, and one that may have been warm-blooded.

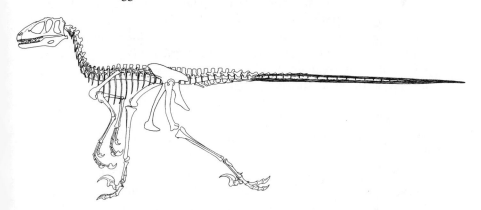

Paleontologist John H. Ostrom's original skeletal reconstruction of the theropod DEINONYCHUS ANTIRRHOPUS, *published in 1969. Ostrom, reinterpreting certain features of the skeleton, particularly in the skull and pelvis, later revised his reconstruction. (Drawn by Robert T. Bakker.)*

~ 29 ~

1838   The ship *Mediator* arrives from London in New York Harbor. On board is former Secretary of the Treasury and United States Minister to England Richard Rush, carrying with him the money bequeathed by James Smithson to fund the Smithsonian Institution.

1947   Edwin H. Colbert departs Ghost Ranch for Chicago and other assignments, leaving the *Coelophysis* quarry in the charge of Carl Sorenson. Sorensen and George Whitaker will continue working the site during this and the following year.

1954 The Saturday-morning kids television series *Space Patrol* telecasts live and in black and white "The Mystery of Planet X," part of a lengthy storyline set around a new planet 5,000 times the size of Earth, the strange domain of evil Prince Baccarratti (played by associate producer Bela Kovacs), the so-called Black Falcon. Commander Buzz Corry (Ed Kemmer) and his Space Patrol crew journey to Planet X where their spaceship *Terra V* is promptly crippled by a meat-eating dinosaur (a stiff moved model). More prehistoric perils will follow on Saturdays to come.

~ 30 ~

1918 Samuel Wendell Williston, who collected dinosaur fossils at Como Bluff, Wyoming, and Garden Park, Colorado, and became one of the foremost authorities on fossil reptiles, dies. While a professor at the University of Chicago, Williston amassed a great collection of Permian amphibians and reptiles that would first be displayed at the university's Walker Museum and later at the Field Museum of Natural History.

1938 Karl P. Schmidt publishes a paper in which he describes various new crocodilian taxa from the Upper Paleocene of western Colorado.

1997 Joe Dasso and Gina Tatom's Dawn of Time Art Gallery has its gala opening in Lake Forest, California. The gallery exhibits original art by "paleo artists" including Mark Hallett, Douglas Henderson, Josef Moravic and Karl Huber, and sculptors Bob Morales, Michael Rusher and Tony Merrithew. Among items sold at the gallery is "Jurassic Java," the establishment's exclusive brand of coffee.

~ 31 ~

1931 Bryan Patterson publishes a paper on the occurrence of *Allognathosuchus*, a crocodilian genus of the Lower Oligocene period of North America.

1982 Scientists in Nairobi, at a press conference held at the Kenya National Museum, announce the discovery by acting museum director Richard E. Leakey and Professor Hidemi Ishida of the University of Osaka, Japan, of a jawbone possibly 8 million years old. Belonging to an unnamed hominid, the fossil may provide new data regarding mankind's origins. "We consider it a critical specimen," Leakey tells reporters. "At 12 million years you do not have any upright specimens on Earth, but at 4 million years you do have an upright specimen. Although the data of the latest find is unsure, we suspect to find it about 8 million years old. It fills that fossil gap." The specimen has quite hominoid characteristics and is the only specimen that belongs to this group from that time period. "It is not like anything we have had before," Leakey proudly adds.

"Dinny the Dinosaur," a bigger-than-life APATOSAURUS *model residing at the Calgary Zoo. Courtesy Browarny Photographs, Ltd.*

SEPTEMBER

~ 1 ~

Previously unpublished photo of author Edgar Rice Burroughs in his office seated before a favorite painting, done for his novel THE CAVE GIRL (1925 Grosset & Dunlap edition) by artist J. Allen St. John. © 1998 Edgar Rice Burroughs, Inc.

1875 Edgar Rice Burroughs is born in Chicago, Illinois. Burroughs will have many careers, including cowboy, gold miner and railroad policeman, before he becomes a writer of heroic adventure, fantasy and science-fiction tales in 1911. Many of Burroughs' novels and short stories will be set in exotic lost lands populated by dinosaurs, prehistoric mammals, primitive peoples or evolved variations thereof. His most famous hero, Tarzan the Apeman, will encounter prehistoric creatures in various stories, including *Tarzan the Terrible* (1921), in which the jungle man discovers the lost African land of Pal-ul-Don. Burroughs will author two entire series of "lost worlds" novels featuring some of his best work, one set in a world inside a hollow Earth (beginning with *At the Earth's Core*, first published in 1914), the other on Caspak, an island where evolution has run wild (starting off with *The Land That Time Forgot* in 1918). Also, his stories will be the basis for countless movies, comic strips and books, radio and television shows, pastiches and imitations. (Dies March 19, 1950.)

1904   Elmer S. Riggs publishes his paper on the Brachiosauridae, a family of gigantic sauropod dinosaurs having, among other distinguishing features, front legs longer than the hind legs. The family is founded upon *Brachiosaurus*, a genus named and described by Riggs the previous year.

1959   Joe Jusko is born on the birthdate of one of his future idols, Edgar Rice Burroughs, in New York, N.Y. Inspired by the work of Frank Frazetta, Jusko will illustrate two sets of Burroughs-related trading cards and, by the mid–1990s, produce more than 120 Burroughs-related paintings, many of them featuring prehistoric creatures. In 1996 a collection of these paintings titled *Joe Jusko's Art of Edgar Rice Burroughs* will be published by FPG.

~ 2 ~

1922   The train of automobiles conveying members of the Central Asiatic Expedition of the American Museum of Natural History reaches a vast, eroded Gobi basin composed of red sandstone that will be unofficially dubbed the "Flaming Cliffs" of Shabarakhu Usu. The site is so named because the setting sun illuminates the towering red rocks in a way that makes them appear to be on fire.

1990   A beautifully preserved skull of a Pleistocene dire wolf is recovered from the reopened Pit 91 at Rancho La Brea by Gary Takeuchi, a geology student at Cal State Los Angeles. Eric Scott, chief excavator at the site, describes the find as "Spectacular" in a September 6 interview printed in the Los Angeles *Times*. The worn teeth on the specimen reveal that the wolf had lived until old age.

~ 3 ~

1994   The first meeting of fans of Japanese movie monsters (especially Godzilla) meets in Chicago. The two-day gathering — including discussions, film screenings and buying and selling related merchandise — will evolve into "G-Con," a much bigger annual convention. This and future events are spearheaded by the Godzilla Society of North America and notable "Kaiju" movie fans such as J. D. Lees, editor and publisher of the fanzine *G-Fan*.

~ 4 ~

1879　William H. Reed and E. G. Ashley discover two huge adult sauropod skeletons in the Morrison Formation at Como Bluff, Wyoming. The more complete skeleton lacks a skull and is found much in the position the animal was in when it died sometime during the Late Jurassic period. Shortly after this discovery this very year, Othniel Charles Marsh will quickly name the more complete specimen *Brontosaurus*, later having the skeleton mounted at Yale's Peabody Museum of Natural History. Marsh will refer the other skeleton to *Apatosaurus*, a genus he had named earlier this year, as the new species *A. amplus*. Although *Brontosaurus* will become what remains probably the best known dinosaur name of all, it will also, in later years, be properly referred to *Apatosaurus*.

1915　A huge block containing numerous bones of Ice Age animals is dragged by mules out of Pit 81 at Rancho La Brea. The entire block, the largest single chunk of matrix excavated at La Brea, will later be exhibited at the George C. Page Museum of La Brea Discoveries.

1931　Paleontologist Karl P. Schmidt publishes a paper in which he describes a new fossil turtle found in Peru.

1958　*Teenage Caveman* (American International Pictures) is released starring actor Robert Vaughn in one of his earliest screen roles. Though clearly no longer a teenager, Vaughn appears in the titled role, a curious young man coping in an apparently ancient world (actually, it is revealed to be the distant future). Producer/director Roger Corman prefers his own title for the film *Prehistoric World*. Judiciously spliced into the movie at various spots are more ubiquitous scenes from *One Million B.C.*

~ 5 ~

1857　Charles Darwin outlines the basic points of his theory of evolution, planned as a major book, to American botanist Asa Gray. Darwin will also correspond on this matter with other scientists, including Sir Joseph

Dalton Hooker, the Director of Key Gardens, who will encourage him to complete the project. Gray, the first American scientist to accept Darwin's theory, will arrange to have the work published in the United States.

1940   Raquel Welch is born in Chicago, Illinois. Welch will become an international movie star with the 1967 release of *One Million Years B.C.*. A poster of the actress as cavegirl "Loana the Fair One" will become a 1960s icon. Continuing the cave tradition, Welch will do a voice-over role in the Hanna-Barbera Productions 1996 "Flintstones" television movie *Hollyrock-a-Bye Baby*.

1953   *Space Patrol* telecasts "The Trap on Planet X." In this installment of the continuing saga of bad Prince Baccarratti's (Bela Kovacs) prehistoric world, Space Patrollers Major "Robbie" Robertson (Ken Mayer) and Tonga (Nina Bara) get stranded in the Valley of the Dinosaurs.

1978   The Institut de Paléontologie du Muséum National d'Histoire Naturelle in Paris hosts the First Symposium on Mesozoic Continental Ecosystems.

The "new" Tumak (John Richardson) and Loana (Raquel Welch) in One Million Years B.C. *(1967), a remake of 1940's* One Million B.C. *(© Hammer Films/20th Century–Fox).*

~ 6 ~

1906   Morris F. Skinner is born in Springview, Nebraska. Beginning in 1933 and for the next 40 years, Skinner will work as a paleontologist at the American Museum of Natural History, preparing and studying fossils, his time divided between working in the laboratory and the field. In 1973, after leaving New York, he will be made Research Affiliate of the Nebraska

State Museum by the University of Nebraska. Skinner will publish over 20 papers during his career, most of them after 1965. However, his most important contribution to the field of paleontology will be the enormous amount of data he compiles documenting Childs Frick's vast collection of fossil mammals housed at the American Museum, some of this material having been recovered by Skinner himself. (Dies December 15, 1989.)

~ 7 ~

1829 Ferdinand Vandiveer Hayden is born in Westfield, Massachusetts. A future physician-turned-paleontologist, Hayden will be one of the first scientists to explore the territories west of the Mississippi River. During these explorations, Hayden will collect teeth that he believes to be those of giant lizards, but which actually belong to different kinds of dinosaurs. Joseph Leidy will later describe these teeth, their names (including *Palaeoscincus*, *Trachodon*, *Troödon* and *Deinodon*) being among the earliest published names for North American dinosaurs.

1935 William Ritt and Clarence Gray's *Brick Bradford* comic strip, which introduced the science-fiction concept of time travel to comics, starts "The Land of the Lost" storyline featuring prehistoric and other exotic creatures. The collected strips will be reprinted in 1981 by Pacific Comics.

1953 *Life* magazine's new series "World We Live In" begins. The article is illustrated with a reproduction of Rudolf F. Zallinger's preliminary cartoon for his mural "The Age of Reptiles" made for the Peabody Museum of Natural History, Yale University. The article, especially the eye-catching cover detailing Zallinger's *Apatosaurus*, will inspire the big "dinosaur craze" of the 1950s.

1974 Three Saturday-morning television series geared toward children premiere: Krofft Entertainment's videotaped *Land of the Lost* (NBC) is the continuing saga of the Marshall family who, while exploring the Colorado River by raft, are propelled through a time warp to another dimension inhabited by dinosaurs including Big Alice the *Allosaurus*, Emily the *Brontosaurus* (or *Apatosaurus*), Dopey the baby "brontosaur" and Grumpy the *Tyrannosaurus*, brought to life via stop-motion animation and rubber hand puppets by Wah Chang and Gene Warren's Excelsior Animated Moving Pictures. Humanoid denizens of this land are the apeish Pakuni and insect-like Sleestax. *Korg: 70,000 B.C.* (ABC) depicts the struggle in a Stone Age world for survival

Grumpy the T*YRANNOSAURUS* menaces *"Pakuni" boy Chaka (Phillip Paley), and Will (Wesley Eure), Holly (Kathy Coleman) and Rick (Spencer Milligan) Marshall in the children's television series* L*AND OF THE* L*OST (1974).* © *Krofft Entertainment, all rights reserved.*

by a Neandertal family. *Valley of the Dinosaurs* cartoon (CBS) is about another modern family, the Butlers, who, while exploring an Amazon river canyon, are swept back through time to the titled valley. In trying to survive alongside a family of friendly cavemen, both primitives and moderns learn much from each other. Both *Korg* and *Valley* originate from Hanna-Barbera Productions.

Promotional art piece for the television cartoon series V*ALLEY OF THE* D*INOSAURS (1974).* © *Hanna-Barbera Productions, all rights reserved.*

1991 The new, revised and now shot-on-film *Land of the Lost* television series (ABC) begins, featuring a different family and co-produced by Chiodo Brothers Productions, which also handles the show's special stop-motion and hand-puppet effects and masks. The Sleestax are now reptilian instead of insect-like creatures and the main dinosaur villain is a *Tyrannosaurus* appropriately called Scarface. A juvenile dinosaur named Tasha is also part of the regular cast.

1995 A heavily-worn and somewhat broken incisor tooth belonging to Great Britain's oldest prehistoric man, found by Laura Basell at Boxgrove, beneath the Sussex Downs (Britain's most ancient archaeological site), is praised as one of the most important archaeological discoveries ever made. Basell, an archaeology student at Bristol University, comments in an article about the find in the next day's *Daily Mail*: "I'd found deer teeth earlier. I was trowelling along and suddenly saw it. I thought it might be humanoid but dismissed it."

Same day: F.A.O. Schwartz, New York's largest toy store, starts a major Godzilla promotion that will continue through the holiday season. Most prominent is Trendmasters' new line of Godzilla merchandise. To attract customers, a huge moving and roaring figure of the Japanese monster, with glowing eyes, looms above the popular shop.

1996 Dinotour, led by Philip J. Currie, leaves Canada, taking dinosaur enthusiasts through China and Mongolia, visiting fossil localities and museums.

~ 8 ~

1970 John H. Ostrom correctly identifies another specimen of *Archaeopteryx*, this one having been on exhibit at the Teyler Museum in Haarlem, Netherlands, since 1860. The specimen consists of a slab and counterslab and preserves a finger claw with its horny sheath, as well as faint feather impressions. Found in 1855 in a quarry near Riedenburg, Bavaria, it seems to be the second specimen of this genus ever found. The specimen was first identified by Hermann von Meyer (who would, ironically, name and originally describe *Archaeopteryx* in 1861) as the flying reptile *Pterodactylus*, a designation it would keep for well over a century.

1973 *The Flintstones Show*, another incarnation of the classic television cartoon series, premieres on CBS. New episodes will continue through January 26 of next year.

1981   Charles M. Sternberg, the last surviving collector from the pioneer or "golden years" of dinosaur hunting in western Canada, dies in Canada.

1988   The International Symposium on Vertebrate Behavior as Derived from the Fossil Record commences at the Museum of the Rockies in Bozeman, Montana.

~ 9 ~

1823   Joseph Leidy is born in Philadelphia in a financially secure family. Leidy will have an interest in anatomy and the intention to become a medical doctor, but will eventually turn to paleontology. Planning to go into the Western territories to collect fossils in 1852, Leidy will find his career changed somewhat when the University of Pennsylvania's professor of anatomy becomes fatally ill and Leidy is asked to replace him. Here, and subsequently at the Academy of Natural Sciences for which he will eventually become Curator, Leidy will do much work on fossils collected by other people. He will become famous as the scientist who, in 1858, will name and describe *Hadrosaurus foulkii*, the second dinosaur to be named in North America. (Dies April 30, 1891.)

1967   Hanna-Barbera Productions' animated *Moby Dick and the Mighty Mightor* series debuts on CBS. "The Mighty Mightor" segments feature television cartoon's first prehistoric superhero. Meek prehistoric teenager Tor (voice of Bobby Diamond), by means of a magical power club, transforms into Mightor (Paul Stewart), a powerful flying superhero. Likewise, Tor's dinosaur pet Tog metamorphoses into a prehistoric flying dragon.

1972   *The Flintstones Comedy Hour*, a new Saturday-morning cartoon series from Hanna-Barbera, begins on CBS television. This incarnation comprises a number of shorter segments, most notably those about the continuing escapades of the Flintstone and Rubble families.

1978   Hanna-Barbera Productions' half-hour *Godzilla* television-cartoons debut on NBC as part of the *Godzilla Power Hour*. This original 13-episode series presents Godzilla (voiced by Ted Cassidy) as a green fire-breathing hero accompanied by a cute, flying "infant relative" named Godzooky (voice of Don Messick), both of which battle various menaces — including dinosaurs — on a weekly basis. The cartoons will prove popular enough to spawn another 13-episode season, this time paired with the popular *Jonny Quest*.

~ 10 ~

1873   The 21st Indiana State Fair and Exposition opens in Indianapolis. Henry Ward's company has a display of fossil casts managed by Professor Franklin C. Hill. The display includes Ward's skeletons of *Megatherium*, *Glyptodont*, *Plesiosaurus* and other familiar Ward's catalogue items.

1898   Bessie Love is born. She will become the first movie heroine to be menaced by a dinosaur in a feature-length movie, *The Lost World* (1925). (Dies April 26, 1986.)

1907   Fay Wray is born. Actress Wray will be best remembered for her starring role in *King Kong* (1933), wherein she is menaced by a *Tyrannosaurus*, *Elasmosaurus*, *Pteranodon* and the titled giant gorilla. In both her film and Bessie Love's (immediately above), the prehistoric creatures have been sculpted by Marcel Delgado and animated by Willis O'Brien.

1966   "Dino Boy" becomes part of Hanna-Barbera Productions' new *Space Ghost and Dino Boy* cartoon series (CBS). Dino Boy (voiced by Johnny Carson) is a modern youth named Tod stranded in a prehistoric world. His friends are caveman Ugh (Mike Road) and "Bronty," a young "Brontosaurus" (*Apatosaurus*) which he rides.
Same day: Rankin-Bass' *King Kong* series begins, in which the famous giant ape, home-based on the prehistoric island Mondo, will be in conflict with the evil Dr. Who, as well as monstrous menaces including dinosaurs.

~ 11 ~

1903   The Carnegie Museum of Natural History acquires the famous Bayet Collection of fossils.

1966   *It's About Time*, a prime-time "sitcom" series featuring cave people and dinosaurs (the latter mostly stock footage from the movie *The Beast of Hollow Mountain*), debuts on CBS television. The premise: two American astronauts, Frank (Frank Aletter) and Hector (Jack Mullaney), breaking the time barrier in a rocket, crash land in a prehistoric era and befriend a Stone Age tribe including friendly caveman Gronk (Joe E. Ross), his mate Shad (Imogene Coca), attractive young Mlor (Mary Grace) and Cave Boss (Cliff Norton). In the second half of the first (and only) season, the astronauts will return to their own time with their cave friends tagging along.

1971 *Pebbles and Bamm Bamm*, the first animated *Flintstones* spin-off, starts on the CBS television network. Emphasis is on the teenaged children, Pebbles Flintstone and the unusually strong Bamm Bamm Rubble.

1977 *The Last Dinosaur*, a movie made for television, premieres on ABC. It stars Richard Boone as a big-game hunter stalking a live *Tyrannosaurus* in a lost world under the Earth's polar ice cap. The movie was made by Tsuburaya Productions, the Japanese company responsible for the special effects in the first series of Godzilla movies, which explains why the tyrannosaur's roar sounds suspiciously like that of the famous Japanese monster.

1982 Don Glut gives his first presentation of the lecture "Fantasy Dinosaurs of the Movies" at the second annual Dinosaur Days held at the Field Museum of Natural History in Chicago.

1984 The International *Archaeopteryx* Conference begins in Eichstätt, West Germany, near the site where the first specimens of this rare fossil animal were discovered. When the conference is over, the consensus will be that *Archaeopteryx* is indeed a bird, though not necessarily the direct ancestor of modern birds, and that the animal was capable of at least limited flight.

1991 *Dinosaur!*, a television mini-series starring retired CBS news commentator Walter Cronkite, debuts on the Arts & Entertainment Network. In addition to interviews with paleontologists, visits to dig sites and other educational features, the series also boasts new state-of-the-art animation effects to bring dinosaurs to life. The entire series will later be released on home video cassette.

~ 12 ~

1940 In Lascaux, near Montignac, France, a pet dog falls through a crack in the ground and lands in a cavern hundreds of feet below. The four young schoolboys with the animal attempt to rescue it, inadvertently discovering a vast underground chamber, the walls of which are decorated with beautifully preserved color artwork painted by Cro-Magnon humans. Animals depicted on the paintings include bison, deer and horses (one of them shown to be pregnant). The cave will become the country's fourth most popular tourist attraction until, in 1963, it will be closed because of damaging effects of algae.

1948 A menacing *Tyrannosaurus* enters the *Mandrake the Magician* comic strip written by Lee Falk and drawn by Phil Davis. The monster chases Mandrake and friend Lothar through the jungle with more prehistoric thrills awaiting in succeeding installments.

1952 More scenes and outtakes from 1940's *One Million B.C.* turn up in *Untamed Women* (United Artists), a movie in which a World War II bomber crew become stranded on an island populated by a lost race of lovely female Druids, brutish "hairy men" and familiar prehistoric animals.

1953 Commander Buzz Corry (Ed Kemmer) and comical sidekick Cadet Happy (Lyn Osborn) meet more prehistoric terrors in "The Primitive Men of Planet X" on television's *Space Patrol*. This time the menace is a ruthless primitive tribe of cavemen who trap the heroes inside a vast cavern.

Paleontologist Othniel Charles Marsh as the subject of an 1890 PUNCH *cartoon.*

~ 13 ~

1890 Professor Othniel C. Marsh is the subject of a *Punch* cartoon. The cartoon depicts Marsh as a circus ringmaster standing atop a *Triceratops* skull while conducting a troupe of prehistoric skeletons he has described.

1938 Composer Deems Taylor, who will host the movie *Fantasia*, suggests to Walt Disney that Stravinsky's "Rite of Spring" be given a prehistoric theme.

1954 "Through the Time Barrier," the first color episode of the syndicated television series *Adventures of Superman*, sends the Man of Steel (George Reeves) and his *Daily Planet* friends back to the Stone Age. Writer David Chantier's script was based on the comic-book story "Caveman Clark Kent!" drawn by Al Plastino and published in *Action Comic* no. 169 (June 1952). The illustrated adventure featured dinosaurs, which were unfortunately beyond the budget of the television version.

1997   An exhibition of 59 original paintings by James Gurney, from his books *Dinotopia* and *Dinotopia: The World Beneath*, opens at the Carnegie Center for the Arts in Three Rivers, Michigan. The exhibition, which also includes theatrical and interactive activities, will remain until November 16.

~ 14 ~

1942   A farewell tea for retiring Curator of Paleontology Elmer S. Riggs is given by staff members of the Field Museum of Natural History. As a going-away gift and show of appreciation, Riggs' Department of Geology colleagues present him with three large volumes recording his accomplishments during his 44 years of service at the museum.

~ 15 ~

1942   Elmer S. Riggs officially retires from his position at the Field Museum of Natural History where he has remained for most of his professional career.

Full-scale TYRANNOSAURUS *and* TRICERATOPS *models made by Elbert H. Porter in Orderville, Utah, soon to travel to their new home, the Dinosaur Gardens outside the Utah Field House of Natural History, Vernal. Courtesy State of Utah Division of Parks and Recreation.*

1977   A collection of life-sized prehistoric-animal figures arrive — greeted by a parade with a band and the local news media — at their new permanent home on the grounds of the Utah Field House of Natural History in Vernal. The fiberglass models, including a *Diplodocus* and *Tyrannosaurus*, were made during the early 1960s by Utah sculptor Elbert H. Porter and his crew, including Robert Cook, Jack Jarvie, Harold Poole, Twila Rockwell and Norene Porter. Before coming to Vernal, the models were first displayed next to Porter's studio in Draper, Utah; for six years as a tourist attraction in West Yellowstone, Montana; then to the small town of Orderville, Utah, where they remained for seven years. In 1984, to commemorate the models' residence in their final home, the Dinosaur Gardens behind Field House museum will sell a miniature plaster model based on Porter's giant *Diplodocus*.

1993   Bonhams auction house in London puts up for bid fossils from China including 100-million-year-old dinosaur eggs, coprolites and amber preserving insects. One clutch of eggs is auctioned off to an American collector for 50,600 pounds.

~ 16 ~

1901   The Imperial Academy of Sciences expedition to retrieve a frozen mammoth in Siberia reaches its goal. Most of the skin of the head has already been eaten by wolves and bears, and the trunk is gone. Nevertheless the great beast will be collected.

1997   The movie *Dinosaur Valley Girls* officially debuts as a rental item at video stores. Two versions are made available from EI Cinema — the sexier "director's cut" and a toned-down "family edition."

~ 17 ~

1950   Pete Von Sholly is born in New York, N.Y. Von Sholly will spend much of his professional career as a story-board artist, working on such movies as Disney Studios' multi-million-dollar dinosaur epic begun in the late 1990s. His credits will include creating *Tyranostar*, a book-character superhero in a land of evolved prehistoric animals, illustrations for various dinosaur books, calendars and posters, and being part of the Iridium Band (including playing lead and rhythm guitar), which records the *Dinosaur Tracks* musical albums. In 1992 he will co-produce the highly successful movie *Prehysteria!* for which his wife Andrea sculpts the dinosaur models, and its two sequels. (Son Peter, born on July 15, 1987, can easily say "*Micro-pachycephalosaurus*" at age one.)

1954   A dramatic serialized adaptation of *Gojira*, produced by Toho Co. and debuting the monster's distinctive roar, is broadcast over Japanese radio to promote the new movie, continuing through September 25.

1985   Godzilla, in the person of a human being wearing a rubber suit, strolls the Magnificent Mile in Chicago, Illinois, and does interviews with reporters to promote his comeback movie *Godzilla 1985*.

~ 18 ~

1885   Charles M. (Mortram) Sternberg is born in Lawrence, Kansas. "Charlie" is the second son in what will be a family of very successful fossil collectors, led by his father Charles H. Sternberg, and including brothers George and Levi. Although he does not originally intend to become a paleontologist, his will become one of the field's greatest names. He will assist his father looking for and bringing back fossils from the Kansas chalk and then the Laramie Formation of Wyoming. Inspired by such new and astonishing finds as the famous mummy of a duckbilled dinosaur (now known as *Edmontosaurus*), Sternberg will realize his life's vocation. Hired by the Canadian government to compete with American Museum of Natural History paleontologist Barnum Brown in collecting dinosaurs, Sternberg, mostly working for the Geological Survey of Canada and National Museum of Canada (now the Canadian Museum

Paleontologist Charles M. Sternberg in his 90s photographed outside his Ottawa, Canada, home on June 18, 1976. Photo by Philip J. Currie.

of Nature), will become one of history's greatest collectors of dinosaur remains in Canada. Following the death of Lawrence Lambe in 1919, Sternberg will take advantage of an opportunity and begin to write descriptive papers, mostly about dinosaurs, though his field work will continue. Although his Ph.D. will be an honorary one, he becomes an unrivaled field man who will make numerous discoveries and usually study the specimens where he finds them. Sternberg's accomplishments, both in field and laboratory, will be virtually countless; among the ones of which he will be most proud is his discovery of narial passages within the crest of a specimen of crested duckbilled dinosaur. In 1956 Sternberg will become instrumental in the Alberta government's establishment of the Dinosaur Provincial Park in the Steveville-Deadlodge Canyon badlands.

First issue (1953) of artist/writer/editor Joe Kubert's series which, with issue number 2, was retitled simply TOR, *named for its caveman hero.* © St. John Publishing Company and Joe Kubert, all rights reserved.

1926 Joe Kubert is born in Poland but grows up in Brooklyn, New York, where he will enter the comic-book field as an artist while only a teenager in high school. Eventually he will become a writer, editor and publisher of comic books, later teaching and founding his own school for other comic-book artists. An enthusiast of prehistoric life, Kubert will manage to work dinosaurs, cave people and other primitive creatures into various comic-book genres including superhero, jungle and war, all in his own distinctive drawing style. Many of Kubert's fans will consider his greatest creation to be the comic-book series which debuts in 1953 as *1,000,000 Years Ago* and is retitled *Tor* with its second issue (printed in a three-dimensional process), a series starring compassionate caveman hero Tor, who struggles to survive in an anachronistic prehistoric world populated with brutal early humans and also animals from earlier time periods, including dinosaurs. Beginning in the 1960s Kubert will contribute cover and interior art to many of DC Comics' "War That Time Forgot" stories published in various comic books pitting soldiers against prehistoric creatures. In 1974 Kubert will edit as well as often write and illustrate a new series of *Tarzan* comic books for DC Comics, with many of the stories featuring prehistoric creatures.

Artist William Stout with the skull (cast) of an ancient friend. Photo by Richard Trimarchi.

1949   William Stout is born in Salt Lake City, Utah. A lover of prehistoric life since childhood, Stout will become an artist known for his illustrations of dinosaurs and other fantastic creatures. His first major dinosaur art will be featured in his *Prehistoric Portfolio* (1976), then in the books *The Dinosaur Scrapbook* (1980) and *The New Dinosaur Dictionary* (1978). His illustrations for *The Dinosaurs* (1981), which present the Mesozoic reptiles in new, dynamic and innovative ways, will inspire and influence many future artists. In the late 1980s Stout will spend much time in Antarctica, his experiences there leading to "Lost Worlds," a major art exhibition of paintings depicting life on that continent in ancient and present times.

~ 19 ~

1948   The *Feg Murray* Sunday comic-strip feature, written and drawn by Murray, highlights the new "lost world" movie *Unknown Island*, released this year. The large, single-panel feature depicts the actors from the film

Still from the movie UNKNOWN ISLAND (1948) featuring CERATOSAURUS vs. giant ground sloth (Ray "Crash" Corrigan), this photo the basis for the artwork in a FEG MURRAY comic-strip feature. © Film Classics.

watching as the *Ceratosaurus* (here called a *Tyrannosaurus*) and gigantic ground sloth battle to the death.

~ 20 ~

1941 Paul O. McGrew names and describes a new procynoid — one of a group of small, carnivorous arboreal mammals including rac-coons — from the Miocene of Nebraska. Same day, McGrew describes a new Miocene lago-morph (a group including rab-bits and hares).

~ 21 ~

1923 Walter Hall Wheeler is born in Syracuse, New York. Among Wheeler's future accomplishments as a geologist and paleontologist will be serving as Chairman of the Southwestern Section of the Geological Survey of America, President of the Carolina Geological Society and President of the American Institute of Professional Geologists. In 1960 and for the next six years, Wheeler will edit the *Journal of the Elisha Mitchell Scientific Society.* (Dies November 21, 1989.)

1949 Kenneth Carpenter is born in Tokyo, Japan. Inspired as a child by the movie *Gojira* (U.S. title: *Godzilla, King of the Monsters!*), Carpenter will become a vertebrate paleontologist. The early years of his professional career will be largely spent as a fossil preparator. In the early 1980s he will revamp the Philadelphia Academy of Natural Sciences' fossil hall, including mounting what is considered by many colleagues as the most accurately mounted skeleton of *Tyrannosaurus rex* in the world. Carpenter will become a leading authority on theropods (carnivorous dinosaurs) thyreophorans (armored dinosaurs including stegosaurs and ankylosaurs) and will name and describe a number of new dinosaurian taxa. Among his achievements will be publishing numerous scientific papers on dinosaurs and co-editing such books as (with Philip J. Currie) *Dinosaur Systematics: Approaches and*

Perspectives (1990) and (with John R. Horner and Karl F. Hirsch) *Dinosaur Eggs and Babies* (1994).

~ 22 ~

1926 Otto Zdansky announces his discovery of two fossil teeth that appear to be human at a meeting held in Peking to honor the visiting Crown Prince of Sweden. The teeth had been found on a hill near the village of Choukoutien, China. Zdansky names the teeth *Homo* sp. The find will lead to the discovery of Peking Man next year.

~ 23 ~

1989 Edwin H. Colbert is honored at the Symposium on Southwestern Geology and Paleontology held in Flagstaff, Arizona.

1991 The first Joint Symposium on Volcanism and Early Terrestrial Biotas is held as a combined meeting of the Royal Society of Edinburgh and National Museums of Scotland in Edinburgh. The symposium centers around animal and plant fossils of Carboniferous age found in volcanogenic deposits at East Kirkton, Bathgate, Scotland. Faunae at this site include the oldest known reptile and first amphibian assemblage (the oldest known, entirely terrestrial tetrapods) found in the British Carboniferous. Also found at this site are the earliest known arthropods — including a scorpion measuring one meter in length — and excellently-preserved plant fossils.

~ 24 ~

1901 The Imperial Academy of Sciences team begins to recover its Siberian mammoth. Otto F. Hertz records in his diary: "To my great surprise I found well-preserved food fragments between the teeth, which proves that our mammoth, after a short death struggle, died in this very position. The fact that what we found was food, and not substance carried into the mouth recently, was later proved by comparing it with the stomach contents."

1930 After a series of operations, William Diller Matthew, called the "Father of Mammalian Paleontology" by biographer Edwin H. Colbert (*William Diller Matthew: Paleontologist*, 1992), dies in Berkeley, California.

1931 Sharat Kumar Roy and Carey Cronies publish a joint paper describing a worm of the Silurian period and associated fauna.

1937 Christiane Helene Mendrez-Carroll is born (*née* Mendrez) in Paris, France. During her future brief career as a paleontologist she will teach genetics and physical anthropology, then go on to specialize in Pleistocene mammals. Her major work, a study of South African therocephalian reptiles, will be left unfinished when she dies in Paris in November 1978.

~ 25 ~

1901 The Imperial Academy expedition continues collecting its mammoth, exposing the thick hair on the underside. Dr. Hertz writes, "The colour of this hair on the under side of the leg is roan, while that on the outer and inner side, up to the middle of the foreleg, is dark brown — somewhat lighter at the ends."

1949 Marc R. Gallup is born. Gallup will become a paleontologist who, among other accomplishments, will discover previously unknown details regarding the foot of the sauropod dinosaur *Pleurocoelus*.

1985 The Tyrrell Museum of Palaeontology (later to be called the Royal Tyrrell Museum of Palaeontology), on the banks of the Red Deer River in Drumheller, Alberta, Canada, opens to the public. The museum, a major research institution for the study of prehistoric life, houses the most impressive permanent display of dinosaur bones, comprising both original material and casts, in the world. Some 35 dinosaur skeletons are displayed as well as skeletons of other kinds of reptiles, birds, fishes, amphibians and mammals. Behind the building are badlands that continue to yield a wealth of dinosaur fossils.

~ 26 ~

1867 Winsor McCay is born (*né* Zenas G. Winsor McCay) in Ontario, Canada (birth date according to census reports; McCay's tombstone inscription gives the date as 1869 and he once claimed to have been born in 1871 in Spring Lake, Michigan). McCay, a future cartoonist and pioneer cartoon animator, will create the first classic character ever designed for a motion picture cartoon, an *Apatosaurus* with human-like feelings who stars in the short film *Gertie* (aka *Gertie the Dinosaur*). As originally presented in 1912, the film will be a projected background for McCay's live stage appearance, the dinosaur responding to his words. In 1914 McCay will release *Gertie* theatrically with an added-on framing sequence featuring himself, other cartoonists and scenes shot at the American Museum of Natural History. *Gertie* will inspire one of the first sequels in movie history, *Gertie on Tour*, which McCay will make in 1917. McCay also, on occasion, will draw dinosaurs into his printed newspaper comic strips. In 1905 a live *Apatosaurus* skeleton will act like a racehorse in McCay's *Dreams of the Rarebit Fiend* feature, while in 1913 a pink sauropod looking suspiciously like Gertie will appear in the strip *In the Wonderful Land of Dreams*. (Dies 1934.)

1901   Otto F. Hertz writes of the continuing mammoth recovery: "I searched the vicinity for bones of other animals, and found horns of the northern deer lying about everywhere."

1930   A meeting takes place at the University of California at Berkeley to honor the late paleontologist William Diller Matthew, who had recently taught there. The meeting, attended by numerous colleagues and co-workers, is held in Bacon Hall where Diller had worked and studied while a professor at the university. The group will sign a resolution pledging their "continued interest in the aims he has set so high, and in the plans which he has left for us to complete."

1980   "The Flintstones' New Neighbors" airs on *The Flintstones* NBC television cartoon special. The titled neighbors are the Frankenstones, a prehistoric family patterned after modern horror-movie characters (and influenced by *The Munsters* sitcom series). After being spooked, Fred Flinstone finally accepts the weird but friendly Frankenstone family.

~ 27 ~

1901   Collection of the Siberian mammoth continues. Dr. Hertz writes, "A very interesting discovery was made at a distance of 5 in. from the upper edge of the sole of the right hind-foot — the very hairy end of the tail, which was thawed out and examined."

1949   Gregg E. Ostrander is born in Chadron, Nebraska. At the age of six interested in rocks and fossils, Ostrander will become a paleontologist spending most of his career working at the Museum of Geology, South Dakota School of Mines and Technology, and later as collections manager at the Division of Vertebrate Paleontology of the Museum of Natural History, University of Kansas. He will have already published 10 papers and be working on others when he dies in 1988.

~ 28 ~

1838   Charles Darwin, influenced by rural English vicar Robert Malthus' use of the term "struggle for survival," explains how individual creatures are naturally selected. According to Darwin: Organisms which survive are those best adapted to the environmental conditions in which they live. These surviving organisms pass on to their descendants those characteristics useful for survival. In later generations selection occurs. If selection continues over a long period of time, the degree of being best adapted increases, the result being that the organism becomes better adapted to its environment. This idea will be popularly known as the "survival of the fittest."

1851   Captain Lorenzo Sitgreaves discovers a vast "petrified forest"—so described because of the countless logs and pieces of logs of fossilized trees scattered about — in southeastern Arizona. The logs will later be dated as of Late Triassic age, the area will yield a wealth of fossil material, including vertebrate and invertebrate animals, and will become known as the Petrified Forest.

1901   Otto F. Hertz decides to build a heated shed over the mammoth carcass in which the animal can be dismembered after the coming of the severely cold weather.

1905   Edwin H. (Harris) Colbert is born in Maryville, Missouri. Colbert will become a paleontologist specializing in fossil mammals though his name will become associated with dinosaurs. In 1933, after doing field and preparation work at the University of Nebraska, Colbert will become assistant curator at the American Museum of Natural History working under Henry Fairfield Osborn. Following Osborn's death in 1935, Colbert becomes Curator and eventually Chairman of the Department of Fossil and Recent Reptiles and Amphibians. While in this position, Colbert will write a number of books about dinosaurs, starting with *The Dinosaur Book* in 1945, and work with the media regarding dinosaurs, these activities forever linking his name with the Mesozoic reptiles. Colbert's formal association with the American Museum will end in 1968 when he and wife Margaret move to Flagstaff, with his becoming Curator of Vertebrate Paleontology at the Museum of

Northern Arizona. Colbert will author myriad scientific and popular articles about fossil vertebrates, write numerous books about dinosaurs, the history of dinosaur discoveries and about his own life and experiences. He will name and describe new taxa (such as the primitive armored dinosaur *Scutellosaurus* in 1981). He will be most proud of his work done in the late 1940s at the *Coelophysis* quarry at Ghost Ranch, New Mexico, and that in the late 1960s in Antarctica, where he will discover firm evidence supporting the idea of continental drift, leading to the modern concept of plate tectonics.

1914   Fossil collector Charles H. Sternberg, competing in the badlands of Alberta, Canada, with American Museum of Natural History collector Barnum Brown, hauls in his last load of fossils for the season. Exhausted from the demanding physical work, Sternberg is pleased to behold a phenomenon of nature which he will describe in his book *Hunting Dinosaurs in the Badlands of the Red Deer River, Alberta, Canada* (1917): "Suddenly, as if to relieve our tiresome journey, God's moving pictures, the Northern Lights, burst upon us in all their glory."

~ 29 ~

1901   Otto F. Hertz collects specimens of mountain flora which he plans to use in determining the mammoth's diet.

1950   Everett Claire Olson publishes a paper in which he describes the temporal region of *Diadectes*, a large and clumsy Permian reptile distinguished as one of the first terrestrial plant-eating animals.

1983   "Dinosaur Jim" Jensen is a subject of the *Ripley's Believe It or Not!* newspaper comics feature. According to its text, the Brigham Young University paleontologist, over a period of 30 years, has collected over 100 tons of fossil bones.

1990   *Rimshot*, a comedy play involving dinosaurs, written by Nina Giovannitti and directed by Robert Schrock, opens at The Complex, a theatre in Hollywood, California.

~ 30 ~

1900   W. E. (William Elgin) Swinton is born in Kirkcaldy, Scotland. Swinton will join the British Museum (Natural History) as a paleontologist in 1924, becoming curator of the collection of dinosaur fossils. Also a popularizer of science, he will author numerous magazine articles and books (among them *The Dinosaurs*, published in 1934), appear on radio and television programs and give lectures about extinct animals. His scientific papers will deal with such subjects as dinosaurs, pterosaurs, fossil crocodiles and marine reptiles. In 1961, after leaving England, Swinton will join the staff of the Royal Ontario Museum in Toronto, first as director of life sciences, then in 1963 as overall director. Swinton's other interesting accomplishments will include being commanding officer of James Bond creator Ian Fleming while serving in British Naval Intelligence during World War II, climbing Mount Everest in the 1950s and teaching natural history to young Princess Elizabeth, the future Queen of England. (Dies June 12, 1994.)

1901   Dr. Otto F. Hertz contemplates comparing the plants he has collected with the mammoth's stomach contents to determine if they are the same.

1960   *The Flintstones*, which will become Hanna-Barbera Productions' most successful cartoon series, starts its long television run on ABC. The show spoofs situation comedies and is most specifically an imitation of *The Honeymooners*, depicting modern day life through a Stone Age setting. Most stories will take place in the prehistoric town of Bedrock and center around the foibles of Fred Flintstone (voice of Alan Reed), friend Barney Rubble (Mel Blanc) and their long-suffering wives Wilma (Jean Vanderpyl) and Betty (Bea Benaderet), respectively. Fred has a pet dinosaur named Dino (voice of Chips Spam) that behaves more like a dog than a prehistoric reptile. Reruns, spinoffs, comic books and strips, merchandise and even live stage shows will follow. *The Flintstones*, a live-action movie based on the series, will be released in 1994.

1995   *PaleoWorld*, a half-hour cable-television documentary series about various aspects of paleontology, debuts on The Learning Channel. The show will prove popular enough to warrant renewal for several additional seasons. Highlights will be visits to excavation sites and interviews with scientists. The premiere episode "Hunting Dinosaurs" features Paul C. Sereno and his field team working in the Sahara Desert of Morocco.

OCTOBER

~ 1 ~

1862   The first skeleton of *Archaeopteryx* is acquired by the British Museum (Natural History) at a cost of 700 pounds. This fossil, which will come to be known as the "London specimen" of *Archaeopteryx*, is articulated and includes preserved feather impressions.

1872   J. Allen St. John is born in Chicago, Illinois (though he later gives his birth year as 1875). St. John will become an artist with a rugged, heroic and almost dreamlike romantic style that establishes him as the premier illustrator of Edgar Rice Burroughs stories of the 1920s. He will create numerous cover paintings and black and white interior illustrations, many of them (e.g., *At the Earth's Core*, 1922) featuring prehistoric creatures. Also, he will illustrate pulp magazine dinosaur-related stories not written

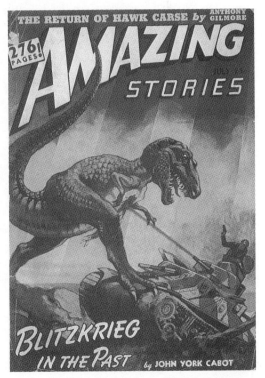

One of many illustrations made by artist J. Allen St. John for the pulp magazines, this one dated 1942, TYRANNOSAURUS based on a mural by Charles R. Knight. © Ziff-Davis Publishing Company.

by Burroughs, like the "Jongor" tales appearing during the 1940s in *Fantastic Adventures* and "The Lost Warship" (1943) and "Dinosaur Destroyer" (1949) in *Amazing Stories*. St. John's influence will be seen in the work of future artists illustrating Burroughs' fantastic tales. (Dies May 27, 1957.)

1901 The Imperial Academy team moves from their tents into a newly constructed building designed to keep out the cold weather.

1989 Four postage stamps of Mesozoic reptiles featuring paintings by artist John Gurche, staff artist at the Smithsonian Institution, are issued by the United States Postal Service. The stamps depict individual scenes of the dinosaurs *Tyrannosaurus*, *Stegosaurus* and *Apatosaurus* and pterosaur *Pteranodon*. Though identifying *Apatosaurus* by its incorrect name *Brontosaurus* is controversial, the Postal Service explains that more people are familiar with the latter. Establishing a precedent, the Postal Service will join forces in September with a private company, MCA (parent company of Universal Pictures), the two mounting a multi-million-dollar ad campaign that will both promote the new stamps and MCA's home video release of the 1988 animated hit movie *The Land Before Time*. The tie-in is also intended to increase sales of the "dinosaur" stamps during National Stamp Collecting Month.

~ 2 ~

1836 The *Beagle* docks at Falmouth, England. Aboard ship is homesick Charles Darwin, his long global voyage completed. From the fossils and living organisms he has observed on the trip, Darwin now understands that the similarities and differences of life are products of a steady process of change and that the present inhabitants of Earth all descended from common ancestors. Darwin will collect his facts for two decades before publishing the great theory this voyage has helped to inspire.

1901 Back in Siberia, the timber has been cut for the mammoth shed. Of the dead beast Dr. Otto F. Hertz comments, "Although the mammoth is frozen it smells abominably."

1909 Alexander Gillespie Raymond, or simply Alex Raymond as he will be known, is born in New Rochelle, New York. Raymond will become one of the most respected (and copied) adventure strip cartoonists from the 1930s to 1950s. One of his most successful strips will be *Flash Gordon*, which he both writes and illustrates, and which, despite the futuristic setting, features plenty of prehistoric-type creatures. Another Raymond hero, the star of the *Jungle Jim* comic strip, will meet his own share of prehistoric animals and men in several movies based on the character made by Columbia Pictures in the 1940s and '50s. Raymond's career will end when, in September 1956, he is killed in an automobile accident near Westport, Connecticut.

1951 Daniel J. Chure is born in Passaic, New Jersey. Chure will become a paleontologist specializing in dinosaurs of the Upper Jurassic Morrison Formation and in dinosaur footprints. He will be made Park Paleontologist at Dinosaur National Monument. Among Chure's credits will be a definitive reference work, *A Bibliography of the Dinosauria (Exclusive of the Aves), 1677–1986* (1989), co-authored with John S. McIntosh. In 1995 Chure will name and describe the giant theropod *Saurophaganax maximus* (which will later be referred to as a new species of *Allasaurus*).

1992 Dinodon Music publishing company (BMI) is established. Most of the music featured on Fossil Records' *Dinosaur Tracks* albums will be published by Dinodon.

~ 3 ~

1901 Taxidermist M. E. V. Pfizenmayer brings the transport equipment to be used in hauling back the frozen mammoth.

1910 Miguel Crusafont-Pairo is born in Spain. As a paleontologist he will name and describe many new genera and species of fossil mammals. Among his interests will be the concept of evolution, culminating in co-authoring the book *La Evolución* (1966), featuring 28 scholarly papers on the topic by various authors. (Dies August 16, 1983.)

1980 Anticipating Halloween, another horror-films inspired *Flintstones* television special is aired on NBC, this one titled "The Flintstones Meet Rockula and Frankenstone." The show will inspire "Fred and Barney Meet the Frankenstones," an episode of *The New Fred and Barney Show* (NBC, 1979), and become a regular feature on *The Flintstone Comedy Show* (NBC, 1980).

1997 Paleontologist Paul C. Sereno ("NIU alumnus ... discovered the world's oldest dinosaur") and his entire family are the subject of a full-page advertisement for Northern Illinois University.

~ 4 ~

1901 The Imperial Academy of Sciences team begins to thaw out the frozen mammoth tail, which is eight and one half inches long with inch long hairs. "We soon had to stop," writes Dr. Otto F. Hertz, "as all the hair threatened to fall off."

1905 Henry F. Osborn names and describes the new giant theropod *Tyrannosaurus rex* and, in the same paper, *Dynamosaurus imperiosis*, which he believes possesses armor. The dinosaurs were collected in Montana and Wyoming, respectively, by Barnum Brown. In future years *Dynamosaurus* will be referred to *Tyrannosaurus*, the armor correctly identified as ankylosaurian.

1915 United States President Woodrow Wilson officially declares the rich dinosaur quarry in the Upper Jurassic Morrison Formation, located within an 80-acre area including part of Colorado and Utah, to be Dinosaur National Monument. (As the quarry was located on federal land opened to settlement, the Carnegie Museum of Natural History took steps to protect the site.) Less than a year later the Monument will become part of the new National Park System.

First Dinosaur Quarry excavations in progress during 1910, utilizing blasting powder and hand tools, at the locality that will be called Dinosaur National Monument. Courtesy United States Department of Interior, National Parks Service.

1994   The movie *Jurassic Park* is released on home video supported by a dinosaur-sized $65 million advertising campaign. (Many fans must first sign onto a waiting list to ensure getting their copy the day the video hits the stores.)

1996   The Field Museum, with financial support from McDonald's and Disney Enterprises, acquires the *Tyrannosaurus rex* skeleton known as "Sue" at an auction held at Sotheby's Auction House in New York City for $8.4 million, the highest price ever paid for a fossil. The specimen will be prepared in the museum's spacious Stanley Field Hall where, by 1999, mounting of it should be completed. Casts of the specimen will be given to McDonald's and Disney for their own exhibitions.

1997   The Field Museum opens the temporary exhibit "*Archaeopteryx*: The Bird That Rocked the World," displaying the seventh specimen and second species (*A. bavarica*) of this Jurassic animal collected in 1992. The event marks the first time an *Archaeopteryx* specimen has been exhibited outside of Europe.

~ 5 ~

1787   Caspar Wistar, an anatomist who will later become a professor at the medical school in Philadelphia, and "radical Whig" Timothy Matlack offer a report (unpublished) to the American Philosophical Society on the discovery of a large bone, said to be a "thigh bone," from Gloucester County, New Jersey. This may be the first reported North American dinosaur fossil. Possibly it represents a hadrosaur as the place of its discovery is not far from Upper Cretaceous sediments in New Jersey where duckbilled dinosaurs will later be collected. Unfortunately the specimen will become lost.

1986   Dinamation International Corporation's robotic dinosaurs go on display at the Houston Museum of Natural Science.

~ 6 ~

1953   *Creature from the Black Lagoon* begins shooting in three dimensions. When released in 1954, the movie will become a hit spawning two sequels, *Revenge of the Creature* (1955, also in 3D) and *The Creature Walks Among Us* (1956, in standard 2D).

1984 The Fernbank Science Center in Atlanta, Georgia, hosts a display of Dinamation International Corporation's robotic prehistoric reptiles and mammals sponsored by Friends of Ferbank. Though not all of the reptiles in the show are dinosaurs, Fernbank advertises the exhibition with the headline "Dinosaurs Roam Again."

1989 The Lawrence Hall of Science, in Berkeley, California, and the San Diego Natural History Museum launch a dinosaur field trip to the People's Republic of China.

1997 "The Ceratopsia: The Life and Times of the Horned Dinosaurs" exhibit opens at the Mesa Southwest Museum in Mesa, Arizona.

~ 7 ~

1900 In its cover story the Chicago *Times-Herald* proudly announces to the world the discovery of a giant dinosaur found in Colorado, and which will find its new home in the city's Field Columbian Museum: "Chicago has the largest land animal that ever lived." In three years this dinosaur will be named *Brachiosaurus*.

1948 The Columbia comedy short film *I'm a Monkey's Uncle* is released starring the Three Stooges (Moe Howard, Larry Fine and Shemp Howard) as cavemen. Their mates are played by Virginia Hunter (Aggie), Nancy Saunders (Maggie) and Dee Green (Baggie).

1997 The traveling "Great Russian Dinosaurs Exhibition" has its North American debut at the Mesa Southwest Museum in Mesa, Arizona.

1955 The television series *Science Fiction Theatre* airs "Dead Storage," about a baby woolly mammoth reviving after being frozen in suspended animation since the Ice Age, and the efforts of a scientist and a reporter to keep it alive. The mammoth, called Tobey, is played by a live baby elephant dressed up with hair and prop tusks.

~ 8 ~

1901 In Siberia, the mammoth shed is almost completed. The party removes the skull and Dr. Otto Hertz writes, "We were then able to take out the remnants of food from between the molars on the left side. These remnants appear masticated and apparently contain not parts of pine or larch needles, but only bits of various grasses. The imprint of the tooth crenations is well preserved upon the half-chewed food. There is also a small quantity of food upon the well-preserved tongue, but I can secure this only when the lower jaw is removed."

1914　The new helmet-crested duckbilled dinosaur *Corythosaurus* is named and described by paleontologist Barnum Brown, established on two almost complete skeletons, one with skin impressions preserved, both found by him earlier this year in Alberta, Canada.

~ 9 ~

1901　Otto F. Hertz takes the chief measurements of the frozen mammoth.

1905　Llewellyn Ivor Price is born in Santa Maria, Rio Grande do Sul, Brazil. "Llew" will become a research assistant of Alfred S. Romer and, having talent as an artist, provide some illustrations for Romer's classic book *Vertebrate Paleontology*. Displaying an unusual knack for finding fossils in the field, Price will work alongside many notable scientists and serve on numerous geological and paleontological commissions, particularly in South America, collecting numerous specimens. Unknowingly he will win — ironically, on the date of his death, March 14, 1980 — the Jose Bonifacio Gold Medal of the Brazilian Society of Geology for his paleontological researches.

1966　In "Night of Terror," an episode of the 20th Century–Fox science-fiction/adventure television series *Voyage to the Bottom of the Sea* produced by Irwin Allen, the *Seaview*'s captain and a geologist are trapped on a prehistoric island ruled by a giant monitor lizard sporting a ceratopsian-like neck frill — stock scenes from Allen's version of *The Lost World* (1960), but apparently also new footage utilizing a similar lizard wearing the same left-over frill.

~ 10 ~

1953　More prehistoric perils await Commander Buzz Corry (Ed Kemmer) and Cadet Happy (Lyn Osborn) in the *Space Patrol* episode "The Ice Demon of Planet X." Our heroes become trapped in a pit in the frigid area of the mysterious planet where Prince Baccarratti (Bela Kovacs) unleashes his Ice Demon to devour them. The Ice Demon is a kind of sauropod with two long fangs. The miniature model is not convincing; the wire working its neck is plainly visible and, in one embarrassing on-camera moment, the model plops over. With live TV there are no retakes!

1964 Television's *Voyage to the Bottom of the Sea*, still being filmed in black and white, airs the episode "Turn Back the Clock" in which the crew of the super-submarine *Seaview* is trapped on a prehistoric world. Re-use of actors (including star David Hedison), sets and props from *The Lost World* (1960 Fox version) have allowed for the incorporation of substantial stock footage — featuring live lizards outfitted with rubber horns, fins and other dressings — from that movie.

1995 The Denver Museum of Natural History celebrates the forth-coming opening of its "Prehistoric Journey" exhibit with a lecture by famous invertebrate paleontologist Stephen Jay Gould, who discusses how the Earth has changed over millions of years.

1997 The Field Museum displays one 12-inch-long tooth belonging to the *Tyrannosaurus rex* specimen called "Sue," the rest of the skeleton to follow at a later date.

Paleontologist Robert A. Long with the skull of DICERATOPS HATCHERI, *which John Bell Hatcher discovered in the Upper Cretaceous of Wyoming. Photo by R. A. Long and S. P. Welles (neg. #73/200-32), courtesy National Museum of Natural History, Smithsonian Institution.*

~ 11 ~

1861 John Bell Hatcher is born. Hatcher will begin his work as a paleontologist as an assistant to O. C. Marsh and then as one of Marsh's collectors. Based at Carnegie Museum, Hatcher will work mostly in the Upper Cretaceous Lance Formation east of the Rocky Mountain Front Range. In 1887 in the Lance Forma-tion of Wyoming, Hatcher will find an enormous horned skull that Marsh, two years later, will name

Triceratops. Subsequently, Hatcher will collect numerous dinosaur specimens and become a paleontologist in his own right, authoring many scientific articles and co-authoring (with Marsh and Richard Swann Lull) in 1907 the classic monograph "The Ceratopsia." (Dies July 3, 1904.)

1901   The roof of the shed for the Siberian mammoth is completed.

1957   Paul C. Sereno is born in Aurora, Illinois. Sereno will grow up in Naperville, Illinois. A kind of "street kid," he will develop an interest in science upon discovering his ability to draw. Sereno will become one of the foremost modern vertebrate paleontologists specializing in dinosaurs. Eventually based at the University of Chicago where he will be made an associate professor, Sereno will become a champion of the cladistic method of classification. Possessing a knack for finding dinosaur specimens, Sereno will spend much time in such locations as China, South America and Africa, making significant and oftentimes spectacular discoveries in the field. In 1988 Sereno and Alfredo Monetta will discover in Argentina a new skull of *Herrerasaurus ischigualastensis,* the study of which will lead Sereno to become an authority on this very primitive dinosaur. Sereno will publish numerous

Paleontologist Paul C. Sereno in 1996 clinging to a sandstone cliff in the Moroccan Sahara while uncovering a jaw of the 90-million-year-old theropod dinosaur Carcharodontosaurus saharicus. *© Hans Larsson.*

technical papers, some of them dramatically revising dinosaurian phyloge-nies, others naming and describing new genera and species such as the theropods *Afrovenator abakensis* and *Deltadromeus agilis*, and what may be the earliest known theropod or dinosaur of any kind, *Eoraptor lunensis* (all three co-authored). Sereno's work, plus his having a look and personality that plays well to video and film cameras, will make him one of the relatively few paleontologists to achieve media-celebrity status.

1995   A symposium on the evolution and ecology of life on Earth is held at the Denver Museum of Natural History to herald the institution's "Prehistoric Journey" exhibition, which opens in ten days. Speakers at the symposium include Stephen Jay Gould.

~ 12 ~

1953   Mike Jones is born. Jones will become a sculptor of models of prehistoric animals, his work sold through museums and distributors of dinosaur art. Jones will be the main sculptor of horned dinosaurs for "The Ceratopsia: The Life and Times of the Horned Dinosaurs" exhibition (1997). Also, he will sculpt dinosaurs and other extinct animals for motion pictures, including *Carnosaur* and Disney Studios' in-production dinosaur project.

1958   The movie *Monster on the Campus* (Universal-International) opens in theatres, a Jekyll-Hyde type story in which the violent side of a sci-entist's nature is made manifest in the form of a brutal prehistoric man.

~ 13 ~

1901   The Imperial Academy team experiments with heating the shed without directly exposing the mammoth to the fire, low as it may be.

1994   Paul C. Sereno announces the new theropod dinosaur *Afrove-nator abakensis* at a news conference held at the University of Chicago's downtown center. The large meat-eater, superficially resembling the North American genus *Allosaurus*, is known from an almost complete skeleton found the previous year by Sereno and his field team in the Sahara Desert. Sereno unveils a reconstructed cast of the dinosaur's skeleton. Announced also at the event is the discovery of remains of an as yet unnamed sauropod apparently related to the rather common North American genus *Cama-rasaurus*. Sereno points out that similarities between the African and North

American dinosaurs suggest that the continents were connected by a land bridge that remained in existence at least 15 million years longer than once thought.

~ 14 ~

1900   The Boston *Journal* runs a cover story proclaiming H. W. Menke's discovery of a new sauropod near Grand Junction, Colorado. "The Monster of All Ages," the headline declares. "He Has Been Discovered in Colorado in the Fossilized Remains of a Dinosaur Seventy-Five Feet Long and Twenty-One Feet High." The accompanying illustration depicts the animal sitting on its rear end in a Washington, D.C., street. The sauropod will later be named *Brachiosaurus* by Elmer S. Riggs.

1901   The mammoth shed being too dark for working, the Imperial Academy team makes a second opening near the door.

1935   The first *Sinclair Dinosaur Stamp Album* is announced over the airwaves on the *Sinclair Minstrel Program*. The album is free and has spaces to stick in 24 stamps of prehistoric reptiles and birds to be given away free on a weekly basis at Sinclair Service stations. Artwork for the stamps is by James E. Allen under the direction of Barnum Brown, the latter also having written the booklet's text. In the years to come this item will become highly collectible.

~ 15 ~

1878   The huge but relatively slender sauropod dinosaur *Diplodocus* is named by paleontologist Othniel Charles Marsh, based on some tail vertebrae found in 1877 by Samuel Wendell Williston in Garden Park, Colorado. When more complete specimens are later found, *Diplodocus* will be known as one of the longest dinosaurs.

1901   Determined Dr. Hertz and his team work at cleaning the dirt off the mammoth. They also collect some of the under wool and bristles of the right cheek. "The colour varies from black to pale blonde. The black hairs predominate and are lighter toward the ends," he writes.

1904   Edgard Casier is born in Shaarbek, Belgium. In his future long career as a paleontologist, Casier will specialize in fossil fishes. He will author

52 works, though he may best be known for a 1966 publication, "L'Ichthy-ologique du London Clay." He will die (on February 25, 1976) before finishing a paper, written in collaboration with Jacques Herman, on the evolution of teeth of salachian fishes.

1915   Arthur Conan Doyle's science-fiction novel *The Lost World* has its first North American book publication.

~ 16 ~

1869   Two laborers digging a well on the farm of William "Stub" Newell, near the village of Cardiff in upstate New York, uncover what appears to be the "fossil corpse" of a sepia-colored, giant and apparently prehistoric man, 10 feet four and one half inches tall and weighing 2,990 pounds. For obvious reasons the scowling figure is dubbed the Cardiff Giant.

1901   Dr. Hertz's mammoth collectors in Siberia expose some of the badly decomposed food in the animal's stomach.

1947   The cornerstone is laid for the Utah Field House of Natural History in Natural History State Park, Vernal, Utah, the name suggesting that this is to be a museum "in the field." Plans for the museum had officially begun in 1942 when Vernal-based Arthur G. Nord, Supervisor on the Ashley National Forest, became disturbed that out-of-state institutions were collecting and removing important specimens from the area. Nord then organized the Vernal Lion's Club Museum Committee which promoted his idea for a local museum, resulting in the State Legislature unanimously passing a bill in 1945 approving of the project.

1982   The Premier Congrès International de Paléontologie Humaine, Palais des Expositions, Nice, France, begins at the Institut de Paléontologie Humaine in Paris.

~ 17 ~

1901   Dr. Hertz's team remove the Siberian mammoth's left shoulder blade and some ribs, then clean part of the stomach containing a huge quantity of remains of food. "The walls of the stomach first exposed were dark coffee-brown, almost black, and were badly decayed and torn," Hertz writes. Then they amputate the left foreleg.

1916   Eugene S. Richardson is born in Germantown, Pennsylvania. Richardson will become one of the leading paleontologists specializing in invertebrate fossils. Among his achievements will be the publication of numerous papers about extinct animals without backbones and joining the Field Museum of Natural History in 1946 as Curator of Fossil Invertebrates. (Dies January 21, 1983.)

1992   James Gurney's *Dinotopia* exhibit, based on the bestselling fantasy book he wrote and illustrated, opens at the Natural History Museum of Los Angeles County. Original artwork from the book is displayed.

~ 18 ~

1901   The Imperial Academy of Sciences party skins the left side of the mammoth carcass, then the head. Later the left shoulder will be removed. Dr. Hertz: "The flesh from under the shoulder, fibrous and marbled with fat, is dark red and looks as fresh as well-frozen beef or horse-meat. It looked so appetizing that we wondered for some time whether we would not taste it. But no one would venture to take it into his mouth, and horseflesh was given the preference." The dogs, however, enjoy their meal of mammoth.

1994   The mounted skeleton (cast) of *Afrovenator abakensis* goes on temporary display at the Harold Washington Library Center on Chicago's State Street. The exhibit will remain on view for three months.

~ 19 ~

1869   A Syracuse newspaper announces the Cardiff Giant to the world with the headline "A Wonderful Discovery." Exhibited as a 50 cents per view attraction, the figure will attract the attention of scientists and other authorities, some believing it an authentic fossil, others declaring it a hoax (O. C. Marsh, in November, declaring it to be "a very remarkable fake!"). It will also interest master showman Phineas T. Barnum, who will unsuccessfully try to buy it. Undaunted, Barnum in 1871 will commission Syracuse sculptor Professor Carl C. F. Otto to manufacture his own Cardiff Giant which Barnum then exhibits at a museum in Brooklyn. Inevitably the original figure will be revealed to be a hoax perpetrated by failed cigar-maker George Hull who, annoyed by clergymen always stating that there "were giants in the Earth" in "Genesis" times, had one cut from a block of gypsum, then appropriately "aged" and buried. The fraud had cost Hull $2,200 and netted him $35,000.

1901 The mammoth collectors continue dismembering the carcass and recovering some of its frozen blood. Hertz writes, "The stench is not nearly so bad as it was; perhaps because we have grown accustomed to it."

1951 Seeking out a new world capable of supporting human life, the crew of the spaceship *Polaris*—on the NBC television series *Tom Corbett, Space Cadet*—land on a recently discovered planet in the Alpha Centauri star system, finding a world resembling Earth during the Mesozoic Era. The dinosaurs the crew encounter are actually models, including a *Dimetrodon* and *Apatosaurus*, produced by Messmore and Damon in conjunction with the company's "World A Million Years Ago" attraction. The fact that the creatures do not move is helpful when the spacemen zap them into a motionless state with their "parallo-ray" guns. The show stars Frankie Thomas as Tom, Al Markham as cadet Astro, Jan Merlin as cadet Roger Manning and Ed Bryce as Captain Strong.

1953 *Life* magazine continues its "World We Live In" series with a special feature about prehistoric mammals. Again the illustrations are by Rudolf F. Zallinger from another painting ("The Age of Mammals") displayed at Yale University's Peabody Museum of Natural History.

1988 The "Dinosauria Lecture Series" begins at the Utah Museum of Natural History in Salt Lake City.

1990 The Wagner Free Institute of Science, in Philadelphia, Pennsylvania, hosts a dinosaur symposium held in honor of the 100th anniversary of the lectureship of paleontologist Edward Drinker Cope at this institution. Varied programming is geared both to scientists and children.

~ 20 ~

1882 Bela Lugosi is born Béla Blaskó in Lugos, Hungary (now Romania). Lugosi will become an actor famous for playing vampire Count Dracula, but he will also play characters, usually mad scientists, involved with prehistoric themes. In *Murders in the Rue Morgue* (Universal 1932) Lugosi will be mad Dr. Mirakle who tries proving Darwin right by mixing an ape's blood with a woman's. *Island of Lost Souls* (Paramount 1933) will cast him as a wolflike creature created from an animal, the product of a vivisectionist's attempt to speed up the natural evolutionary process. *The Ape Man* (Monogram 1943) will feature the actor as a hapless scientist who, through his own unexplained experimenting, regresses himself to a half-man, half-ape stage. In the non-sequel *Return of the Ape Man* (Monogram 1944) Lugosi will play another mad doctor, this one reviving a prehistoric caveman to whom he gives a brain transplant. One of Lugosi's last movies will be the comedy *Bela Lugosi Meets a Brooklyn Gorilla* (Jack Broder Productions, 1952), in which he again proves evolution by regressing humans into the form of gorillas. (As a note, Lugosi will also play "first man" Adam in a 1922 run of the play *Az Ember Tragédiája*—"The Tragedy of Man"—opening on April 8 at New York's Lexington Theater and co-produced by the actor.) (Dies August 16, 1956.)

1901   The Siberian mammoth recovery team reaches a part of the body that has, until now, been inaccessible, still in the frozen soil three and one half inches lower than the left foreleg. Dr. Hertz writes, "It proved to be the protruded male genital, 33½ in. long above, and 41 in. long below, four inches above the urinary meatus. The diameter of the flattened out penis is 7½ in."

1968   Edwin H. Colbert, now at the Museum of Northern Arizona, departs from Flagstaff for Antarctica, an expedition during which he will find fossils of *Lystrosaurus*, a reptile whose remains had previously been found in Asia and Africa. This discovery will constitute more evidence supporting the theory of "continental drift."

Paleontologist Edwin H. Colbert (right), with Dave Elliott, finds more bones of the reptile LYSTROSAURUS *on a slope in Antarctica in 1969, a discovery pivotal in proving the theory of "continental drift." Courtesy Edwin H. Colbert.*

1979   The Carnegie Museum of Natural History designates today "Dinosaur Day," commemorating the 70th anniversary of the discovery of the skeleton of *Apatosaurus*. Also today, the Carnegie becomes the first museum to remove the

Camarasaurus lentus skull from its mounted *Apatosaurus* skeleton and replace it with the proper skull. The discovery that skeletons of this dinosaur had traditionally been mounted with the wrong head was made by Carnegie Museum paleontologist David S. Berman and John S. McIntosh, who also identified the correct skull, publishing their findings in a joint paper in 1978.

Composite photograph of the skeleton of APATOSAURUS EXCELSUS, *formerly sporting a* CAMARSAURUS *skull, now wearing the correct one. Courtesy The Field Museum (neg. #G84382).*

1991 Paleontologists discover fossil bones, including a large claw, belonging to the largest dromaeosaurid theropod dinosaur yet found. The discovery is made in the (Early Cretaceous) Gaston Quarry in eastern Utah through research directed by paleontologists James I. Kirkland and Donald Burge, the latter of the College of Eastern Utah Prehistoric Museum, Price, and Dinamation International Society. The first material seen is uncovered by Carl Limoni of the Prehistoric Museum. In 1993 the formal description of this new dinosaur, named *Utahraptor*, will be published.

~ 21 ~

1874 Charles R. (Robert) Knight is born in Brooklyn, New York. Knight (or "Toppy" as daughter Lucy will someday call him) will become an artist specializing in animal life both living and extinct, recreated in all media, combining scientific accuracy with fine art. He will first master modern animals, believing that these must be known before extinct animals can be attempted. To ensure accuracy in restoring the latter, Knight will work closely with scientists, first Edward D. Cope in the late 1800s, and later his mentor Henry Fairfield Osborn. Knight's drawings, paintings and sculptures of dinosaurs, fossil mammals, early man and other extinct creatures will grace many of the finest institutions where fossils are displayed, some of these being the American Museum of Natural History, The Field Museum (his murals here being what Knight will consider his magnum opus), and the Natural History Museum of Los Angeles County. His restorations, some of them photographically realistic, will set the standard and for more than half a century impart to the world its impression of what these ancient life forms were like. During this time most such art produced by others will be either influenced by or copied from Knight's work. As Edwin H. Colbert, who knew Knight, will one day say, "he had so much imagination that he could project himself back in time and feel that he was on a cliff with one of those monsters." Also, Knight will author books including *Before the Dawn of History* (1935), *Life Through the Ages* (1946) and *Prehistoric Man: The Great Adventurer* (1949). (Dies April 15, 1953.)

The young artist Charles R. Knight with his sculpture of Edward D. Cope's new pelycosaur "NAOSAURUS" (a chimera of EDAPHOSAURUS and DIMETRODON done before the genus EDAPHOSAURUS was fully known).

1901 In Siberia, the Imperial Academy of Sciences recovery team removes more of the mammoth including the left side of the pelvis. The flesh underneath the pelvis is still frozen solid.

1986 Paleontologist John R. Bolt of The Field Museum announces the discovery (made in 1985 by geologists Robert McCay and Patrick McAdams of the Iowa Geological Survey) in southeastern Iowa of very rare, remarkably well-preserved fossils of lizard-like animals that may be among the oldest North American tetrapods, or four-footed land vertebrates, yet found (about 340 million years old). Bolt tells Chicago *Sun-Times* reporters that "They're the best tetrapods found in North America, in terms of the quality and abundance of specimens."

1995 The Denver Museum of Natural History, after six years of renovation and a cost of $7.7 million, unveils to the public "Prehistoric Journey," the largest and most ambitious permanent exhibit in the Colorado museum's history. Included are some of the museum's dinosaur skeletons newly mounted to reflect modern paleontological thought. Prominently displayed is the recently acquired cast of a *Tyrannosaurus rex* skeleton, mounted in a dynamic "action" pose, up on one foot, under the direction of paleontologist and active dinosaur advocate Robert T. Bakker.

~ 22 ~

1901 The left hindlimb is cut off the Siberian mammoth and also more hair. "The colour of the hair of the right hind-femur varies from rust-brown to black," writes Hertz. "The best preserved of all the hair was that in the fold of skin between the penis and the left hind-leg."

1944 David Allen is born in Hollywood, California. Allen will become a stop-motion animator whose work in bringing prehistoric creatures to life will be seen in such movies as *When Dinosaurs Ruled the Earth* (1971), *Flesh Gordon* (1972), *The Crater Lake Monster* (1977), *Caveman* (1981), *Doctor Mordrid* (1992) and *Prehysteria!* (1993).

1951 The *Polaris* crew is trapped by attacking dinosaurs on the *Tom Corbett, Space Cadet* television series.

1981 An expedition—led by Herman Regusters, an engineer at the Jet Propulsion Laboratory in Pasadena, California, and his wife Kia—sets out for the Pygmy village of Boa in the African Congo, seeking out a supposedly live sauropod dinosaur. The natives of Boa had reported seeing a giant *Apatosaurus*-like animal which they call Mokele-Mbembe.

~ 23 ~

4004 B.C. The Earth is "born" at 8:00 p.m. on this fine Sunday — or at least this is our planet's "creation" day as calculated in 1654 from the Book of Genesis by the Episcopal clergyman James Ussher, Archbishop of Armagh and Primate of all Ireland. Although incorrect by some billions of years, contemporary people will generally believe Ussher, for the date (and time) will become a marginal note in the King James version of the Bible.

1901 Having removed 270 pounds of flesh, Otto Hertz's busy team begins to raise the mammoth's abdominal skin, under which they find the entire tail. "The joy that possessed us at this new find was so great that, lowering the skin to the ground again, we gave three loud cheers."

1925 John E. Guilday is born in Pittsburgh, Pennsylvania. Interested in zoology and osteology from an early age, Guilday will become a paleontologist who does field work for the Pennsylvania Mammal Survey and an assistant preparator at the Carnegie Museum of Natural History. His contributions to the field of paleontology will be many, his most significant being demonstrating that changes in Late Pleistocene climate resulted in extensive changes in animal and plant life throughout the Eastern Seaboard. (Dies November 17, 1982.)

1956 At the Chicago Natural History Museum and after two years of work in the geology lab, Dr. Clifford C. Gregg, the museum's Director, uses a golden knife to cut the last piece of black shale collected from the Mecca Quarry in Indiana. Staff paleontologist Rainer Zangerl supervises to ensure the precision of Gregg's cut.

1963 The Natural History Museum of Los Angeles County opens its new vertebrate paleontology wing where research, mostly pertaining to marine mammals, birds and Ice Age vertebrates, is conducted. A major Mesozoic hall will be announced about this time, but does not become a reality for decades.

~ 24 ~

1991 *A Revision of the Parainfraclass Archosauria Cope 1869, Excluding the Advanced Crocodylia* is made available by author George Olshevsky through his company Publications Requiring Research. In this document Olshevsky has reorganized archosaurian classification according to his own vision, and also introduces some new taxa.

~ 25 ~

1877 Othniel Charles Marsh announces the new dinosaur names *Apatosaurus* and *Allosaurus* before the National Academy of Sciences in Washington, D.C.

1894 Elizaveta Ivanova Belajeva is born in Russia. She will become a paleontologist specializing in fossil mammals. In her long career Belajeva will carry out the work of systematizing, housing and cataloguing the vertebrate fossils in the collections of the Palaeontological Institute of the USSR Academy of Sciences. Also, she will author more than 80 scientific papers. (Dies March 21, 1983.)

1922 John A. Dorr, Jr., is born in Grosse Point, Michigan. "Jack's" career as a geologist and paleontologist will begin in summer 1947 with his discovery of a dentary of the primitive ungulate *Thryptacodon australis* in the Hoback Basin of Wyoming. Most of his work will deal with fossil mammals, especially uintatheres. In 1966 he will be elected president of the Society of Vertebrate Paleontology. (Dies April 1986.)

~ 26 ~

1963 Dino, the 60 feet long *Apatosaurus* balloon made by Goodyear Aerospace Company in Georgia and intended for the next Macy's annual Thanksgiving Day Parade, is successfully test flown in Akron, Ohio. The balloon has been made from 350 square yards of neoprene-coated nylon painted with 60 gallons of light green paint and inflated with 7,000 cubic feet of helium.

1996 The Natural History Museum of Los Angeles County officially unveils "The Dueling Dinosaurs"—skeletons of *Tyrannosaurus* and *Triceratops* mounted in dynamic battle poses by Peter May in its main foyer. Both skeletons comprise much original fossil material that has long been in the museum's collections. The *Tyrannosaurus* skull, too heavy for the mount and one of the largest ever found belonging to this dinosaur, is exhibited separately in a glass case.

The "Dueling Dinosaurs" exhibit— TYRANNOSAURUS REX *versus* TRICERATOPS PRORSUS*— mounted by Peter May. Photo by Don Glut. Courtesy Natural History Museum of Los Angeles County.*

~ 27 ~

1981   The expedition into the Congo led by Herman Regusters gets a first look at the live dinosaur they have been hunting — or so John Sack, the group's spokesman, will later claim in the December 16 edition of the Chicago *Sun-Times*. The creature is supposedly spotted in the swamps of Lake Tele, near the village of Boa. "It's dark-brownish in color," says Regusters. "The skin appears slick and smooth. It has a long neck and small snakelike head."

~ 28 ~

1862   Earl Douglass is born in Minnesota. In 1902 Douglass will join the staff of the Carnegie Museum of Natural History, his main interest being fossil mammals, most of his work involving collecting. Douglass' most important accomplishment will be made in 1908 when, exploring with Carnegie Museum director W. J. Holland the terrain along the Green River, north of Jensen, Utah, he discovers a huge femur. The bone belongs to the giant dinosaur *Diplodocus* and the site, later to be designated Dinosaur National Monument, will become known as the greatest single deposit of fossil dinosaur bones in the world. Douglass, his assistants and successors will work this site for many years, collecting some of the best Late Jurassic dinosaur specimens ever recovered.

1901 The body of the Siberian mammoth is made ready for transport to St. Petersburg, Russia. Parts of the beast are hauled away on ten horse-drawn sledges while smaller pieces are carried by some of the men.

1942 (John) Michael Crichton is born in Chicago. A future doctor of medicine, Crichton will also author novels including his most successful, *Jurassic Park* (1990), about dinosaurs cloned from DNA in the blood of insects preserved in Mesozoic amber. First advance comments will include this one from *Kirkus Reviews*: "A tornado-paced tale.... Fast, furious, and suspenseful.... A vastly entertaining science thriller.... A sure-fire bestseller." Indeed, that prediction will prove accurate, as over 10 million copies go into print. The book's success (and also the pleas and suggestions of readers) will inspire Crichton to write a sequel *The Lost World* (1995), so named in reference to the original novel of that title by Arthur Conan Doyle.

1981 Kia Regusters — she and her husband Herman reportedly having seen the large dinosaur-like animal they have been searching for on five separate occasions — snaps a photograph of it from a small boat floating on Lake Tele. According to her the picture is taken just as the creature descends back into the water. Herman Regusters records a 20-second audiotape claimed to be the "huge roaring trumpeting noise" that he and his wife have frequently heard in the lake. However, neither picture nor tape yet convince scientists that a dinosaur lives in the Congo.

~ 29 ~

1831 Othniel Charles Marsh is born in Lockport, New York. As a teen an amateur fossil collector, O. C. Marsh will soon receive a sizable amount of money in 1852 from his uncle, wealthy George Peabody, which the young man will use to finance his intellectual pursuits. In 1865 Marsh will arrange to get himself appointed Yale University's first Professor of Paleontology. From his office at Yale, he will dispatch collectors West where a wealth of new dinosaurs and other Mesozoic animals, to be named and described by Marsh, will be brought back. Much of this will be displayed at Yale's Peabody Museum of Natural History for which Marsh was mostly responsible. A major work will be his 1896 monograph "The Dinosaurs of North America." Although famous for his well publicized feud with Edward D. Cope, Marsh will be more noted for his many accomplishments. In addition to introducing the world to some of its best known dinosaurs, Marsh will become the first Vertebrate Paleontologist of the United States Geological Survey and president of the National Academy of Sciences. Marsh will die on March 18, 1899, one of the most well-known and respected scientists of his day.

1948   The Utah Field House of Natural History opens in Vernal. The museum building was completed in July of this year, beginning construction two years earlier from $200,000 of Department of Publicity and Industrial Development funds made available by Utah Governor Herbert B. Maw. Among the exhibits are fossil specimens from the Uinta Mountain and Basin area of Eastern Utah, skeletal casts by the Ward company (including a *Uintatherium* made from recycled paper money) and also numerous paintings of prehistoric life by Ernest Untermann, son of museum director G. E. Untermann. "Dippy," a cast of the Carnegie Museum's *Diplodocus carnegii* skeleton, graces one lawn. In later years the front lawn will display life-sized cement models of *Ceratosaurus*, *Stegosaurus* and *Camarasaurus* sculpted by Millard Fillmore Malin, and the back lawn a suite of full-scale models of extinct animals by Elbert H. Porter.

1950   *Two Lost Worlds* (Eagle-Lion Classics) opens, an adventure movie combining pirates with prehistoric animals. Most of the action consists of stock footage and outtakes, the enlarged reptiles and volcanic eruption once more originating with the original *One Million B.C.* of 1940.

~ 30 ~

1935   Elmer S. Riggs publishes a paper describing the skeleton of *Astrapotherium*, a hoofed mammal measuring about 9 feet in length, from the Oligocene of South America.

1951   John Gurche is born. Gurche will become an artist of ancient life specializing in dinosaurs and early man, much of his work done for the Smithsonian Institution, the National Geographic Society and the Denver Museum of Natural History. His illustrations will be seen in books, on posters, post cards and even postage stamps. Gurche's work will display a unique photographic quality that makes his restorations particularly life-like. In the 1980s he will pioneer and perfect the reconstruction of faces over skulls, utilizing this technique to recreate the countenances of early humans and other hominids.

~ 31 ~

1876   Edward D. Cope reads before the Academy of Natural Sciences of Philadelphia his paper naming various new species of carnivorous dinosaurs: *Aublysodon lateralis, Paronychodon lacustris, Laelaps incrassatus, L. explanatus* and *L. falculus*; the duckbilled dinosaurs *Dysganus encaustus, D. haydenianus, D. bicarinatus* and *D. peiganus*; duckbills *Diclonius pentagonus, D. perangulatus* and *D. calamarius*; horned dinosaur *Monoclonius crassus*; turtles *Compsemys imbricarius, C. variolosus* and *Polythorax missuriensis*; amphibian *Hedrosuchus sternbergii*; fishes *Ceratodus eruciferus, C. hieroglyphus* and *Myledaphus bipartitus*. The paper will be published on November 13. In later years some of these species will be referred to other genera.

1936   Bryan Patterson publishes a paper on the internal structure of the ear in some notoungulates (a group of hoofed mammals).

1939   Elmer S. Riggs publishes on a new specimen of the long-necked marine reptile *Elasmosaurus serpentinus*.

1954   The movie *Creature from the Black Lagoon*—utilizing its $18,000 Gill-Man costume—wraps up shooting, a good reason to celebrate Halloween.
Same day: There is no time for Space Patrollers to enjoy Halloween in the *Space Patrol* episode "The Iron Eaters of Planet X." Once again Tonga (Nina Bara) has been left to die in the Valley of the Dinosaurs!

1970   Angola issues a dozen postage stamps featuring indigenous fossils and minerals. These include the stromatolite *Stromatolites*, plant *Gondwanidium*, sand dollar *Rotula*, ammonite *Nostoceras*, shark *Procarcharodon*, lungfish *Microceratodus* and mosasaur *Angolasaurus*.

1993   Dinosaurs, though inaccurately depicted by 1990s standards, appear in the *Mark Trail* informational comic strip, prompting Gregory S. Paul to write a critical letter to his newspaper carrying the feature. The same day a far more accurate depiction of dinosaurs appears in Bill Watterson's *Calvin and Hobbes*, a humor strip which regularly features such animals.

NOVEMBER

~ 1 ~

1831   The Belfast Museum opens at College Square North in Northern Ireland, with an opening speech by Dr. Drummond. Most items displayed are natural history specimens collected by the Belfast Natural History Society. In 1929 the Museum will relocate to a new building, be renamed the Ulster Museum and become a national museum for Northern Ireland. Among the new displays will be mounted skeletons of the Great Irish Deer *Megaloceros* and the duckbilled dinosaur *Edmontosaurus*.

1950   *Prehistoric Women*, a low-budget "Stone Age" movie from Eagle-Lion, opens, starring Laurette Luez as sultry cavegirl Tigri. In addition to cave people of both sexes the movie features a brutish giant (Johann Peturrson), a never clearly seen flying creature and a mammoth (an elephant outfitted with oversized tusks by Ellis Burman).

Cave women 1950s style: (Clockwise) Tigri (Laurette Luez), Lotee (Joan Shawlee), Eras (Judy Landon), Tulle (Kerry Vaughn), Nika (Jo Carrol Dennison), Arva (Mara Lynn) and the Wise Old Lady (Janet Scott), in the camp cult film Prehistoric Women *(1950). © Eagle-Lion Classics.*

~ 2 ~

1903   Charles Whitney Gilmore joins the staff of the Smithsonian Institution. While working at the Smithsonian's new United States National Museum during the teen years of this century, Gilmore, in addition to doing his more technical work, will sculpt a series of ten dinosaur models for museum display. Copies of these models will be sent to museums across the country where they can be viewed by the public.

1989   Paleontologist Mary Wade of the Queensland Museum announces to the press that the fossil skull and crushed skeleton of a possibly new species of 100-million-year-old, 16-foot-long pliosaur — a short-necked plesiosaur — had been found by scientists in Australia. According to Wade, the skull constitutes one of the best-preserved fossils ever found on this continent.

~ 3 ~

1954   The movie *Gojira*, Toho's moody black and white, science-fiction movie about a mutated prehistoric reptile revived by atomic testing, opens in Japan. In this original version — inspired in part by the recently re-released *King Kong*, but more so by *The Beast from 20,000 Fathoms* — the monster is an allegory representing the atomic attacks on Japan in World War II. Godzilla is impossibly huge and sprays radioactive breath. In real life Godzilla is actor Haruo Nakajima wearing a very hot rubber suit and photographed in slow motion by Japanese special-effects maestro Eiji Tsuburaya. The movie will become an international sensation, smashing box-office records as Godzilla smashes Tokyo, and establishing Toho as a major player in the global film community. Though Godzilla is shown disintegrated in the climax of the film by an "Oxygen Destroyer," the movie spawns at least 21 sequels, the largest number of any single monster-movie series.

~ 4 ~

1927   Richard J. Seltin is born in Chicago, Illinois. Seltin will become a paleontologist, spending much of his early career at the then named Chicago Natural History Museum, where he will study Permian vertebrates under the supervision of Everett C. Olson, becoming Olson's field assistant in the Permian red beds of north-central Texas. In later years Seltin will be named Professor Emeritus of Natural Science at Michigan State University and Adjunct Curator of Vertebrate Paleontology at the MSU Museum. (Dies of heart disease, June 22, 1997.)

1985   An agreement is signed between the Ex Terra (or "From the Earth") Foundation of Edmonton, Canada, and the Chinese Academy of Sciences in Beijing, People's Republic of China, to launch a scientific exchange program between the two countries. This event will lead to a joint expedition to be called the Dinosaur Project, led by Philip J. Currie of the Royal Tyrrell Museum of Palaeontology, and Dong Zhiming of the Chinese Academy, to hunt fossils in both Canada and China. The expeditions will eventually yield a new wealth of dinosaurian remains including bones, eggs and nests, and a world-touring exhibition of the specimens collected.

1988   Universal Pictures releases the movie *The Missing Link*, the odyssey of a prehistoric hominid, the last of his species.

1997   The hit movie *The Lost World: Jurassic Park* makes its home-video debut.

~ 5 ~

1895   The Carnegie Museum of Natural History, named after Pittsburgh industrialist and philanthropist Andrew Carnegie, opens at a dedication of buildings housing the Carnegie Library of Pittsburgh, Carnegie Museum Hall and six galleries each for the exhibition of museum specimens and fine arts, every component having its own entrance.

1973   Paleontologist Alfred Sherwood Romer dies an accidental death, having been active in his beloved chosen field until the end.

~ 6 ~

1812   The first ichthyosaur (or "fish lizard") specimen — a well-preserved, 17-foot-long skeleton with skull — is dug from cliffs between Lyme Regis, a popular seaside resort and a place known for fossil "crocodiles," and Charmouth, England, and will be described two years later by Sir Everard Home. The specimen, at first thought to be a crocodile, is removed from the cliff by workmen hired by the Richard Anning family of Lyme Regis. According to local legend, the specimen was found in 1910 by Mary Anning, then just 11 years old. She was the daughter of Richard Anning who had been supplementing the family income by selling fossils to visitors to Lyme Regis (and who died in November of that same year). The two children, Mary and older brother Joseph, continue to collect and sell fossils to support their widowed mother, also named Mary. In 1847 Joseph's son will state that Joseph discovered the skull in 1811 and that he had told his sister where to look for the remainder of the skeleton so that she could take credit for the discovery.

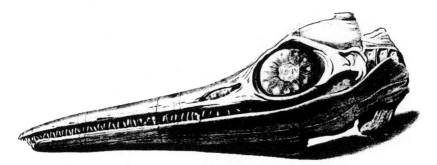

The first icthyosaur skull ever collected as illustrated in a paper by Sir Everhard Home, published in the PHILOSOPHICAL TRANSACTIONS OF THE ROYAL SOCIETY *for 1814.*

One of many prehistoric scenes painted by the prolific Ernest Untermann, Sr., this one depicts life during Morrison (Late Jurassic) times, with dinosaurs including (background) BRACHIOSAURUS *and* DIPLODOCUS, *and (foreground)* ORNITHOLESTES, STEGOSAURUS *and* ALLOSAURUS. *From a Dinosaur National Monument post card.*

1864   Ernest Untermann is born in Soldin, Brandenberg, Prussia. Untermann will work as a seaman, captain, author, translator, adventurer, geologist and fossil collector before finding his true vocation. While a young sailor, he will begin painting pictures, later getting a formal art education at the Chicago Art Institute, Layton School of Art in Milwaukee, and under artist William Heine. Moving to Vernal, Utah, in 1919, he and his son G. Ernest Untermann will become mine examiners at the Dyer Mine. While in Vernal, Untermann, Sr., will be best known as a painter of extinct reptiles, mammals and plants, but also known for present-day scenes of the Uinta area of Eastern Utah (some including cryptic images of prehistoric animals), the latter earning him the sobriquet "Artist of the Uintas." Untermann will produce over 100 pieces of art, all done in his own unique and somewhat quaint style, most of them for the Utah Field House of Natural History where he will serve as an unsalaried staff artist. (Dies January 10, 1956.)

1867   Richard Swann Lull is born in Annapolis, Maryland, into a military family (his father being on the teaching staff of the United States Naval Academy). Instead of following his family's wishes that he pursue a military career, Lull will instead gravitate toward science and athletics, eventually becoming an entomology teacher at Massachusetts Agricultural College. Intrigued by the great collection of Triassic tracks from the Connecticut Valley housed at nearby Amherst College, Lull will enter paleontology and

Slab containing Upper Triassic dinosaur footprints from the Connecticut Valley displayed at Amherst College, specimens such as this having inspired a young Richard Swann Lull. Photo by James O. Farlow.

achieve much success in this field. Working for the American Museum of
Natural History in 1899, he will dig fossils at Bone Cabin Quarry, Wyoming,
and help recover an *Apatosaurus* skeleton. At Yale University he will become
O. C. Marsh's successor, first as a Professor of Paleontology and then Director of the Peabody Museum, there displaying a flair for introducing new
exhibition techniques. Among his many scientific writings will be three classic monographs — "The Ceratopsia" (1907, co-authored with J. B. Hatcher
and Marsh), "Triassic Life of the Connecticut Valley" (1915, much revised in
1953) and "Hadrosaurian Dinosaurs of North America" (1942, co-authored
with Nelda E. Wright). Lull's continuing work on Connecticut Valley fossils will result in the first large body of knowledge concerning the earliest
North American dinosaurs. (Dies April 22, 1957.)

1913   The Natural History Museum of Los Angeles County opens to
the public in Exposition Park. Among the exhibits are some of the museum's
excellent collection of Ice Age vertebrate fossils recovered from Rancho La
Brea in nearby Hancock Park. In the 1970s these specimens will be relocated
to the new George C. Page Museum of La Brea Discoveries.

The fossil hall at the Natural History Museum of Los Angeles County in 1914, the year after the museum opened, includ-
ing in its display mounted skeletons of the ground sloth PARAMYLODON HARLANI and (juvenile) mastodon MAMMUT AMER-
ICANUS. Courtesy George C. Page Museum of La Brea Discoveries and Natural History Museum of Los Angeles County.

1935   Henry Fairfield Osborn, one of the true giants in the history of paleontology, dies peacefully this morning while sitting at his desk at Castle Rock, his expensive home atop a hill across the Hudson River from West Point, in Garrison, New York.

~ 7 ~

1872   Walter Granger is born in Vermont. Granger will become a paleontologist on the staff of the American Museum of Natural History. He will go on to do significant field work, particularly in the wealthy collection of dinosaurs and dinosaur eggs found in Mongolia. Among Granger's accomplishments will be the discoveries of the dinosaur *Alectrosaurus* and giant mammal *Balucitherium* (now *Indricothermium*).

1901   The Imperial Academy of Sciences team arrives at last in Mysova, Russia, with the remains of their prized mammoth.

1924   Henry Fairfield Osborn names the theropod *Velociraptor*. Relatively obscure to the public for almost 70 years, this sickle-clawed meat-eater will become one of the most famous dinosaurs of all with the 1993 release of the movie *Jurassic Park*.

1950   Michael K. (Keith) Brett-Surman is born in White Plains, New York. Brett-Surman will become a vertebrate paleontologist specializing in hadrosaurs or duckbilled dinosaurs (for which he will be nicknamed "Hadrosaur Mikey" and later re-nicknamed the more encompassing "Dinosaur Mikey"). He will name and describe new taxa including the duckbilled dinosaurs *Gilmoreosaurus* and *Secernosaurus*. Among his other accomplishments, Brett-Surman will curate 'the collection of dinosaur type specimens at the National Museum of Natural History. Also, he will co-edit (with James O. Farlow) *The Complete Dinosaur*, a comprehensive book published in 1997.

1955   *Life* magazine begins a new series of special cover features, "The Epic of Man," this one about early humans. The premiere article, "Man Inherits the Earth," is supplemented with paintings by Carroll Jones, Simon Greco and Antonio Petruccelli.

~ 8 ~

1981   The Field Museum of Natural History presents Dinosaur Day — a full day of films, lectures, demonstrations and other activities for dinosaur buffs, young and old alike. The event is so popular that an expanded Dinosaur Days will become an annual event and inspires other museums to schedule their own Dinosaur Days.

1986 Archaeologist Melinda Peak of Peak Associates, Inc., announces to the press the discovery of what may be the oldest manmade structure ever found in North America (carbon-dated as at least 9,750 years old) along a tributary of the Stanislaus River in Alpine County, near Bear Valley, California. Peak tells reporters, "It pushes back our knowledge about man and particularly his use of the mountains." The structural remains were found in August by Peak's mother Ann, the company's chief archaeologist, while excavating the site of a hydraulic project. The find may fuel debates as to how long ago humans migrated to North America. According to prehistory specialist Robson Bonnichson of the Center for the Study of Early Man in Orono, Maine, "This find shows that people were living in North America at the tail end of the Ice Age in houses, something we've always expected."

~ 9 ~

1911 Robert H. Denison is born in Summerville, Massachusetts. Future paleontologist Denison will become one of North America's outstanding specialists in fossil fishes, his accomplishments in this area including the two-volume *Handbook of Paleoichthyology*, each volume to be published, respectively, in 1978 and 1979. (Dies September 1985.)

1967 The *Batman* television series (ABC) airs the episode "How to Hatch a Dinosaur" wherein villain Egghead (Vincent Price) tries to hatch a giant dinosaur egg in a museum. The creature that emerges turns out to be hero Batman (Adam West) wearing a dinosaur outfit (actually a dragon get-up left over from the *Lost in Space* television show) over his regular costume. Adding ambience to the museum set are props first seen in the movie *Bringing Up Baby*.

1977 A retirement party is held for Dino, Macy's Thanksgiving Day parade giant *Apatosaurus* balloon, in the spacious entrance hall of the American Museum of Natural History. The Goodyear balloon hovers above the marble floor after six hours of inflation of 8,000 cubic feet of air. For five days Dino will meet reporters, dinosaur experts, even performing clowns and a circus band. When the swan-song festivities are over, Dino will take up permanent residence in Rockmart, Georgia, at a facility of the Goodyear Aerospace Company.

~ 10 ~

1852 Gideon Algernon Mantell dies in London. The door to his home in Lewes will be adorned with a brass plate bearing his name and the phrase, "Dr. Gideon A. Mantell, F.R.S., surgeon and geologist ... lived here. He discovered the fossil bones of the prehistoric Iguanodon in the Sussex Weald."

1878 Werner Janensch is born in Germany. Janensch will become a paleontologist in charge of fossil reptiles at the Berlin Museum. In 1911, accompanied by paleontologist Edwin Hennig, Janensch will begin major field work in the Upper Jurassic rocks of Tendaguru, Tanzania. The four-year expedition will result in the accumulation of 250 boxes of fossil specimens collectively weighing some 50 tons and the recovery of vertebrate skeletons including dinosaurs which, in many ways, are similar to some taxa found in the Morrison Formation of North America. These include the stegosaur *Kentrosaurus*, sauropod *Dicraeosaurus* and a new species of *Brachiosaurus*, which Janensch will name *B. brancai*. He finds evidence indicating that Europe and North America were joined during Jurassic times. A tribute to Janensch's work in the Tendaguru beds will be the enormous composite skeleton of *Brachiosaurus brancai* mounted at the Humboldt Museum für Naturkunde. (Dies 1969.)

1995 A combined French and British team led by ethnologist Michel Peissel, during the fourth week of an exploratory expedition, discover previously unknown "Stone Age" type horses living in a "lost valley" at Riwoche, in northeastern Tibet. The horses are pony-sized, about four feet high, with triangular heads. They have beige coats, bristly manes, black stripes on their backs and black lines on the lower legs. According to Peissel, "They looked completely archaic, like the horses in prehistoric cave paintings. We thought it was just a freak, then we saw they were all alike." The explorers dub the animal the "Riwoche horse."

~ 12 ~

1839 Richard Owen discusses the results of his study of a Pleistocene bone fragment, purchased by Richard Bright for the British Museum (Natural History), in a lecture to the Zoological Society of London. Owen incorrectly believes the bone (actually that of a flightless bird that Owen will later name *Dinornis*) to be that of a giant ostrich. The lecture is successful, its text later published under the title "On the bone of an unknown struthios bird from New Zealand."

1943 The holotype skeleton of the small herbivorous African dinosaur *Dysalotosaurus lettow-vorbecki*—which in 1977 will be made a species of *Dryosaurus*—becomes another war casualty when Allied bombers target the Humboldt Museum.

1988 Former Disney Studios animator Don Bluth's feature-length dinosaur cartoon *The Land Before Time*, released by Universal Pictures, has its world premiere. A group of youthful herbivorous prehistoric reptiles, led by an *Apatosaurus* named Littlefoot, tries to find a valley where they can live in peace, unmolested by the nasty meat eaters. In trying to reach this sanctuary they are pursued by Big Tooth, the *Tyrannosaurus*. The movie will be a big hit followed by a string of successful direct-to-home-video sequels.

~ 13 ~

1902 Gustav Ralph von Koenigswald is born in Berlin. Ralph's future work as a paleoanthropologist will mostly focus on fossil hominids, inspired by observations of Chinese pharmacists selling so-called "dragon bones" and teeth (actually vertebrate fossils) as remedies. A highlight of his career will be his appointment in 1937 to the Carnegie Foundation as a research associate. Koenigswald will name and describe a number of hominoid taxa based upon "dragon" remains, among them the giant *Giganopithecus blacki* (1935), *Sinanthropus officinalis* (1952) and *Hemanthropus peil* (1957), and also a new species of *Pithecanthropus*, which he names *P. dubius*.

1935 The *New York Sun* publishes a poem written by Charles R. Knight in which the artist expresses grief over and admiration for his recently deceased "second father," paleontologist Henry Fairfield Osborn.

1940 Walt Disney's *Fantasia*—with Igor Stravinsky's "Rite of Spring" visualized by Disney as a recreation of the first two billion years on Earth — opens on Broadway, released by Buena Vista. The feature-length cartoon has been filmed in Multiplane Technicolor with stereophonic sound. The movie will not be successful in this original release, music critics generally panning its choice of imagery over classical pieces, audiences apparently expecting something less esoteric from the creator of Mickey Mouse and Donald Duck. In decades to come, however, the film will become quite profitable for the Disney Studios, be re-released many times, acknowledged as both a masterpiece and a classic and declared a national treasure by the United States government.

~ 14 ~

1797 Charles Lyell is born at Kinnordy in Forfarshire, England. Lyell, a future wealthy baronet, will become a geologist and true revolutionary in the scientific community. Among his ideas will be that gigantic ice floes had once washed Europe's coast, this theory being in contrast with the older hypothesis that the so-called "Ice Age" was caused by sudden cooling of large areas of the world. Lyell's greatest work, *Principles of Geology*, to be published in three volumes from 1830 to 1833, will constitute the foundation for a new era of natural science, replacing old notions based on catastrophes, including the biblical Deluge, with concepts of actualism and evolution. (Dies February 22, 1875.)

1992 "Cave art" depicting Stone Age rhinos, horses and bison, praised by historians in 1990 as the most important cave paintings ever found in Europe, are exposed as frauds. Supposed to be 13,000 years old, the pictures had been discovered by history student Serafin Ruiz in a cave in the province of Alava, in the Basque country of northern Spain, the find making a tourist attraction of the area. The paintings are identified as fakes by a team including archaeologists and art experts from the Louvre in Paris, and from Australia and North America. A clue to the fakery is a misplaced horn on one animal, and leaving the legs of spiders and insects in the paintwork, fragile remains that could never have survived a span of 13,000 years.

~ 15 ~

1877 Paleontologist Othniel Charles Marsh names a new kind of dinosaur, the plated *Stegosaurus*, based on a skeleton that more than a century later will neither

STEGOSAURUS, *a plated dinosaur named and described by Othniel C. Marsh. This life-sized model, made by Louis Paul Jonas for the New York World's Fair (1964–65), is now displayed outside the visitors center at Dinosaur National Monument. Courtesy Sinclair Refining Company.*

be fully prepared nor described. Not understanding the kind of animal this is, Marsh has incorrectly interpreted the limb bones of this heavy terrestrial creature as adapted to an aquatic life style, imagining *Stegosaurus* to be an animal that was mainly a swimmer.

1994   The quarry in Haddonfield, New Jersey, where remains of *Hadrosaurus foulkii* were discovered, is designated a National Historical Landmark.

~ 16 ~

1907   Theodore H. Eaton is born in Boston, Massachusetts. Ted's future accomplishments as a paleontologist will include authoring the books *Evolution* and *Comparative Anatomy of the Vertebrates* and over 100 scientific papers ranging in subjects from invertebrates to dinosaurs to recent animals. In 1958 he will become curator of the lower vertebrate collection at the University of Kansas where he will remain until his retirement, and where he will publish exclusively on lower vertebrates. (Dies October 17, 1981.)

1952   David B. Weishampel is born in Lakewood, Ohio. Weishampel will become a paleontologist based at the School of Medicine, Johns Hopkins University, and specializing in dinosaurs. In 1991 he will, with Peter Dodson and Don Lessem, found The Dinosaur Society. After authoring and co-authoring numerous papers on dinosaurs, Weishampel will specialize further in the dinosaurs of Transylvania, and in the life and career of the eccentric Hungarian paleontologist Baron Franz Nopcsa.

~ 17 ~

1877   Samuel Wendell Williston writes to Othniel C. Marsh at Yale University from Como Bluff, Wyoming. Williston is excited about the potential for dinosaur collecting in the area and urges Marsh to begin excavations before men working for Marsh's rival, Edward D. Cope, can move in and start their own digging. Wisely, Marsh agrees.

~ 18 ~

1853   Her Majesty, Queen Victoria of England and her Consort, Prince Albert, visit Benjamin Waterhouse Hawkins' workshop on the Crystal

Palace grounds and inspect his models of prehistoric animals still under construction. According to a November edition of the *Crystal Palace Gazette*, "the Royal visitors were surprised at the antediluvian wonders which they were surrounded, the vestiges and tracing of an earlier world. The colossal Megatherium, gigantic Iguanodon, the Ichthyosaurus, with his screw-propeller tail, several Plesiosauruses, combining beast, bird, fish and reptile; the tapir, the elk, enormous toads and turtles, the inhabitants of this Earth before the abode of our first parent Adam; and many other anomalous creatures to us, filled the workshop." Apparently "We" are impressed.

1901 Construction begins on the main building of the Colorado (now Denver) Museum of Natural History in Denver. The museum had been incorporated the previous year as the Colorado Museum of Natural History. Its original, small yet excellent collection of natural history specimens, amassed by pioneer naturalist Edwin Carter Galbreath of Breckenridge, Colorado, was bought for the new museum by a group of Colorado citizens.

1918 Chow Minchin (formerly Zhou Min-zhen) is born in Shanghai. A future protégé of C. C. Young (aka Yang Zhungian), paleontologist Chow will co-found the journal *Vertebrata PalAsiatica* with Young in 1957 and organize and lead or co-lead numerous fossil-collecting expeditions into many parts of China. Among Chow's other accomplishments will be the publication of more than 100 scientific papers and five monographs on such topics as systematic paleontology, paleoclimatology, paleobiogeography, vertebrate biostratigraphy and Quaternary geology. In 1980 Chow will be elected to the Chinese Academy of Sciences and, succeeding Young, Director of the Institute of Vertebrate Paleontology and Paleoanthropology (IVPP). (Dies 1996.)

1985 Bill Watterson's *Calvin and Hobbes* comic strip debuts in newspapers. Though no dinosaurs are yet featured, the strip will soon become a haven for them. The strip is a humorous one, but Watterson will continue to seek out paleontological information in order to make his dinosaurs as accurate and up to date as possible.

1986 Chiodo Brothers Productions, mostly a special-effects house for motion pictures and television shows but also a production company, is incorporated. Before and after incorporation, the Chiodo brothers (Steven, Ed and Charlie) create effects for many projects utilizing prehistoric animals, including: "Runaway" music video; the television specials *Dinosaurs* and *Son* *of Dinosaurs* (in the latter transforming host Gary Owens into a dinosaur); television's second incarnation of *Land of the Lost* (also co-producers); *Zombie Dinos from the Planet Deltoid* video game; Cup-a-Noodles commercials for Japanese television; the movies *Pee Wee's Big Adventure* and *RoboCop*; and *Dinosaur Adventure*, a 360-degree educational film made for Iwerks Entertainment's Cinetropolis theme park.

Chicago Natural History Museum (now The Field Museum) paleontologists Eugene S. Richardson and Rainer Zangerl examine and chart black shale fossils from the Mecca Quarry, Indiana. Courtesy The Field Museum (neg. #GEO81466).

~ 19 ~

1912   Rainer Zangerl is born in Winterthur, Switzerland. Zangerl will become a vertebrate paleontologist who, in 1945, will join the Field Museum of Natural History as Curator of Fossil Reptiles and Amphibians. Zangerl will publish numerous papers on such animals and also author the popular booklet *Dinosaurs, Predator and Prey* (1956), about the museum's new *Gorgosaurus/ Lambeosaurus* skeletons exhibit. After retiring from the museum, Zangerl will remain relatively active in his field.

1924   Björn Kurtén is born in Vasa, Finland. Kurtén will become one of the leading paleontologists specializing in fossil mammals. He will author numerous popular books on the subject that make him known to the public, these including *The Ice Age*, *The Age of Mammals, Not from the Apes* (all 1972) and *The Cave Bear Story* (1976). He will also venture into fiction with novels such as the Ice Age–set *Dance of the Tiger* (1980) and *Singletusk* (1986). Kurtén will maintain that knowing the living animal is always central to understanding the fossil animal and, in later years, complain about what he calls the "fossil blindness" of some scientists. Among his many awards will be the twice won (1969 and

1980) Finnish state award for popular dissemination of knowledge and the UNESCO Kalinga award (1988) for the popularization of science. (Dies December 28, 1988.)

1993 In his office at the Museum of Northern Arizona in Flagstaff, Professor Edwin H. Colbert accurately and vividly records his memories for the first *Dinosaur Talks* audiocassette album and *Fossil Hunter* video.

1994 Roofing contractor Gary Byrd stops his car on a roadside near Dallas, Texas. He picks through some shale that had been exposed during the construction of a farm road. After 10 minutes of looking Byrd finds remains of the apparently oldest known duckbilled dinosaur in North America.

~ 20 ~

1877 The gigantic sauropod *Apatosaurus*, most familiar of all dinosaurs, is named by Othniel Charles Marsh, founded by him on a sacrum and some vertebrae discovered by Arthur Lakes in the Morrison Formation of Colorado. As the material represents a young animal, it will, for more than a quarter century, be regarded as different from the better known (and mature) *Brontosaurus*, which Marsh names later this year.

1890 Robert Armstrong, who will become a film actor starring in both *King Kong* and *The Son of Kong*, is born. (Dies April 24, 1973.) Coincidentally Bruce Cabot, the future leading man in *King Kong*, is born on this day in 1904. (Dies May 3, 1972.)

1980 *The Flintstone Comedy Show*, yet another spinoff of Hanna-Barbera's popular concept, premieres on NBC television. The new format comprises various regular segments, most prominent being those featuring the Flintstones themselves. Other segments include "The Frankenstones" as well as other recycled Hanna-Barbera features such as "Captain Caveman" (from the 1977 series *Captain Caveman and the Teen Angels*).

~ 21 ~

1947 Mark Hallett is born in Atherton, Australia. Inspired mostly by the artwork of Charles R. Knight, Hallett will become a top illustrator of prehistoric life, specializing in paintings of dinosaurs (especially sauropods) and Ice Age mammals (particularly sabertoothed cats). Original work by

Hallett will appear in myriad publications including *Zoobooks, Fossils, Science Digest, National Geographic* and others, books including *The New Dinosaur Dictionary, Dinosaurs Past and Present* (1987), *Dinosaurs: A Global View* (1991), *Seismosaurus: The Earth Shaker* (1995), *Puzzle of the Dinosaur Bird: The Story of Archaeopteryx* (1996), and *Dinosaurs: The Encyclopedia* (1997), various touring exhibitions and in museums, particularly the George C. Page Museum of La Brea Discoveries for which he does a mural of the Rancho La Brea fauna. Hallett will also become involved in films. His paintings will inspire Steven Spielberg during pre-production of *Jurassic Park*, and in the mid–1990s he will do character design for Disney Studio's dinosaur movie.

~ 22 ~

1988   Raymond A. Dart, among the most important figures in paleoanthropology, dies of a brain hemorrhage at a clinic near Johannesburg, South Africa. Born in 1893 in Toowang, Australia, Dart became an anatomist specializing in neuroanatomy. He revolutionized prevailing ideas about human evolution and demonstrated that Charles Darwin may have been correct in predicting that Africa would someday prove to be the place of mankind's origins. The latter was substantiated by Dart's interpretation in 1925 of a young apelike skull — found by his students the year before in limestone at Cape Province, then believed to be that of a baboon — as that of an early hominid. He named the fossil *Australopithecus africanus*, though it became informally known as the Taung child. For many years Dart's belief that the skull belonged to an ancestor of man was discounted by other scientists wanting to link man's origins to Asia. Future discoveries, however, proved Dart correct, earning him a place in history.

~ 23 ~

1914   Edgar Rice Burroughs starts writing *Pellucidar*, the first sequel to *At the Earth's Core*, set in a prehistoric world beneath the planet's surface.

1953   The so-called Piltdown Man — long a questionable fossil not exactly fitting onto mankind's family tree — is exposed in London as a forgery by anthropologists Kenneth Page Oakley of the British Museum (Natural History), Sherwood L. Washburn of the University of Chicago and J. S. Weiner of Oxford University. After restudying the existing specimens, the scientists have determined that the teeth had been filed rather than naturally worn down and the bone artificially colored. The skull has proven to belong to a fossil man while the jaw is that of a fairly recent anthropoid ape. The animal fossils found with the Piltdown remains have also been exposed as stained. All of the remains had obviously been planted for its "discoverers" to find. News of the fraud will spread rapidly around the world. Though various people will subsequently be suspected for perpetrating this hoax (including Charles Dawson, one of the finders of the original specimen, and author Arthur Conan Doyle), their true identities may forever remain a mystery.

~ 24 ~

1859 Charles Darwin's book *On the Origin of Species by Means of Natural Selection or the Preservation of Favoured Races in the Struggle for Life* is published in London. The book, expanded from an abstract, has taken 13 months and 10 days to write, during which time its author is in ill health. Many of the reviews are favorable, others damning, one of the most praising reviews written by Thomas H. Huxley for the London *Times*. The 1,250 copies of the book will sell out rapidly and the publisher promptly will order a second printing. The book will remain in print, a classic.

~ 25 ~

1825 Gideon Mantell is elected a Fellow of the Royal Society of London largely as a result of his work on the dinosaur *Iguanodon*.

~ 26 ~

1767 Quaker merchant Peter Collinson reports his analysis of the fossils recovered by George Croghan's team at Big Bone Lick at a meeting of the Royal Society of London. According to Collinson, the tusks are similar to those of modern African and Asian elephants, but the teeth "belong to another species of elephant not yet known which is probably supported by browsing on trees and shrubs and other vegetable foods."

1993 Paleontologist Everett Claire Olson dies in his Los Angeles home after a period of deteriorating health following a serious throat operation the year before. "Ole" was born in 1910 in Waupaca, Wisconsin. A student of Alfred S. Romer at the University of Chicago prior to Romer's departure to Harvard, Olson spent 34 years of his professional life at the University. Around 1933-34, unknown to many of his colleagues, he made extra money moonlighting as a barker outside "The World A Million Years Ago" attraction at the Chicago World's Fair. His main focus was upon Permian tetrapods and ecosystems, this interest remaining until his death. Olson's field work with Romer in the Permian of Texas and the challenges it presented led to major changes in the discipline of paleobiology. The symposium volume *A Cold Look at the Warm Blooded Dinosaurs*, edited by Roger D. K. Thomas and Olson, offered papers collectively constituting the first major criticism of the hot topic of endothermic dinosaurs.

~ 27 ~

1906 James Harrison Quinn is born in Ainsworth, Nebraska. In 1930 Quinn will be employed at the Field Museum of Natural History as a preparator and assistant in paleontology. Ten years later he will publish a paper on using liquid rubber for preparing brain casts, an article which is destined to become a standard. Quinn's main interest will be fossil horses, though he will also work with fossil invertebrates and in geology. On September 14, 1977, while attempting to retrieve a mastodon tooth from a ledge on an outcrop in Cherry County, Nebraska, Quinn will be struck in the head by a dislodged rock. Falling, he will die about a half hour later of massive internal bleeding.

1907 L. Sprague de Camp is born. De Camp will become one of the more prominent writers of science fiction and fantasy stories. "A Gun for Dinosaur," first published in the March 1956 issue of *Galaxy* magazine, will be reprinted and adapted to other media such as comic books and radio drama. In addition to fiction, de Camp will also write factual texts on dinosaurs, including the book *The Day of the Dinosaur* (1968), co-authored with his wife Catherine Crook de Camp.

1913 Edgar Rice Burroughs begins writing the caveman novel *Nu of the Neocene* (aka *The Eternal Lover* and *The Eternal Savage*).

~ 28 ~

1894 Otto Zdansky is born in Vienna, Austria. Zdansky will be inspired to become a paleontologist by the 1916 discovery of various fossil mammals in eastern China by Swedish geologist Johan Gunnar Anderson. During the early 1920s, Zdansky will spend much time in China working at the Peking Man Cave site at Zhoukoudian (where he will find hominid fossils), on late Cenozoic mammal faunas from Henan and Shanxi, also Eocene mammals and Jurassic dinosaurs from Shandong. Subsequently he will publish a series of monographs on fossil vertebrates collected by him in China. Zdansky's monographs on fossil mammals, published in *Palaeontologia Sinica*, will be regarded as classics. (Dies December 26, 1988.)

1924 Raymond Dart obtains the fossil skull and brain cast belonging to a juvenile so-called "missing link" from Taung, South Africa.

1954 In "The Tesseract Prison of Planet X," television's *Space Patrol* heroes escape more giant reptiles in the Valley of the Dinosaurs and, utilizing a fourth-dimensional quirk of time travel, manage to capture — at least for now — the nefarious Prince Baccarratti (Bela Kovacs).

1963 Dino, the *Apatosaurus* balloon, makes its debut "flight" high above the streets of New York City in Macy's 37th annual Thanksgiving Day Parade near the American Museum of Natural History. Twenty-two handlers guide the dinosaur's slow journey to Herald Square. Originally intended to make only five parade appearances, Dino will continue to appear — skipping 1971 because of severe ice storms — until his last parade in 1976.

Dino the dinosaur balloon is test flown in Akron, Ohio. Photo by UPI, courtesy Macy's Thanksgiving Day Parade.

1975   Dale A. Russell names and describes a new species of *Globidens*, a mosasaur from the Upper Cretaceous of South Dakota.

1992   Lensing begins on producer Roger Corman's *Carnosaur*, a low-budget horror movie featuring genetically engineered dinosaurs, based on a novel that predates Michael Crichton's similarly themed *Jurassic Park*. Corman's intent is to get his film completed and in release before the movie version of *Jurassic Park*. He will succeed, *Carnosaur* bowing about a week before its big-budget competition and, in that time, grossing some 10 times its cost.

~ 29 ~

1939   In the *Alley Oop* daily comic strip, our time-traveling caveman hero, dressed like a Greek soldier, witnesses the end of the Trojan War. More of Oop's "Odyssey," including meeting Hercules, will follow.

~ 30 ~

1946   The Royal Society of South Africa arranges for a major scientific gathering to honor the return from the United States of Robert Broom, now an honored and world renowned scientist, and to publish a *Robert Broom Commemorative Volume*, all in honor of the man's 80th birthday. The meeting includes a dinner in which Broom is the honored speaker and a visit to the cave where he had collected fossils of early hominids. The commemorative book includes chapters written by the leading figures in anthropology, Broom and his aid writing a chapter on new kinds of mammal-like reptiles.

1996   Kaiju-Con N.Y., a fan convention devoted to "Kaiju" (a Japanese word literally meaning "great strange beast" but usually meaning "monster") movies, is held over a three-day period at the New Yorker Hotel, sponsored by Daikaiju Enterprises & Productions ("Daikaiju" meaning "*big monster*"). Activities include panel discussions, a trivia contest, prizes, guest speakers and movie screenings. Concerning the latter, Toho Co. Ltd., producers of the Godzilla movies, subsequently will file a civil action suit against the organizers of the event for screening *Gojira tai Destroyah*, a movie not yet released in the United States. Toho will claim copyright infringement and argue that the screening has damaged the Japanese company's ability to get an American release for the film.

DECEMBER

~ 1 ~

1879   The world's most famous dinosaur name, *Brontosaurus*, is published by Othniel Charles Marsh, founded upon the almost complete skeleton of an adult animal. Early next century this genus will be referred to *Apatosaurus*, though the public continues to use the "junior synonym" *Brontosaurus* for many decades to come.

Skeleton of the giant sauropod APATOSAURUS EXCELSUS *(formerly called* BRONTOSAURUS*), the first large dinosaur skeleton ever to be mounted, now remounted in the American Museum of Natural History's Hall of Saurischian Dinosaurs. Photo by Don Glut, courtesy American Museum of Natural History.*

1901 Walt Disney is born in Chicago, Illinois. Disney will develop a fascination for dinosaurs and other prehistoric animals reflected in many of the animated and live-action movie and television projects he will produce. His animated feature, *Fantasia* (1940), will include the "Rite of Spring" sequence, a history of life on Earth set to the music of Igor Stravinsky. Disney will feature dinosaurs in the first CinemaScope cartoon *Grand Canyonscope* (1954, starring Donald Duck); on his *Disneyland* (ABC) television show in the episodes "Monsters of the Deep" (1955) and "Disneyland Goes to the World's Fair" (1964); also during the 1950s, on *The Mickey Mouse Club* (ABC). Soon after the closing of the New York World's Fair in 1964, he will relocate the Audio-Animatronics dinosaurs he featured there to his Disneyland theme park. After Disney's death in 1966, the studio will continue this tradition with movies such as the comedy *One of Our Dinosaurs Is Missing* (1976), *Baby... Secret of the Lost Legend* and *My Science Project* (both 1985) and the television sit-com parody *Dinosaurs* (1991). In the mid–1990s the studio will begin production on a major movie featuring computer-generated dinosaurs.

1940 Grayson Meade reports on a new fossil site discovered in Howard County, New Mexico.

1960 A year after anthropologist Mary Leakey's discovery of a robust, 1.75-million-year-old man-ape (to be named *Zinjanthropus boisei*) in the Olduvai Gorge, Tanzania, anthropologist husband Louis Leakey finds the nearly complete braincase of a more humanlike and gracile hominid in the same locality. Louis believes this second find represents a true human rather than an advanced ape. As primitive tools have been found with the specimen (also with *Z. boisei*), Louis Leakey names it *Homo habilis*, meaning "handy" man.

~ 2 ~

1929 The original skull of Peking Man, contained uncrushed within a large matrix block, is excavated by W. C. Pei (Pei Wen-chung) at Choukoutien, China. Another smaller block is also cut away.

1951 Don Lessem is born. The future "Dino Don" and a Knight Science Journalism Fellow at M.I.T., Lessem will become a professional writer specializing in dinosaurs. Lessem will travel the world researching dinosaur digs and interviewing paleontologists. He will author numerous popular articles and some 20 books (e.g., *Dinosaurs Rediscovered*; *The Complete T. Rex*, with John R. Horner; *The Dinosaur Society Dinosaur Encyclopedia*, with the present writer; *Raptors* and others), and work with producers of TV documentaries about these Mesozoic animals. Lessem will be a founder of The Dinosaur Society and organize "The Dinosaurs of Jurassic Park," a popular touring exhibit that generates profits channeled into dinosaur research. *People* magazine will dub him with a second nickname, "Mr. Dinosaur."

~ 3 ~

1967 In "A Time to Die," a final-season episode of TV's *Voyage to the Bottom of the Sea*, the *Seaview* is transported back through time to the Mesozoic Era. Dinosaur stock footage comes courtesy of the movies *The Animal World* (1956) and — yes, again — the 1960 version of *The Lost World*.

~ 4 ~

1941 The holotype skeleton of *Tyrannosaurus rex*, purchased from the American Museum of Natural History, arrives at its new home, the Carnegie Museum of Natural History. The American Museum had originally possessed two skeletons, this one moved for protection in the event of a possible Axis bombing raid on New York City.

1968 Paleontologist James A. Jensen (aka "Dinosaur" Jim) finds the skull of the mammal-like reptile *Lystrosaurus* in Antarctica, this constituting hard evidence supporting the theory of "continental drift."

1984 Chris Mays, President of Dinosaur International Corporation, visits Grand Junction, Colorado, and meets with board members of the Museum of Western Colorado, local businessmen and community leaders to discuss a permanent dinosaur exhibit. This meeting will lead to an eventual permanent facility, Dinosaur Valley, which, among its displays, will be some of Dinamation's robotic creatures.

1991 A cast of the skeleton of the enormous sauropod *Barosaurus* is mounted in the spacious Roosevelt Hall at the American Museum of Natural History. The skeleton has been assembled by former Royal Tyrrell Museum of Palaeontology mount-maker Peter May, rearing up on its hind legs as if protecting its young from an attacking *Allosaurus*. The pose will prove to be controversial, not all paleontologists believing that these giant sauropods could assume such a tripodal stance.

1992 Dennis Etier, Professor of Anthropology at the University of California at Berkeley, announces at an annual meeting of the American Anthropological Association the discovery of two smashed fossil skulls that may help to fill an important gap in man's evolution. The skulls, found by co-worker Li Tianyuan near the Han River in Hubei province, central China, apparently represent large adults, one male and the other probably male. Found with the skulls were various quartz tools and flakes. The find is pronounced the most important remains of fossil man found in China since the discovery of Peking Man.

~ 5 ~

1832 Richard Owen's paper on the armored *Hylaeosaurus*, the third dinosaur and first ankylosaur to be named and described, is published. It has been established on a partial postcranial skeleton with armor found by Gideon Mantell earlier this year in a block of stone in a quarry at Tilgate Forest, Sussex, England.

1916 Two *Corythosaurus* skeletons collected along the Red Deer River in Alberta, Canada, by Charles H. Sternberg are lost during World War I when the *Mount Laurel*, the ship carrying them, is sunk by a German U-boat.

1941 Another shipment of important fossils becomes a casualty of a world war, this time the second. A special United States Marine train transporting the hidden original remains of Peking Man, comprising only a few handfuls of fossil material, sets out from Peking in anticipation of a possible Japanese invasion of this major city. After a series of rail and road connections, the bones' final destination is to be the American ocean liner *President Harrison*, which will transport them safely to the United States.

1996 Pebbles and Bam-Bam, the grown-up children of the Flintstones and Rubbles, respectively, have their first blessed event — twins — in the network premiere of Hanna-Barbera's new animated movie *Hollyrock-a-Bye Baby* (ABC television). Raquel Welch, no newcomer to prehistoric storylines, has provided the voice of one of the characters.

~ 6 ~

1925 The animated cartoon *The Bonehead Age* debuts in movie theaters. Produced by Paul Terry, this short is one of many silent comedy shorts having a prehistoric setting.

1928 Edgar Rice Burroughs starts writing *Tarzan at the Earth's Core*. It will become a favorite of fans of both the Tarzan and Pellucidar series.

1929 The original Peking Man specimen is taken to its namesake city. Here it will be subjected to a series of major studies by Franz Weidenrich. The authority on Asian fossils will author three sizable publications on Peking Man — *The Dentition of Sinanthropus, The Extremity Bones of Sinanthropus* and *The Skull of Sinanthropus*—concluding that it does represent a true, albeit primitive, man.

1942 John M. Harris is born in London, England. Harris will become a paleontologist specializing in fossil mammals. He will be appointed both an administrator and Chief Curator of the George C. Page Museum of La Brea Discoveries.

1969 The significant discovery of remains of *Lystrosaurus*—a genus previously known only from Africa and Asia — in Antarctica is announced in the *New York Times*.

Designer Jack Oehlert inspects a TYRANNOSAURUS REX model, one of the creatures planned for the Lion Country Safari prehistoric animals attraction.

1977 A total of 35 to 40 full-scale fiberglass replicas of dinosaurs and other prehistoric animals are shipped from northern California, where they have been manufactured, to their new home, the entertainment center at Lion Country Safari, a combination wild animal preserve and tourist attraction in Irvine. The figures, designed by Jack Oehlert of Long Beach, California, are intended to be part of a permanent educational exhibit to open in early 1978, then rescheduled to 1979.

~ 7 ~

Louis Dollo's drawing, first published in 1883, of the skeleton of the herbivorous dinosaur IGUANODON BERNISSARTENSIS.

1851 Charles Dickens completes writing the first chapter of *Bleak House* with its *Megalosaurus* reference.

1857 Future paleontologist Louis Dollo is born in Lille, France. An engineer, Dollo will find his real interests in zoology and geology. In 1882 Dollo will travel to Brussels, Belgium. There he will become interested by the many fine *Iguanodon* skeletons being excavated from a coal mine in Bernissart and deposited in the Institut Royal des Sciences Naturelles de Belgique. Nine years later Dollo will be made Conservator at this museum and in 1909 Professor of Paleontology at the University of Brussels. Most of Dollo's professional life will be devoted to the Bernissart *Iguanodon* specimens, arranging for their cleaning, preparation and eventual mounting at the museum in Belgium. Dollo will believe that these specimens represent a second and more robust species — later named *Iguanodon bernissartensis*. Among his discoveries from these remains will be that a spike-like bone identified by Richard Owen as a nose horn is actually a thumb. From Dollo's work on these skeletons, much will be learned about the genus *Iguanodon* and the environment in which it once lived. The skeletons, mounted as a group, will become a lasting monument to his work on this dinosaur. (Dies April 19, 1933.)

1941   The Japanese attack on the United States naval base at Pearl Harbor, Hawaii, will live in infamy for yet another reason — interrupting delivery of the Peking Man fossils to the American ocean liner *President Harrison*. The remains are never seen again, possibly lost aboard a capsized vessel, or confiscated by Japanese who sell them back to the Chinese to be ground up as "dragon bones."

1962   History (and, in a way, prehistory) repeats with another Japanese attack — this one by a new giant prehistoric monster as the movie *Varan the Unbelievable* (Japanese title: *Daikaiju Baran*) opens in the United States. Varan is a Godzilla type reptile played again by Godzilla-actor Haruo Nakajima. In the Japanese version only, the monster flies via winglike membranes revealed under its arms.

1996   The general-audience version of *Dinosaur Valley Girls* premieres on USA cable television's *Up All Night* show, with commercial-break commentary by comedian Gilbert Gottfried.

~ 8 ~

1906   United States President Theodore Roosevelt declares that a vast area of land in southeastern Arizona, best known for its countless specimens of Late Triassic fossil logs, be designated Petrified Forest National Monument, this being the second such monument to be established in the United States. In 1962 the area will become a national park.

1943   *Tarzan's Desert Mystery* opens. Though Tarzan had encountered prehistoric animals in some of Edgar Rice Burroughs' novels and would also meet them in comic strips, comic books and on television, this RKO motion picture is the first and only movie to include them (courtesy of more stock footage and outtakes from *One Million B.C.*).

1954   The Observation Pit, a circular building at the west end of Hancock Park at Rancho La Brea, is dedicated to Chester Stock who supervised its construction shortly before his death. The exhibit allows visitors to look down to view bubbling tar and fossil bones stuck in a partially excavated deposit.

1989   William Stout's "Lost Worlds" exhibition of his artwork depicting prehistoric life debuts at the Art Gallery Store, in Pasadena, California.

Curated by Joan Kahn, the show includes "Set and costume designs, children, comic, and neo-pop illustrations, posters and wildlife paintings."

1994 As rain stalls the excavation of the hadrosaur specimen found last month by Gary Byrd, Charles E. Finsley tells a reporter, "We have a duckbill as old as the one in China. That shows development might have taken place here as well as in China…. It puts Texas in the running for possibly the beginning of the duckbilled dinosaurs."

~ 9 ~

1995 *Gojira tai Destroyah* ("Godzilla vs. Destroyah"), the 19th and last of Toho Co.'s "Godzilla" movies, is released in Japan. The series comes to an explosive end as Godzilla — after killing the monster Destroyah, of course — self destructs, consumed by his own inner radioactive energy. With closure the Godzilla property will shift to other shores as a big-budget North American movie about the character goes into pre-production.

1998 Professor Hilary Deacon of Stellenbosch University, England, announces to the media two important fossil discoveries in South Africa: The first is the skeleton of a gorgonopsid, a 250-million-year-old therapsid — a lizardlike reptile related to mammals — in the Karoo Desert. The second, in a lime quarry west of Johannesburg, is a 3.6-million-year-old skeleton of an *Australopithecus africanus*, a 4-foot hominid.

~ 10 ~

1676 Peter Collinson repeats his report on the fossils found at the Big Bone site before members of the Royal Society of London.

1998 A reconstructed skeletal cast of the newly described, apparently fish-eating dinosaur *Suchomimus tenerensis* goes on display at the Chicago Children's Museum at Navy Pier. This spectacular animal, almost as big as *Tyrannosaurus rex*, was found earlier this year by Paul C. Sereno and colleagues in the Sahara Desert. *Suchomimus* is characterized by such features as a long, crocodile-like head (its name means "crocodile mimic"), large fore-claws and elongated spines above the hip region. Augmenting the display is a painting of the animal in life by artist Michael W. Skrepnick and a model by sculptor Stephen A. Czerkas.

~ 11 ~

1933 Elmer S. Riggs publishes a preliminary description of a new sabertoothed marsupial recovered from Pliocene-age rocks in Argentina.

Same day: Sharat Kumar Roy publishes a paper naming and describing a new trilobite from the Devonian of southern Illinois.

1993 *Gojira tai Mechagojira* premieres in Japan. This latest in the second wave of Godzilla movies is significant for its introduction of new and revamped incarnations of Godzilla's robot double Mechagodzilla, the giant supersonic pterosaur Rodan and also Godzilla's son, "Little Godzilla."

~ 12 ~

1960 Rick Yager's Sunday comic strip *Little Orvy*, about a precocious and very imaginative little boy, begins continuity involving time travel and prehistoric animals.

1992 A mastodon skeleton, with tens of thousands of still-living, 11,000-year-old bacteria in its rib cage, is found in Livingston County, Newark, Ohio. The bones are discovered by workers turning a peat bog into a lake for the Burning Tree Golf Course. The single-cell organisms are believed to be remnants of the mastodon's last meal. Gerald Goldstein of Ohio Wesleyan University's Biology/Microbiology Department will identify two strains of *Enterobactor cloacae*, a bacterium commonly found in mammalian intestinal tracts. This will suggest that the animal had dined on leaves, water lily seeds, moss and swamp grass rather than twigs from spruce trees as commonly believed. In the Associated Press news item carrying the story, Goldstein will state, "This bacteria could be the oldest living organism ever found."

~ 13 ~

1939 Akiko Wakabayashi is born. Wakabayashi will become an actress in Japanese motion pictures. She will be best remembered by fans of prehistoric-monster movies for her roles of the pie-dropping Tamiye in *King Kong vs. Godzilla* and the prophetess Princess Salno in *Ghidrah the Three Headed Monster* (1965), the latter including Godzilla and Rodan on its monster roll call.

~ 14 ~

1858 Academy of Natural Sciences of Philadelphia member William Parker Foulke donates the partial skeleton of the first certain North American dinosaur bones which he had found in a marl pit at Haddonfield, New Jersey, to the Academy. At the same time Joseph Leidy officially begins the study of dinosaurs in North America by proposing the new name *Hadrosaurus foulkii* for the specimen, *Hadrosaurus* thereby becoming the second dinosaur named in North America and the first known from good skeletal material. Leidy states, "*Hadrosaurus* was most probably amphibious; and though its remains were obtained from a marine deposit, the rarity of them in the latter leads us to suppose that those in our possession had been carried down the current of a river, upon whose banks the animals lived." The remains will soon be exhibited at the Academy in open boxes; in 1868 Benjamin Waterhouse Hawkins will reconstruct the skeleton for display at this institution.

1964 A formal ceremony designating Rancho La Brea a National Natural Landmark by the National Park Services, United States Department of the Interior, is held in Hancock Park. The bronze plaque commemorating this event, already installed and dated 1963, states: "This site possesses exceptional value as an illustration of the nation's natural heritage and contributes to a better understanding of man's environment."

This huge TRICERATOPS *was the last of the dinosaur figures to arrive at Lion Country Safari.*

1977 Lion Country Safari in Irvine, California, receives its last shipment of life-sized replicas of prehistoric animals, including an 1,800-pound *Triceratops*. Present to greet the three-horned dinosaur are paleontologists Richard Estes and Robert M. Sullivan. Although the plan is to open this exhibit in early 1978, the opening will never happen. The prehistoric figures will be left to deteriorate gradually in the staff parking lot. Eventually Lion Country Safari itself will suffer extinction.

~ 15 ~

1984   A brand new Gojira ("Godzilla")—after a predecessor had starred in a long series of mŏvies, becoming more friendly, comical and even heroic—makes its Japanese debut in Toho Co., Ltd.'s serious movie *Gojira* (1984). The film, in some ways both a remake of and sequel to the 1954 movie, once again features Godzilla as a menace. Regarding all past Godzilla sequels as if they did not exist, Toho now begins a new (and equally successful) movie series. Special effects are by Teruyoshi Nakano.

1989   The National Geographic Society announces the discovery of a collection of rare, 225-million-year-old (Late Triassic) fossils in Richmond, Virginia. The excellently-preserved fossils, thus far of taxa unique to North America, were found by paleobiologist Hans Dieter-Sues of the National Museum of Natural History and geologist Paul E. Olsen (who found the site while looking for gas and oil in the area) of Columbia University's Lamont-Doherty Geological Observatory. These remains of mammal-like reptiles include eleven tiny (less than a centimeter in length) jaws of cynodonts, reptiles superficially resembling lizards but which seem to be ancestral to mammals. Until now only a few cynodont scraps had been found in the United States, most of the good material collected in Argentina, Brazil and South Africa.

~ 16 ~

1965   *The Munsters* television show runs the episode "Underground Munster." Spot, the family's pet fire-breathing dinosaur, feelings hurt after being scolded by family head Herman Munster (Fred Gwynne), lumbers away from home and hides in the sewers, thereby creating an embarrassment for the town mayor. (Spot is sometimes seen as a prop *Tyrannosaurus* head left over from the 1957 Universal-International movie *The Land Unknown*.)

~ 17 ~

1908   Willard F. Libby, future discoverer of the Carbon-14 method of dating old objects, is born on a farm near Grand Valley, Colorado.

1959   One of the best examples of live lizards portraying prehistoric animals in a movie is seen with today's release of *Journey to the Center of the Earth* (20th Century–Fox), based on the classic science-fiction novel by Jules Verne. Rhinoceros iguanas sporting rubber dorsal fins (and photographed in slow motion) make fairly convincing representations of the Permian period "mammal-like reptile" *Dimetrodon.*

1968 Cryptozoologists Ivan T. Sanderson and Bernard Heuvelmans investigate the so-called Minnesota Iceman, a frozen manlike figure being exhibited by custodian Frank D. Hansen as a carnival attraction. Mystery has enshrouded the Iceman and its origins. A bullet wound suggests that the creature, if real and human, may have been murdered. Though Smithsonian Institution scientists will later declare the Iceman a dummy, Sanderson and Heuvelmans accept the figure as the authentic remains of a species of Neandertal Man. Though only viewing the creature through obscuring ice, Heuvelmans (a Belgian zoologist and author of many books about unknown animals) will designate it a new species in the article "Notice on a specimen preserved in ice of an unknown form of living hominid: *Homo pongoides,*" published in a 1969 issue of the *Bulletin of the Royal Institute of Natural Sciences of Belgium.* Sanderson, in an issue of *Genus* later the same year, will publish a more cautious interpretation of the creature. Soon, the Iceman will no longer be available for examination.

~ 18 ~

1877 The American Museum of Natural History opens its doors to the public. The fourth floor, completed at a cost of $700,000, does not yet have a fossil hall *per se,* although some fossils are displayed among the museum's many geology exhibits. A mastodon skeleton will be acquired by the museum and mounted in 1887.

1879 Harry Govier Seeley announces the new armored dinosaur *Syngonosaurus* based on vertebrae found in the Greensand of Cambridge, England. This genus will later be regarded as a "junior synonym" of *Acanthopholis.*

1892 Sir Richard Owen, who bequeathed the word "dinosaur" to the world, dies in England.

1912 Charles Dawson and Arthur Smith Woodward announce to the Geological Society of London the discovery of what they claim to be the skull and lower jaw of the earliest known human fossil. The remains were found in a shallow gravel pit near Piltdown, a village near Sussex, England. Discovered with the specimen were crude stone implements and fossils of various Ice Age animals. The hominid specimen will be scientifically named

Eoanthropus dawsoni, though the public will call it Piltdown Man. This supposed "missing link" between ape and man seems to confirm the notion of British supremacy in the world with the earliest man having evolved on English soil. This assessment will be dramatically turned around in 1953.

1932   Abel Brillanceau is born at Menomblet, Vendée, France. During his future career as a geologist, he will author numerous scientific articles. Though not a paleontologist, he will become a member of a multinational paleontological expedition to Cameroon, West Africa. In 1989 he will die in the field of spinal malaria caught during that expedition.

1947   Steven Spielberg is born. A future lover of dinosaurs, Spielberg will produce and sometimes direct a number of popular movies featuring such animals, these including the blockbuster *Jurassic Park* (1993) and its sequel *The Lost World: Jurassic Park* (1997), *The Flintstones* (1995) and the animated *Land Before Time* (1988) and *We're Back: A Dinosaur's Story!* (1993). Spielberg will also generously contribute funds for dinosaur research.

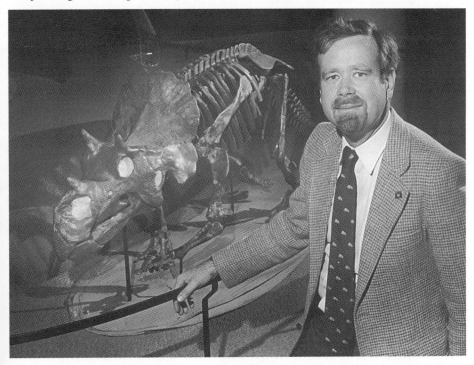

Paleontologist Peter Dodson with the mounted skeleton of AVACERATOPS LAMMERSI, *a small horned dinosaur he named and described. Photo by David Bennett, courtesy Academy of Natural Sciences of Philadelphia.*

1986   Peter Dodson announces *Avaceratops lammersi*, a new 75-million-year-old horned dinosaur he has named and described, at a press conference held at the Academy of Natural Science of Philadelphia. At the same time Dodson unveils a mounted reconstructed skeleton of the animal. The skeleton is seven and a half feet long and three feet high at the hips. The skull has short horns and a solid, fan-shaped frill.

1995   A cave possessing several vast galleries showcasing 300 perfectly-preserved cave paintings of animals made by early man 17–20,000 years ago is found at Valon-Pont-d'Arc in southern France. Among the animals depicted are rhinoceros, reindeer, bear, mammoth, hyena, lion, horse, bison and ox, as well as the first prehistoric depictions of panther and owl. One painting depicts two rhinoceroses of an extinct species rubbing horns. Creatively a bump in the rock wall adds three-dimensional bulk to a picture of a mammoth. A bear skull, set down on a large rock in the middle of one gallery, may be some kind of primitive altar. The find will be hailed as one of the archaeological discoveries of the century.

~ 19 ~

1965   *Kaiju Daisenso* ("The Great Monster War") premieres in Japan. The movie is significant in being the first in which Godzilla travels to another planet where he and fellow monsters Rodan (a huge pterosaur) and Mothra, now serving as gigantic and bizarre "superheroes," battle the three-headed space monster Ghidrah. The movie will be released in the United States on July 20, 1970, as *Monster Zero*.

~ 20 ~

1921   *The Katzenjammer Kids* newspaper comic strip has a story with a dinosaur theme, now written and drawn by Harold H. Knerr. The mischievous Kids, Hans and Fritz, again get themselves into trouble, this time creating a panic while masquerading in a dinosaur costume.

1940   "Tuk, Cave Boy," a comic-strip feature drawn, inked, lettered and possibly written by Jack Kirby, debuts in the first issue of Timely Publishing's *Captain America Comics*. Tuk is a young Cro-Magnon type who must survive alone in a Stone Age world inhabited by more primitive (and savage) kinds of humans.

1962   *Mysterious Island* (Columbia Pictures), a movie based on the novel by Jules Verne, opens in theatres with stop-motion visual effects created by Ray Harryhausen. The island features its share of prehistoric creatures including the flightless bird *Phororhacus* (which audiences generally assume to be a giant chicken) and a coiled nautiloid (similarly mistaken for a huge octopus).

~ 21 ~

1877   John A. Ryder, an anatomist at the University of Pennsylvania, shows his "roughly drawn, life size reconstruction" of E. D. Cope's sauropod *Camarasaurus* to members of the American Philosophical Society in Philadelphia. The reconstruction is based only on the skeletal parts that had been cleaned by Cope's assistant Jacob Geismar. The picture will be criticized in 1919 by Henry Fairfield Osborn and Charles M. Mook. They illustrate how Cope (and also Marsh) often rush their work in order to top each other: "The reconstruction was obviously made after one series of bones was exposed, but before Professor Cope had had time to give them much study. It would not appear that Professor Cope himself seriously studied the reconstruction...." Osborn and Mook then point out the errors.

1889   Sewall Wright is born in Melrose, Massachusetts. In his future occupation as a professor at the University of Chicago, Wright, experimenting with guinea pigs, will conclude that chance affects evolution. His work, presented in a series of brief but succinct publications, will pioneer what will become modern concepts of evolutionary theory. With biochemist John Burdon Sanderson Haldane and mathematician Robert Aylmer Fisher, Wright will conclude the following: 1. Evolutionary transformation consists almost entirely of changes in gene frequency; 2. selection mostly controls the course of transformation; and 3. mutations only furnish random raw material for evolution, rarely if ever determining the path of progress.

1989   *A Claymation Christmas Celebration*, a half-hour holiday television special made by stop-motion animator Will Vinton, premieres on CBS. The offbeat show is hosted by two "Claymation" dinosaur-character commentators based on film critics Gene Siskel and Roger Ebert. The show will be highly praised, winning a four-star (two spiked-thumbs up?) review from the Chicago *Sun-Times*. Vinton had previously made the popular short film *Dinosaurs*, in which never-seen grammar-school students envision, in their own highly imaginative way, life in the Mesozoic.

1995 Paleontologists Mark A. Norell, James M. Clark, Luis M. Chiappe and Demberelyn Dashzeveg publish a joint paper on a quite spectacular dinosaur discovery made in Late Cretaceous deposits of the Gobi Desert, Mongolia — the skeleton of the theropod *Oviraptor* atop a nest of its eggs. Apparently the dinosaur died quickly during a sandstorm. The find constitutes the first evidence of avian-like brooding in dinosaurs, behavior further attesting to the relationship between theropods and birds.

~ 22 ~

1983 Brad Riney, a paleontologist at the San Diego Museum of Natural History, discovers the well-preserved femur of a 70-million-year-old hadrosaur at a construction site in Carlsbad, California. The find constitutes the largest and most complete dinosaur bone yet found in Southern California. It is the second dinosaur bone to be found in San Diego County. The first specimen, a hadrosaur vertebra, was found 17 years earlier, also by Riney.

The mysterious prehistoric sea creature of "Tourist Attraction," an episode of THE OUTER LIMITS *television series.*

~ 23 ~

1963 The science-fiction television series *The Outer Limits* (ABC) airs the episode "Tourist Attraction," about a giant prehistoric fish with reptilian scales caught in waters off South America. The creature, believed to be dead, revives, proving to be an intelligent being able to communicate with other "living fossils" of its species.

1991 After many months of work and a ride in three sections aboard a flatbed truck, a 26-feet-long, metal *Stegosaurus* replica nicknamed "Bob" is assembled and erected 15 feet above US Highway 50, Gateway to Cañon

City, Colorado. The project has been a cooperative effort of the Garden Park Paleontology Society and the Colorado Department of Corrections in Fremont County, the latter supplying both inmates and staff to make the replica. The dinosaur is nicknamed for the project's instigator, psychologist Robert Hubbell.

~ 24 ~

1801 Charles Willson Peale creatively celebrates Christmas Eve by staging a dinner party at his Peale Museum underneath a recently acquired and mounted skeleton. Peale calls this elephant-like specimen (which was collected at the Big Bone site) *Mammut americanus*, believing it to be a mammoth similar to ones being found in Siberia. Later, however, Peale's specimen will prove to be a mastodon, a related but quite different animal.

1924 Raymond Dart exposes the almost complete face of what will become known as the Taung child. The milk teeth and other features identify the skull as that of a juvenile, apelike creature apparently no more than six years old at time of death. Next February he will name the specimen *Australopithecus afarensis*.

1954 Gregory S. Paul is born in Washington, D.C. In some ways inspired by the new ideas about dinosaurs espoused by Robert T. Bakker, Paul will become an artist, paleontologist and self-proclaimed "dinosaurologist." He will be an author of numerous scientific papers and creator of many detailed skeletal and life reconstructions of dinosaurs and other extinct animals, much of Paul's work centering on the ideas that dinosaurs were active endotherms, some of them possibly having feathers. Many of these ideas, as they apply to theropods, will be presented in Paul's book *Predatory Dinosaurs of the World* (1988).

~ 25 ~

1905 The Burke family receives a Christmas present in the birth of John James Burke in Wellsburg, West Virginia. During the 1930s Burke will become a paleontologist who leads various field parties for the Carnegie Museum of Natural History in Pennsylvania, Ohio and West Virginia. In 1967 he will become Curator of Collections at the Cleveland Museum of Natural History and in 1971 Senior Scientist. Among Burke's accomplishments will be his 1968 discovery of a Mississippian-age amphibian which Alfred S.

Romer will name *Greererpeton burkemorani* in his honor. (Dies August 9, 1979.)

1911   Burne Hogarth is born in Chicago, Illinois. Hogarth will study art history and anthropology at Crane College in Chicago and Northwestern University in Evanston, Illinois, and at Columbia University in New York, after which he takes art courses at Chicago's Art Institute. He will go on to become the first illustrator (and writer) of the *Tarzan* newspaper strip, some of his storylines featuring prehistoric creatures.

~ 26 ~

1868   *Punch* publishes "A Little Christmas Dream," George du Maurier's cartoon of a boy, exposed to natural history, pursued by a nightmarish figure of an enormous mammoth.

1965   More stock footage from *The Lost World* (1960) turns up in "Terror on Dinosaur Island," another episode of television's *Voyage to the Bottom of the Sea*. The *Seaview* crew members get stranded on yet another volcanic island populated by familiar modern lizards masquerading as ancient dinosaurs.

~ 27 ~

1831   Inspired by the work of geologist Charles Lyell, Charles Darwin sets sail aboard the ship *Beagle*, thereby launching his scientific career via a long trip around the world that would be hailed as one of the most important voyages in history. From his experiences on this voyage Darwin will formulate his great theory of evolution.

~ 28 ~

1894   Alfred Sherwood Romer is born in Connecticut. "Al" Romer, to become one of the great vertebrate paleontologists, will one day claim that he went into the field because he was bitten by a mad dog. (In truth, young Romer was bitten by his fox terrier, believed to be rabid, and went to New York for treatments, there visiting the American Museum of Natural History where he was inspired by the fossil skeletons on display.) Romer will specialize in fossil vertebrates, becoming an authority on Permian fossil amphibians and reptiles. He will work both in the field and institution, eventually becoming Professor of Zoology at Harvard University and Director of that institution's Museum of Comparative Zoology. Romer will publish numerous scientific papers. His book *Vertebrate Paleontology*, first published in 1933, will go through a series of new editions, becoming a standard and a classic. (Dies November 5, 1973.)

1929 Peking Man is formally announced at a special meeting of the Geological Society of China. Davidson Black expresses the opinion that the skull is that of "a more generalized and progressive type" *Pithecanthropus* and one of an adolescent or young adult.

1937 Bryan Patterson continues to publish on notoungulates, this time on the braincase in some taxa.

1938 A live coelacanth, a fish thought to be extinct since the Cretaceous period, is caught from a fishing boat off the southern coast of Africa.

1940 The Society of Vertebrate Paleontology (SVP) is founded at the Biological Laboratories of Harvard University, Cambridge, Massachusetts. It comprises a group of vertebrate paleontologists who have officially split off from the "Section of Vertebrate Paleontology of the Paleontological Society," the PS being an organization mostly concerned with invertebrates. Present at this charter meeting are 28 original members including George Gaylord Simpson, Charles Whitney Gilmore, Alfred S. Romer and Edwin H. Colbert. The SVP will become an international society made up mostly of professional paleontologists who meet annually to deliver papers, exchange information and socialize. It will publish its own *News Bulletin* and eventually add *The Journal of Vertebrate Paleontology*.

1967 Ralph Baillie and Peter Barrett find a jaw belonging to *Lystrosaurus*, a genus known from other continents, in Antarctica, evidence supporting the theory of "continental drift."

~ 29 ~

1899 Roland T. Bird is born in Rye, New York. In 1932, while on a motorcycle odyssey to see the country, Bird will stop at a site south of Holbrook, Arizona. There he will find the skull of a Triassic capitosaur that will later be named *Stanocephalosaurus birdi* in his honor. This find will

Roland T. Bird's crew in 1938 excavating the dinosaur trackway at the Paluxy River, the sauropod prints later to be named BRONTOPODUS BIRDI in his honor. Courtesy James O. Farlow.

introduce Bird to Barnum Brown for whom Byrd will collect fossils for many years to come. Joining the American Museum of Natural History staff two years later, Bird will make many significant discoveries. In 1934 he will recover sauropod remains from the famous Howe Quarry in the Morrison Formation of Wyoming. His main achievement, however, will be the discovery, collection (by WPA workers in 1938) and interpretation of a number of huge Cretaceous dinosaur footprints and trackways along the Paluxy River, near Glen Rose, Texas. Bird interprets one set of these tracks as the record of a large theropod stalking a sauropod. In 1989 the sauropod trackway will be named *Brontopodus birdi*. (Dies January 24, 1978.)

1941 The Society of Vertebrate Paleontology holds its first official (and organizational) meeting at Harvard University. Alfred S. Romer is elected provisional president and George Gaylord Simpson provisional secretary-treasurer.

~ 30 ~

1965 Henry Horback and Edward J. Olsen jointly publish a catalogue of meteorites — some of which fell to Earth in very ancient times — housed at the Chicago Natural History Museum.

~ 31 ~

1853 A gala New Year's Eve dinner party, hosted by Benjamin Waterhouse Hawkins and Richard Owen, takes place inside the "mould" of Hawkin's *Iguanodon* model at the Crystal Palace grounds. Among the guests are Professor Edward Forbes, Mr. Joseph Prestwick "and 18 other Scientific and Literary Gentlemen of the Crystal Palace." Arrival time is 5:00 P.M. Owen gives a lecture in which he praises fellow scientist Baron Georges Cuvier. The large and elaborate menu, catered by "Mr. Higinbothom of the Anerly Arms and the European Street," includes a variety of soup, fish, fowl, meats, sweets, wines and dessert.

Same day: The *Illustrated London News* publishes a wood engraving depicting Hawkins' "Extinct Animals Model-Room, at the Crystal Palace, Sydenham," cluttered with his sculptures and molds.

Benjamin Waterhouse Hawkins' "Extinct Animals Model-Room" on the Crystal Palace Grounds. In foreground, from left to right, LABYRINTHODON and DICYNODON; background, PALAEOTHERIUM, IGUANODON and HYLAEOSAURUS. From the ILLUSTRATED LONDON NEWS.

1914 Charles Whitney Gilmore's landmark monograph on *Stegosaurus* is published, making this an especially Happy New Year's Eve for him. Though Gilmore had been denied access to the holotype specimen of type species *Stegosaurus armatus* at Yale, still jacketed and mostly unprepared, he was able to base his study mostly on the excellent, virtually complete "road-kill" skeleton of *S. stenops* exhibited at the United States National Museum. Gilmore has correctly deduced from this holotype specimen, found *in situ* and articulated, that *Stegosaurus* possessed two rows of plates arranged in alternating order.

1934 Bryan Patterson publishes a paper describing the auditory region of typotherids (mammals similar in some ways to large rodents) of the Upper Pliocene. Same day, the prolific Patterson also publishes on the upper premolar-molar structure of notoungulates (a group of large mammals with hooves), skull characters of the South American genus *Homalodotherium* (a toxodon) and description of *Trachytheus*, a typotherid from the Deseado Beds of Patagonia.

The affectionate baby APATOSAURUS *brought to life by Ron Tantin and Isidoro Raponi in the movie* BABY ... SECRET OF THE LOST LEGEND *(1985). © Touchstone Pictures.*

Four pleistocene mammals collected at Rancho La Brea as formerly mounted at the Field Museum of Natural History. In tar, the sabertooth cat SMILODON FATALIS *atop the ground sloth* PARAMYLODON HARLONI; *standing, the horse* EQUUS OCCIDENTALIS *and bison* BISON ANTIQUUS. *Courtesy The Field Museum (neg. #GEO79100).*

BIBLIOGRAPHY

With so many dates coming from so many sources it was not easy to assemble a thorough bibliography. Many books contain the same dates, which have been published many times before. The following list of books, then, has been compiled rather subjectively. All entries following contain a number of specific dates that found their way into the present work.

Augusta, Josef, and Zdenek Burian (illustrator). *The Age of Monsters*. London: Paul Hamlyn, 1966.

_____ and _____. *Prehistoric Sea Monsters*. London: Paul Hamlyn, 1964.

Bassett, Michael G. "Formed Stones," *Folklore and Fossils*. Wales: National Musuem of Wales, Geological Series No. 1, 1982.

Bird, Roland T. *Bones for Barnum Brown*. V. Theodore Schreiber, editor. Fort Worth: Texas Christian University Press, 1985.

Brunas, Michael, John Brunas and Tom Weaver. *Universal Horrors*. Jefferson, N.C.: McFarland, 1990.

Colbert, Edwin H. *Digging into the Past: An Autobiography*. New York: Dembner Books, 1989.

_____. *The Little Dinosaurs of Ghost Ranch*. New York: Columbia University Press, 1995.

_____. *Men and Dinosaurs: The Search in Field and Laboratory*. New York: E. P. Dutton, 1968. (Reprinted by Dover as a trade paperback in 1984 as *The Great Dinosaur Hunters and Their Discoveries*.)

_____. *William Diller Matthew, Paleontologist: The Splendid Drama Observed*. New York: Columbia University Press, 1992.

Culhane, John. *Walt Disney's Fantasia*. New York: Harry N. Abrams, 1983.

Czerkas, Sylvia Massey, and Donald F. Glut. *Dinosaurs, Mammoths and Cavemen: The Art of Charles R. Knight*. New York: E. P. Dutton, 1982.

Desmond, Adrian J. *The Hot-Blooded Dinosaurs: A Revolution in Paleontology*. New York: The Dial Press/James Wade, 1976.

Digby, Bassett. *The Mammoth and Mammoth Hunting in Northeast Siberia.* New York: D. Appleton, 1926.

Dingus, Lowell. *Next of Kin.* New York: Rizzoli International Publications, 1996.

Dinosaurs Return: Elbert H. Porter, Dinosaur Sculptor. [Utah]: Davis Printing, 1982.

Essoe, Gabe. *Tarzan of the Movies.* New York: Citadel Press, 1968.

Fischer, Stuart. *Kids TV: The First 25 Years.* New York: Facts on File Publications, 1983.

Glut, Donald F. *The Dinosaur Scrapbook.* Secaucus, N.J.: Citadel Press, 1980.

Good, John M., Theodore E. White and Gilbert F. Stucker. *The Dinosaur Quarry: Dinosaur National Monument.* Washington, D.C.: National Park Service, 1958.

Gross, Renie. *Dinosaur Country: Unearthing the Badlands' Prehistoric Past.* Saskatoon, Saskatchewan: Western Producer Prairie Books, 1985.

Harris, John M., and George T. Jefferson, editors. *Rancho La Brea: Treasures of the Tar Pits.* Los Angeles: Natural History Museum of Los Angeles County, Science Series 31, 1985.

Howard, Robert West. *The Dawnseekers: The First History of American Paleontology.* New York: Harcourt Brace Jovanovich, 1975.

Howe, S. R., and H. S. Torrens. *Ichthyosaurs: A History of Fossil "Sea Dragons."* Wales, U.K.: National Museum of Wales, 1981.

Keel, John A. *Strange Creatures from Time and Space.* Greenwich, Conn.: Fawcett, 1970.

Lenburg, Jeff, Joan Howard Maurer, and Greg Lenburg. *The Three Stooges Scrapbook.* Secaucus, N.J.: Citadel Press, 1982.

Lentz, Harris M., III. *Science Fiction, Horror & Fantasy Film and Television Credits.* 2 vols. Jefferson, N.C.: McFarland, 1983.

Long, Robert A., and Phillip A. Murry. *Late Triassic (Carnian and Norian) Tetrapods from the Southwestern United States.* New Mexico Museum of Natural History & Science, Bulletin 4, 1995.

Lupoff, Richard A. *Edgar Rice Burroughs, Master of Adventure.* New York: Ace Books, 1968. (Revised paperback edition; original hardcover edition published in 1965 by Canaveral Press.)

Maltin, Leonard. *The Disney Films.* New York: Crown, 1973.

Marshall, Richard. *America's Great Comic Strip Artists.* New York: Abbeville Press, 1989.

McCarthy, Steve, and Mick Gilbert. *The Crystal Palace Dinosaurs.* London: The Crystal Palace Foundation, 1994.

McGinnis, Helen J. *Carnegie's Dinosaurs: A Comprehensive Guide to Dinosaur Hall at Carnegie Museum of Natural History, Carnegie Institute.* Pittsburgh: The Board of Trustees, Carnegie Institute, 1982.

Moore, Ruth. *Man, Time, & Fossils.* New York: Alfred A. Knopf, 1953.

Pitts, Michael R. *Horror Film Stars.* Jefferson, N.C.: McFarland, 1981.

Rottensteiner, Franz. *The Science Fiction Book: An Illustrated History.* New York: New American Library, 1975.

Rudwick, Martin J. S. *Scenes from Deep Time.* Chicago: University of Chicago Press, 1992.

Sternberg, Charles H. *Hunting Dinosaurs in the Bad Lands of the Red Deer River, Alberta, Canada.* Lawrence, Kansas: The World Company Press, 1917.

_____. *The Life of a Fossil Hunter*. New York: Henry Holt, 1909.

Stock, Chester. *Rancho La Brea: A Record of Pleistocene Life in California*. Los Angeles: Los Angeles County Museum of Natural History, Science Series No. 20, Paleontology No. 11, 1930.

Swinton, W. E. *The Dinosaurs*. London: George Allen & Unwin, 1970.

Terrace, Vincent. *The Encyclopedia of Television Programs 1947–1976*. 2 vols. Cranbury, N.J.: A. S. Barnes, 1976.

True, Webster Prentiss. *The Smithsonian: America's Treasure House*. New York: Sheridan House, 1962.

Untermann, G. E., and Billie R. Untermann. *Guide to Dinosaur Land and the Unique Uinta Country*. Vernal, Utah: G. E. and B. R. Untermann, 1972.

Variety Film Reviews 1938–1942. New York: Garland, 1983.

Variety Obituaries 1969–1974. New York: Garland, 1988.

Wallace, Irving. *The Fabulous Showman*. New York: Alfred A. Knopf, 1959.

Warren, Bill. *Keep Watching the Skies!* 2 vols. Jefferson, N.C.: McFarland, 1982 and 1986.

Weaver, Tom. *Poverty Row HORRORS!* Jefferson, N.C.: McFarland, 1993.

Wendt, Herbert. *Before the Deluge*. Garden City, N.Y.: Doubleday, 1968.

_____. *Out of Noah's Ark*. Cambridge, Mass.: The Riverside Press, 1959.

INDEX

Page numbers in *italics* refer to pictures and picture captions.